AF600532

Capitalism for All

Capitalism for All

Realizing Its Liberal Promise

Neil E. Harrison
John Mikler

Cover image of political cartoon from Adobe Stock.

Published by State University of New York Press, Albany

Printed in the United States of America

For information, contact State University of New York Press, Albany, NY
www.sunypress.edu

Library of Congress Cataloging-in-Publication Data

Names: Harrison, Neil E., author. | Mikler, John, author.
Title: Capitalism for all : realizing its liberal promise / by Neil E. Harrison and John Mikler.
Description: Albany : State University of New York Press, [2022] | Includes bibliographical references and index.
Identifiers: ISBN 9781438486970 (hardcover : alk. paper) | ISBN 9781438486994 (ebook)
Further information is available at the Library of Congress.

10 9 8 7 6 5 4 3 2 1

Contents

Illustrations

Figures

Tables

Acknowledgments

We have long been interested in environmental problems and how they are related to capitalism and corporate power. The question we have kept coming back to as we have discussed the problems, and climate change in particular, is this: Must they be addressed by a radical revolution in economic systems, or by working *within* these systems? As an American and an Australian, this has had us turning our minds to liberal capitalism in particular, given that we are both supposed to live in countries that are examples of it. One result of this was our 2014 edited collection *Climate Innovation: Liberal Capitalism and Climate Change*. But as it was being published, we realized we were increasingly questioning just how liberal the variety of capitalism really is in countries like ours, and also whether the world economy may be described as such. We are told all the time that it is, for better or for worse—for example, the benefits or the evils of globalization, depending on whom one asks—yet the changes to our countries and the world order have only become more apparent with the passing of the years. We have seen the rise of populism, and along with it the rise of nationalist sentiment. We have also seen the consolidation of power by nonliberal capitalist states, like China, whose government outwardly proclaims an ongoing commitment to Marxism but in reality seems to have embraced state control for other ends. Increasingly, the "left" derides liberalism as responsible for all the world's ills, equating it with neoliberalism, a term employed by many radical critics in a manner that can only be regarded as a swear word. The "right" also derides liberalism, often identifying anyone who proclaims values associated with it as a socialist who wishes to attack capitalism.

Where has liberalism gone? Liberal values were meant to be woven into the political fabric of our world, and Western society in particular, yet are now derided and under attack from all sides. To be truly a liberal, in deed as well as word, is a courageous standpoint to proclaim. As liberals ourselves, we realized that we had become unusual and often regarded as radical by others. This is really odd! Rather than adherents to the status quo, we realized that we were now out of step with it. Therefore, a book on liberal capitalism would not be one that described the world as it exists, nor the countries that are supposedly liberal in their political institutions. Instead, it would be one that revealed how they were not, how they could be, and why moving toward being so might be desirable.

In writing this book, we have benefited from the support, advice, and (mostly) constructive criticism of so many people it is impossible to name them all here. Here are some of them: Ainsley Elbra, Hannah Murphy-Gregory, Barry Hughes, Karsten Ronit, Tabitha Benney, Philippe Le Prestre, Robert Geyer, Diarmuid Maguire, Rodney Smith, Adam Morton, Kate MacDonald, Christian Hendriksen, Christian May, Stewart Jackson, Genevieve LeBaron, Lian Sinclair, Elizabeth Thurbon, Linda Weiss, Nicola Phillips, Tony Payne, Shahar Hameiri, Tom Chodor, Damien Cahill, Madison Cartwright, Phillip Lawrence, Paul Thurloe, Jim Leeper, Paul Sanderson, Ben Clarke, Lachlan Habgood, Jacqui de Jager, and Digby Beckley. Also the late David Held and James Rosenau. For bearing with us, as always we thank our families and in particular our life partners Ursula Harrison and Kara Mikler.

We have also greatly enjoyed supporting and, most importantly, arguing with each other as we wrote the book. It has been such a pleasure to constructively debate the issues, and if doing so more widely were more possible many of the world's problems might be more easily solved. The opportunities for face-to-face discussion were ruled out in 2020 as the COVID-19 pandemic swept the world and locked down our countries and societies. Yet with this dreadful disease, as with all things, there was also an upside in that we were able to be locked in our respective rooms on opposite sides of the world with nowhere to go and nothing else to do but get it finished! We hope that some of our ideas are useful to anyone who wishes to imagine a better world as we emerge from, and deal with, the pandemic's aftermath. A world that is not of MegaCorps, by MegaCorps, and for MegaCorps but one that is made for the empowerment of individuals and their societies. A world that embraces Liberal Capitalism rather than CorpoCapitalism.

—Neil E. Harrison and John Mikler
Fort Collins, USA, and Sydney, Australia
21 January 2021

Chapter 1

The Fading Promise of Capitalism

Capitalism has been extraordinarily beneficial to most of humanity. Wherever capitalism has been adopted it has improved lives, lifted many out of poverty, and increased the rate of innovation and economic growth. Yet, there is a rising tide of extremist populism spreading like a stain across Europe and North America. Extremists, often from the right of the political spectrum, have become more powerful or have been elected in Hungary, Poland, Austria, and Italy, and have brought extremist parties to power. The United Kingdom (UK) was driven by populists to elect to leave the European Union (EU) after four decades of increasing integration, with no plan to survive outside the EU. The United States (US) managed to elect a member of the capitalist class who promised workers a land of "milk and honey" but further entrenched the power of capital. Despite the rising wealth of the rich nations "the natives are restless" and only demagogues spouting simplistic, often hateful, solutions are receiving a hearing.[1] Many explanations for this disconnect have been offered and local conditions in each country cannot be ignored.[2] But clearly capitalism is failing to keep its promise of a better life for all.

It is popular to complain about capitalism. In this book we, too, point out the many failings of modern capitalism as practiced in the rich countries. Our central argument, however, is that capitalism has become unmoored from the principle that gave it birth. As originally conceived capitalism was intended to free the people to pursue their personal interests. An increase in the wealth of nations was an unintended consequence of the exercise of that freedom that would encourage monarchs to accept the change in economic structure. But the demands of giant corporations aided and abetted by governments have usurped this original purpose all in the name of economic efficiency and growth. As governments increasingly worship these false corporate gods, they are less able to prepare for challenges like the scourge of automation, which may allow corporations to cast aside millions of workers, and the existential threat of climate change. We explain that returning capitalism to its philosophical roots would enable the personal pursuit of wellbeing even as nations can effectively combat these two massive challenges.

We recognize that capitalism has always brought forth the bad with the good. It has doubled life spans; brought technological wonders like electricity, indoor plumbing, cars, computers, and planes; and launched humans into space. But we also see that it has given us enormous inequality, "satanic mills," industrial wastelands, and a warming climate. These and many more are legitimate causes for complaint about the impacts of modern capitalism. In addition, the distribution of the fruits of modern capitalism are increasingly enjoyed by the rich and powerful rather than spread more widely. In the last four decades, even as the rich nations have become richer, most of their workers have seen their incomes stagnate. Technological innovation, a feature of capitalism that once always improved everyone's lives, now threatens democracy and freedom and disproportionately enriches those already wealthy and a handful of entrepreneurs. Governments are delivering fewer services, economic growth is stalling, and private and government debts are rapidly increasing. In the rich countries overflowing with the benefits of capitalism and its constant innovation, people are lining up for the latest smartphone or to buy new cars while a growing number are voting for politicians offering to radically change the economic system that produces so many new baubles. With the aid of these "negative" populists, voters are increasingly worried about the social "bads" spawned by capitalism while they thoughtlessly enjoy its supposed "goods."

As assailants attack it from all sides, the social and environmental consequences of capitalism's failures have become glaringly obvious. Scholars and pundits offer no consensus on what caused these problems or how to solve them. Thomas Piketty in his magisterial work *Capital in the Twenty-First Century* tells us that inequality in wealth and income is a natural consequence of modern capitalism. A natural positive feedback of wealth-to-income-to-wealth creation constantly grows capital's share of the economy as labor loses power, income, and wealth. Piketty proposes extensive redistribution by governments but because he is an economist does not explain the politics by which this could be achieved.

Others do though. From the right, crusaders want to shrink government, entirely remove it from the economy, and double down on the "free-market" principles that caused the problems. Concerned with the immorality of inequality, and the class relations that produce them, neo-Marxists demand a radical restructuring of the economy that includes substantial public ownership of the means of production. Most environmentalists would harness the power of government to regulate industrial processes and consumer markets to reduce toxic emissions and the consumption of the environment. Some press for abolition of industrial activities such as coal-fired electricity generation and radical restriction of others. A few argue that we need to embrace the concept of "degrowth," to produce less but share it better to prevent the sinking of "Lifeboat Earth" on which we live.[3] This calls into question many processes of production and consumption that are fundamental to the constant growth on which capitalism feeds, essentially negating it.

A common refrain from the left, and from academia, is that "neoliberalism" is the cause of the present parlous state of capitalism. It is a slippery idea. Even its most trenchant critics cannot nail it down. Colin Crouch, for example, considers it a derivative of liberalism but it really is a huge distortion.[4] Where liberalism aims at individual liberty, neoliberalism is only concerned with liberty of the market and, as we shall demonstrate, of the largest corporations. It has been disparaged as "capitalism with the gloves off."[5] Since about 1980 the idea of neoliberalism has become embedded in policymaking in many countries, and used to justify a shrunken government and weak "safety net" that does little to mitigate the potential harms, now realized, of rampant untamed capitalism.

The idea that capitalism should be untamed was conceived more than a century ago. In the late nineteenth century a group of economists gathered around the idea that all economic activity started with the desires and behaviors of individuals. From this the "Austrian School," which would now be considered "libertarian," concluded that governmental interference in markets reduced individual freedom. Horrified by the carnage of World War I initiated by governments, a group of Austrian economists led by Friedrich Hayek and Ludwig von Mises gathered in Geneva in the 1920s to work out how to protect capitalism from governments and the people.[6] Democracy, they thought, was a threat. It would lead to calls to distribute wealth more equally, weaken essential property rights, and nationalist politics would impede the global flow of goods that classical economic theory says makes all nations wealthier. They advocated construction of supranational institutions to make and enforce the rules of a free global market. Rather than democratically elected governments, they crafted a convincing narrative in which "the free market . . . is advanced as the only rational, fair, and democratic allocator of goods and services."[7] In other words, they and their neoliberal disciples did not want to liberate markets but to "encase" them by "redesigning states, laws, and other institutions" to insulate markets from hostile politics.[8] Actually, from politics in general.

In some ways, the EU comes close to this neoliberal ideal with power allocated to a European council of government leaders, unelected Brussels technocrats to implement policies, and a toothless European parliament. These features also make it supranational as well as international in nature. Yet, interestingly, many scholars of international relations (who often are liberal minded) also support strong international institutions and the rule of law applied at the global level.[9] In an international system without a government, they argue, governance through a "liberal world order" of rules, institutions, and norms keeps the peace. But it also protects and encourages "free" trade, leaving to national governments the task of combating any negative effects of globalization such as income inequality, unemployment, and climate change.

That is all very well in theory. What is the reality though? In this book, we start by showing why capitalism in its current form is neither liberal nor neoliberal. While neoliberalism promises efficient markets free of government interference, massive corporations now dominate most industries. This hands-off approach has allowed a small number of very large multinationals corporations—which we call "MegaCorps"—to dominate most industries within countries and in global trade.[10] MegaCorps have accumulated so much economic and political power that governments cater to their interests and accede to their demands. This is capitalism of, by, and for corporations—what we call "CorpoCapitalism"—in which governments have enabled and empowered the rich and powerful and the corporations that they own or manage. The losers are the great majority of the people and the natural environment. The most important consequence of what is supposedly a neoliberal strategy has thus been a massive growth in corporate power coupled with a political capture of the state. Not only is there nothing neoliberal, and certainly nothing liberal, about this as an ideological stance; there is also nothing neoliberal or liberal about the outcomes produced.

Nowhere has this transition to CorpoCapitalism proceeded farther or faster than in the US. Therefore, throughout this book we use the US as the lodestar that most rich countries are following, though at a slower pace and in varied ways. For a while after CorpoCapitalism took hold in the US and many other countries around the world, inflation fell, and economic growth increased. Apart from financial crises in peripheral countries like Thailand and Russia a "Great Moderation" seemed to have settled in.[11] But then CorpoCapitalism delivered the Great Recession, banking crashes, a massive increase in public and private debt, and rising income inequality, while it accelerated climate change. Now the concern is that economies are again stagnating. Lawrence Summers has argued the problem is excessive savings and reduced demand.[12] Because of the concentration of wealth, ageing populations, and a dearth of investment opportunities, he sees a future of "secular stagnation" punctuated by periods of debt-infused booms followed by deep recessions. A different version of secular stagnation suggests the cause is the ability of consumers and producers to "game" economic institutions constructed around a strategic policy.[13] Robert Gordon worries that economic growth has stagnated because we have plucked the low-hanging fruit of technological innovation, and that technology is not improving people's lives.[14] In his view electricity, mass production, fossil-derived energy, and science increased living standards and ended common diseases, but today's innovations are more entertaining than life enhancing. And information and communications technology (ICT) and nascent artificial intelligence (AI) are beginning to rule our lives as much as enhance them and destroy many low-skilled jobs while creating a few high-skilled jobs.

There are many explanations, or theories, but in total they suggest that the stagnation may be the ultimate gift of CorpoCapitalism. MegaCorps do not need innovation: to protect their position they can crush nascent competitors with their financial might, or just purchase them. In principle they support free competition, but in practice they prevent it. They sell hedonism, prioritize profits, and manage markets with the assent or support of governments. They may privately deliver social welfare to their employees (sick and parental leave, health care, wellness programs, etc.), relieving governments of that task, while increasing automation and outsourcing substantial work to contractors who can be dropped at will in this "gig" economy.

Liberalism and Capitalism

To find a better way, it is necessary to return to first principles. Scholars and policymakers want to "play with parameters," which Donella Meadows disparaged as tinkering at the periphery, tweaking a policy here or establishing an institution there.[15] Yet, to develop a comprehensive approach to capitalism we must start with the question of the purpose of the economy before we consider which form of economy is optimal. *What is the economy really for?* Should the economy float freely, unattached to society or the environment and unconcerned about its effects on either, as neoliberals recommend? Separating it from society in this way simplifies analysis with mathematical models and glib political platforms that avoid difficult debates about values and ethics not amenable to quantitative analysis. But it also means the economy, especially a market economy, serves no purpose beyond existing.

As we explain in chapter 2, liberal political philosophy was the foundation both of capitalism and of the United States. Yet, in recent years both have become unmoored from that vital guiding light. Liberalism is not, as commonly understood in the US and many other countries, a form of socialism. It is instead the ancient idea that the purpose of the economy and of its governance is *as far as possible to secure for each of its members the opportunity to pursue their wellbeing as they see it*. Liberal capitalism does not guarantee a good life for all; it offers opportunities for each to improve their life. "Deaths of despair" from suicide and opioid addiction show that capitalism as currently practiced fails by that measure alone.[16]

The premise for this economic purpose is the values represented by the liberal philosophy that gave rise to capitalism in the first place. Despite—perhaps because of—two centuries of social change, the principles of liberal philosophy have become ever more relevant. Political elites have forgotten—or been misled about—the principles of liberalism that brought forth capitalism out of feudal monarchy. The tradition of liberalism inspired Adam Smith's *The Wealth of Nations*, founded the United States, freed slaves, grew more food, delivered medical innovations that lengthened lives, gave us the forty-hour work week, increased personal security, and broadened the same democracy that populists now threaten. But nor has the average person understood what liberalism entails for them, why they need it, and what their responsibilities would be in a genuinely liberal capitalist economy.

The founding documents of the United States clearly reflect a sense of liberty as "freedom from" the intrusions and restraints of government. This idea of rights-based individualism championed by thinkers such as John Locke fitted the moment as the US was attempting to throw off the shackles of colonial British rule. Similarly, Adam Smith in his *Wealth of Nations* explained how commerce could reject the rule of the monarchy. The classical liberal philosophy of John Locke, Adam Smith, and John Stuart Mill has progressively adapted over the years to the reality of advanced industrial societies, making it still relevant today and in the future. Unfortunately, espousing an extreme version of this philosophy, of which the Austrian economists would approve, Margaret Thatcher declared that there is no such thing as society. For her "there are individual men and women and there are families."[17] She then proceeded to espouse a libertarian view that people should help themselves and each other and not look to government entitlements. But that is not the only logical conclusion from her statement. For example, the strand of liberalism that emerged from the French Revolution adds a "common good" delivered through moral and ethical leadership, democracy, and equality.[18] While government does not have a duty to deliver the "good life" to all, it does have a responsibility to create "life chances" or opportunities through which everyone can pursue their wellbeing in their own way. Yet, CorpoCapitalism directly supports the wellbeing of corporations, or rather the elites who benefit most from their wellbeing, but only indirectly and sparingly the wellbeing of the vast majority of men, women, and their children.

If capitalism is to become more liberal there is not just the need to correct the errors of the recent past, but also to do so while adapting to changing economic and social conditions going forward. In chapter 3 we explain three modern challenges to liberalism. First, it must correct the social harms caused by CorpoCapitalism. There is ample evidence that there is a yearning for a better quality of social life, not just for more goods and services offered by modern economies. Anyone born into a rich capitalist country is taught from the cradle that things bring happiness, that possessions display our worth to the world.[19] In other words, capitalism has so affected perception that most adults in many rich countries have a severely distorted understanding of how to find happiness or wellbeing. Wellbeing is the lifelong process of exploring and developing personal possibilities. Not only does CorpoCapitalism drown out wellbeing with hedonism (delivering pleasures and satisfying emotions) but it also is notoriously poor at enabling or supporting it, which is the true goal of liberalism. Indeed, it counters or distracts us from most of the ways we can increase our wellbeing. Thus, liberalism demands that space must be created *within* capitalism, for communities to secure their environment and individuals to pursue their personal wellbeing.

Second, the present and growing threat of climate change reduces the personal security of millions, even in the rich countries. Many atmospheric scientists are becoming increasingly alarmed about the potential for social collapse as the climate changes.[20] If governments are responsible for the security of citizens individually and collectively, then they are derelict in that duty for doing too little to prevent dangerous climate change or help communities adapt to its effects. This means that governments must create a space within capitalism for communities and individuals to build resilience and flourish in a low-carbon but warmer world. Third, the world of work is already changing, and this transformation will accelerate. Automation and artificial intelligence will cause mass unemployment, increase the wealth of the rich, and grow inequality, yet further straining the bands of common purpose that hold societies together.

As we explain in chapters 4 and 5, armed with the ideology of "free markets"—as if free markets exist anywhere in the universe free of the rules and institutions that political processes provide—MegaCorps have accumulated so much economic and political power that governments generally cater to their interests and accede to their demands. CorpoCapitalism means that, in effect, the profit motivations of MegaCorps have come to rule policy. One result is the collapse of the welfare state. As we explain in chapter 6, all rich countries have some form of welfare state to support the weak and powerless, the unemployed and unskilled, the halt and the lame. Some do much more than this, but in a liberal context this is what welfare is supposed to be about. Yet, in supposed liberal countries they no longer do, because they are designed for the challenges of the past and do little to improve wellbeing, reduce inequality from automation, or to mitigate climate change. They patch the scars of CorpoCapitalism as they are designed to prevent a further decline in living standards but not to increase opportunities for wellbeing. In chapter 7 we look at how governments raise the revenues and manage the distribution of social welfare benefits. We assess the social and personal harms (despite social welfare systems) caused by CorpoCapitalism in chapter 8. Where it has advanced furthest it has increased inequality, reduced social mobility, and even halted the advance in longevity.

If the economy is to support, protect, and improve society and the lives within it, what should liberal capitalist economies provide to society and its members? Technological innovation is widely accepted as a primary way to combat climate change. The current innovation systems rely heavily on the serendipity of market innovation largely directed by the search for private profit. Chapter 9 assesses how technology might mitigate dangerous climate change and direct it toward social improvements rather than solely private gain. Then in chapter 10 we consider several potential changes to the distribution of opportunities for wellbeing and the sources of revenues that would support them. Liberal capitalism demands many and substantial changes to institutions that MegaCorps will oppose. As chapter 11 explains, institutions that are constructed to oppose or delay change must themselves evolve to change the underlying ideology from CorpoCapitalism to Liberal Capitalism.

Climate change is a unique threat to capitalism. Despite the efforts of the United Nations, three decades of international negotiations have not produced an effective agreement to avoid dangerous climate change. In chapter 12 we propose a different approach that emphasizes building global resilience through localized acceptance of the required radical lifestyle changes. Finally, in chapter 13 we sketch the principles by which the people might take back their governments from the MegaCorps and move toward *Liberal* Capitalism.

Part I

The Promise of Liberalism

In 2014 we published *Climate Innovation: Liberal Capitalism and Climate Change* but did not delve too deeply into what the term "Liberal Capitalism" really meant today in reality, as opposed to in theory. After its release, in 2015 Poland followed Hungary and lurched toward authoritarian rule with the election of the Law and Justice Party. Then in 2016 some EU countries closed their borders to Syrian refugees, the UK voted to withdraw from the EU, and the US elected Donald Trump. Meanwhile scholarly interest in the growth of income and wealth inequality grew rapidly.

These changes led us to think about what Liberal Capitalism is and how it compares to what we experience in our daily lives. Is today's economy really a product of Liberal Capitalism or is this term some meaningless pablum to mislead the masses? Is Liberal Capitalism only an idle dream of cloistered scholars? What is freedom (or liberty) and should it have limits? Whose freedom should be limited, who should limit it, and under what conditions? How do we balance individual freedom with collective progress and the common good?

If governments of the rich countries in Europe, North America, Asia, and Australasia adopted the tenets of liberal philosophy as guiding principles for the governance of capitalism, how would life change in those countries and beyond? Would life as experienced by most people be measurably better? Looking to the future, could a truly Liberal Capitalism meet the existential challenge of a warming climate and protect humanity from harm? And how may Liberal Capitalism prevent the social harm from job-destroying automation that gives yet more power to capital over labor?

Chapter 2

What's Been Lost

The Dream of Liberalism

The political philosophy of liberalism is the original foundation of most modern capitalist democracies. Its central idea, found throughout history at least since the Ancient Greeks, is that the freedom of individuals is valuable. In modern history, Thomas Hobbes, John Locke, and other seventeenth-century Enlightenment philosophers constructed from this basic idea a political philosophy in which the purpose of social collectives, communities, and nations is to increase the freedom of individuals and limit the arbitrary reign of autocratic monarchs. The liberal Scottish philosopher Adam Smith similarly attacked the reign of feudal monarchs in 1776 when he described in *The Wealth of Nations* how the economic activity within a nation may be organized to optimize both individual freedom and collective efficiency. It would do so by putting the "invisible hand" of the market in charge, rather than the visible hand of the state, and enabling the freedom of merchants, rather than feudal lords. Then, if everyone were free to better their condition rather than having what was good for them dictated by their rulers, trade among them would increase the wealth of the whole world as well as the nation. The French Revolution added "equality" and "fraternity" (which implies collective good) to the "liberty" of classical British liberalism, which focuses more on political and economic rights. While freedom of the individual is central to both strains of liberalism, the British version has been more widely accepted and followed—particularly in the UK and US, and to a lesser extent in other "Anglo-Saxon" countries—and is central to our discussion in this chapter.

The United States was founded in the same year that Smith published his economics text. It is a delicious irony that British liberal philosophy underpinned the US's desire for independence from Britain and provided the ideological basis for its constitution. But Smith himself considered his work on liberal *philosophy* to be more important than his views on economics.[1] In his *The Theory of Moral Sentiments*, he wrote that everyone wants "to be observed, to be attended to, to be taken notice of with sympathy, complacency, and approbation," which is why we try to better our condition. So, liberalism is evidently about liberty: of the economy and of individuals in society. Yet, what does that mean in practice? In this chapter we discuss the ways in which liberty, or more simply freedom, may be understood. From that discussion we derive four "guiding ideas" or core values that have continually adapted liberalism to the political and economic reality for more than two centuries. The interplay of these guiding ideas and the process of continually balancing them can most effectively guide capitalism in the future.

About Freedom

Liberalism is wholly concerned with freedom.[2] But that is an elastic concept. One version of freedom is the theme of *Churchill and Orwell: The Fight for Freedom* by Thomas Ricks.[3] This freedom is the opposite of totalitarianism. Both men fought with words against the oppressive state authority of Nazi Germany during World War II and against the Soviet Union after. Churchill's oratory prevented Britain from suing for peace after the fall of France. After the war he quickly saw the threat that the Soviet Union posed to liberty and warned that, "from Stettin in the Baltic to Trieste in the Adriatic, an iron curtain has descended across the continent." This was a world, he said, where "the power of the State is exercised without restraint, either by dictators or by compact oligarchies operating through a privileged party and apolitical police."[4]

From his experience in Spain during the Civil War, Orwell had earlier recognized the oppressive nature of the Soviet Union. In his earliest writings he had opposed capitalism and its offspring, colonialism, for building wealth and global commerce on the backs of so many to whom basic freedoms were denied. But in Spain he barely escaped with his life when Soviet operatives, nominally supporting the socialist government forces, began exterminating volunteers like him that they thought were not sufficiently communist. From his experiences in Spain, where he also was wounded in battle, and the war years, he crafted his two most famous warnings about the power of the state. *Animal Farm* is a warning about how revolution may lead to autocracy. The leaders of the revolution slowly create a state even more oppressive than before, as they ostensibly determine what is good for their citizens but which is really what is good for them. In *1984* the state determines what is true and what is false, everyone's actions are monitored, and even thought is "policed." In both books Orwell uses fiction to warn of the power of the state, its capacity to wield authority underpinned by surveillance, and thereby its potential for oppression of individuals and the subjugation of liberty.

World War II was fought to save the world from the totalitarian state and to protect "freedom from" the state. In the euphoria of victory, the Universal Declaration of Human Rights endorsed the broader concept of "freedom to" fulfill our needs and choose our lives. This essential idea is also reflected in the concept of sustainable development, first defined in 1987 in the United Nations' World Commission on Environment and Development report *Our Common Future*. Development is only sustainable if it "meets the needs of the present without compromising the ability of future generations to meet their own needs."[5] As we today cannot know what those needs will be, we must ensure that we leave as good and as much of natural, physical, and human resources to enable future generations the "freedom to" organize their lives.

John Rawls further developed the idea of "freedom to" in his densely argued philosophical treatise *A Theory of Justice*. He elaborated a "justice of fairness" based on equality of treatment by government and access to opportunities. Everyone should have equal rights and any inequalities "must be attached to offices and positions open to all under conditions of fair equality of opportunity; and second, they must be to the greatest benefit of the least advantaged members of society."[6] As social and economic inequalities arise, emphasis should be on equal access to opportunities to advance and succeed. As in all liberal thinking, there should be equality of inputs and fair processes, rather than equality of defined outputs or outcomes.

In France, World War II stimulated a literature about a third understanding of freedom. For existentialists like Sartre, Camus, de Beauvoir, and Merleau-Ponty freedom is created within the individual and external conditions are less important. Even in prison, we have choices in how to survive imprisonment. In France, many people accepted the German occupation and gave up much of their liberty as long as they were left alone to continue their lives. Sartre and Camus, however, were active in the Resistance, reflecting their belief that all humans are "free" to create themselves through their actions. To exist is to face the absolute freedom (and necessity) to choose who you are. Whatever the external conditions, each of us must choose what to believe and how to act on those beliefs. But we also must accept responsibility that the choices we make should be general principles. So, we may act in a situation exclusively from self-interest (as we each define it) while knowing that our choice will harm or burden others, or society at large, but then we must accept that others may choose likewise. Simone de Beauvoir made this responsibility for actions in the world clear in her study of the Marquis de Sade.[7] However heinous our behavior we must grant to others the right to behave similarly, even if it harms us. Adam Smith hoped for something similar. Like other Enlightenment thinkers he envisaged a society of respectable, responsible individuals rationally making decisions about what was in their interests.[8] This was preferable to having their choices constrained, or made for them, by overlords in a manner that is both morally indefensible as well as economically inefficient.

These different conceptions of freedom all imply different liberalisms. The "freedom to" offers a more expansive view of governance than "freedom from," while existentialism proposes freedom as a natural imposition with which each of us must struggle, but which encourages individuals to "make themselves" through their chosen actions throughout their lives.

Liberalism, Democracy, and Capitalism

Several recent commentaries on liberalism have argued that there is an essential tension within liberalism that will lead to its destruction. They commonly conclude that it has failed because they erroneously treat liberalism as identical with democracy or capitalism. However, the reality is that democracy and capitalism have different roles in social identity and coherence, and different purposes. For example, Edward Luce's *The Retreat of Western Liberalism* argues that liberalism only survived this long as a political philosophy because it has generated economic growth. He argues that the slowing of mature economies is the cause of the current crisis in liberalism:

> We are taught to think our democracies are held together by values. Our faith in history fuels that myth. But liberal democracy's strongest glue is economic growth. When groups fight over the fruits of growth, the rules of the political game are relatively easy to uphold. When those fruits disappear, or are monopolized by a fortunate few, things turn nasty.[9]

If both democracy and capitalism seem to need growth to maintain themselves, the trick, from a normative point of view, is to reconcile the desirability of liberal democracy with the socially destabilizing forces of unbridled capitalism.

The problem today is that illiberal, undemocratic capitalism appears to be working, or rather, thriving, while liberal, democratic capitalism appears to be under attack. In addition to slowing growth, both governments and corporations have privatized risk to employees and customers to the extent that "to one degree or another—most sharply in the US and UK—societies are creeping back to the days before social insurance. What was underwritten by government and employers has been shifted to the individual."[10] On top of that, bankers whose reckless greed caused the Great Recession were able to offload their costs to taxpayers. While this may have made economic sense in the midst of a crisis, ten years later it only highlights a continual risk transfer from big capital to individuals, so that capitalism *as it currently exists* is harming democracy, rather than the other way around.

Every rich country has institutionally managed the natural tension between democracy and market capitalism in its own way. In examining the institutional variations between states as they attempt to reconcile market capitalism and democracy, Esping-Andersen recognized that the link between the two is neither natural, nor necessarily liberal.[11] Democratic countries have differed in their institutional choices guided by their interpretation of liberalism. For example, the US is primarily concerned with "freedom from" government authority. The American fixation on the rights of the individual (as mandated in its constitution) against the power of the state is a minimalist "freedom from" version of liberalism rooted in eighteenth-century thinking. In contrast, European countries lean more toward "freedom to" achieve equality of opportunity and outcomes and have historically been more interventionist and have provided more social benefits paid for with higher taxes.

Though capitalism historically emerged from liberal foundations, not all capitalist states are democratic or liberal. For example, China has a "state-led" version of capitalism. Nobody would claim that there is not a thriving capitalist economy alongside the state-owned, or more accurately effectively state-controlled, corporations that have emerged from the ashes of Mao Zedong's communism. But China is neither liberal nor democratic and has adopted capitalist markets to generate the economic growth it needs to maintain the authority of its president and Communist Party, as well as the passive support of its citizens.

For some critics, liberalism generates its own destruction by reinforcing self-interest. For example, Patrick Deneen eloquently argues that "liberalism has failed because liberalism has succeeded. As it becomes fully itself, it generates endemic pathologies more rapidly and pervasively than it is able to produce Band-aids and veils to cover them."[12] Because of the need for authority to enable capitalism yet prevent its excesses, the power of modern capitalism draws forth excessive governmental authority over personal choices. Another pathology is that the increasing individualism fostered by capitalism, as founded on liberalism, leads to destruction of community ties, trust, and even family relations.

Liberalism, according to Deneen, has attracted attention and support because it "ingratiates by invitation to the easy liberties, diversions, and attractions of freedom, pleasure, and wealth."[13] This leads us to believe the worst of human nature and that by nature humans are corrupt and solely self-interested. Such beliefs encourage self-interested and untrusting behaviors: if we believe everyone is out for themselves in any way possible, with no regard to moral sentiments, then we need to follow the same path in order to protect ourselves and pursue our interests. We agree that liberalism's success has bred the demons of its own demise, but we demur that there is no solution. Indeed, we argue in this book that liberalism, properly understood, is the solution that is needed but that CorpoCapitalism has eroded its own liberal foundation. So, while Deneen, like others, argues that liberalism has produced "endemic pathologies" such as equal rights with inequality, a need for collective action with individualism, and growing state authority with personal autonomy, we see Deneen's error. This is that, like others, he confuses CorpoCapitalism with true Liberal Capitalism. He, and they, read the label on the box rather than examine its actual contents.

Liberalism as an Idea

Liberalism is an ideology in so far as it is a "system of ideas and ideals, especially one which forms the basis of economic or political theory and policy."[14] Unlike most *-isms* such as communism, socialism, or even fascism, it is more concerned with inputs and processes than in specific outputs such as a classless society, ownership of the means of production, or an excessively ordered, ultranationalist society sharing a common vision. Its only goal is to maintain and expand the liberty of the individual, which as we have shown is quite an amorphous and deliberately ill-defined objective.

The idea of personal freedom is as old as the tribe. Edmund Fawcett complains that it would be helpful "if liberals themselves agreed on what liberty amounted to and why it mattered in politics. But they do not."[15] So, let's define it. While much debated, we use the term liberty as *optimization of the space within which individuals may choose their lives*. We take this to combine the "freedom from" that protects from overweening governmental authority, the "freedom to" that offers to improve everyone's "life chances" and recognizes that each of us must make ourselves our own way.[16] Beyond these values, liberalism does not ground itself in morals or ethical action for, as John Rawls wrote, "as a practical political matter no general moral conception can provide a publicly recognized basis for a conception of justice [that would guarantee personal freedom] in a modern democratic state."[17]

The problem is that in the rich countries that are supposed to be democratic and implicitly meritocratic, inequality has grown, opportunities have shrunk (especially for many of the poorest), and social mobility has decayed. And liberalism, which is held to blame, is now under siege from populists. However, to be more accurate, it is not so much liberalism that populists attack as the status quo, which we show in the following chapters is actually *not* liberal. Although populism was once for the people (and liberty) against the constraints of the elite, now it takes its starting point as the description of a terrifying world that must be rectified through radical political means. This is worrying for where it might lead. Starting as it is from CorpoCapitalism, it is more likely to lead to an authoritarian state than back to liberalism.

Yet, liberalism has survived challenges before. The massive movement from villages to the cities at the start of the British Industrial Revolution created desperate living and working conditions. Liberalism reduced the mass misery of rapid industrialization and laissez-faire capitalism and supported those injured by it. In the US, the robber barons of the late nineteenth century trampled workers but the Progressive Era effectively stifled them and broke up their trusts. And it has survived financial booms and crashes, world wars, cold wars, and technological changes. The story of liberalism has been its ability to change and adapt to conditions.

Its strength is its essential flexibility. Edmund Fawcett comprehensively demonstrates this in *Liberalism: The Life of an Idea*. From his masterly review of the literature, he offers four "guiding ideas" that underpin it: *conflict mitigation*, *power prevention*, *personal and collective progress*, and *respect*. In liberal states, these frame the structure of institutions and the shape of the political process.[18] The heart of the project is to maintain "peaceable competition" while restraining individual behavior to prevent civic fragmentation. As he puts it: "To liberals, competition in the town square, laboratory or marketplace encouraged bargaining, creativity, and initiative, whereas social harmony stifled or silenced them."[19] Particularly destructive would be the social harmony enforced by the state as in Orwell's *1984*.

Conflict Mitigation

Conflict mitigation recognizes that people will disagree about what they value. Liberals accept that conflict over values is normal, and that government may need to intercede, or regulate interactions, to prevent violence and maintain order. In a free society people will always compete over their beliefs in the role of the press, religious rights, workers' rights and employment, the right to hold and use property, and the ability to speak one's mind, among many others, as much as they compete in the economy for income and wealth. After all, if we all thought the same, we would be living in Orwell's Oceania in *1984*. To be liberal is to accept that this competition is inevitable, indeed desirable, and that it should be tolerated until it becomes destructive. Political processes, guided by the goal of liberty, determine when and how to cut off destructive conflict.

Yet, neither side in these competitions of values should "win" because there is more freedom in keeping debate open than closing it down. This competition need not necessarily be individualist. It may as readily be between self-organizing groups within society. Concord may be reached between them, but whether it occurs is not the goal or function of government. Likewise, on the same issue there may be agreement in one country but not in another from the different construction of institutions or from differences in shared interests. For example, in the US there is bitter contestation over abortion and climate change, two issues over which in other countries—for example, the UK, Germany, and many others in the EU—there is a general agreement across the political spectrum. Indeed, across the rich world there now is concern that conflict may not always be beneficial and that capitalism has not "achieved a wished-for steady-state of concord in discord."[20]

This means that even after economic activity is freed from the grip of an avaricious sovereign, civil power will be required to ensure justice and preserve liberty. As Smith recognized:

> In the race for wealth, and honours, and preferments . . . he may run as hard as he can, and strain every nerve and every muscle, in order to outstrip all his competitors. But if he should justle, or throw down any of them, the indulgences of the spectators is [*sic*] entirely at an end. It is a violation of fair play, which they cannot admit of.[21]

Therefore, he reasoned that when capital exists, civil government is *needed*.[22] In other words, capitalism itself causes the need for the exercise of governmental authority. As we show in chapters 4 and 5, today we have as much to fear from MegaCorps spewing a free-market ideology while coercing government to protect their dominance or technology "platforms" enjoying network effects as we do from government. As capitalism has diverged from liberalism, it has increased civil discord.

Power Prevention

This is the big one. Simply put, power prevention means that no organization (including government) or person should be able to dominate individuals, groups, or society at large. Smith recognized the power of mores and social control:

> Nature when she formed man for society, endowed him with an original desire to please, and an original aversion to offend his brethren. She taught him to feel pleasure in their favourable, and pain in their unfavourable regard.[23]

Yet the need for the power of civil government to regulate social interaction was broadly accepted by Smith and his contemporaries. For example, Edmund Burke, who was a conservative Irish member of the British Parliament, commented in 1791 that

> men are qualified for civil liberty in exact proportion to their disposition to put moral chains upon their own appetites; . . . Society cannot exist unless a controlling power upon will and appetite be placed somewhere, and the less of it there is within, the more there must be without.[24]

As we noted earlier, liberals support the liberty of individuals guided by an ingrained ethic of personal responsibility and restraint rather than unbridled hedonism, and concern for others, without which behavior must be regulated by some external power.

The power of government is especially necessary to prevent the accumulation of great power by elites, and the organizations they control, such as MegaCorps. Liberalism recognizes a natural tendency of human behavior, which is that the acquisition of power usually leads to attempts to control or regulate others in order to use them for power's purposes. In essence, superior power, whether political, economic, or social, of some people over others often tends to arbitrariness and domination unless opposed and prevented. Only government can check excesses of economic or social power, and within government the excessive power of any one branch (legislative, executive, or judicial) should be checked by the other branches. A free press is also essential to speak truth to the power of government. Such checks on excess power are expressly written into the US Constitution, as they are in many other liberal democracies that have a separation of powers either formally or informally recognized.

Liberalism is not an ideology with an all-encompassing vision of the perfect future. Instead, it is a process with a singular continuing purpose: to protect and expand personal freedom. In other words, it is about inputs to political, economic, and social processes more than outputs from those processes. So, it has been misrepresented in many national political systems across the world. Authoritarian Americans of the right wing, many of whom are acolytes of Ayn Rand and anti-tax campaigner Grover Norquist, charge that "liberal" is a "four-letter word" for wasteful government spending and social control. Their libertarian ideal of minimalist government—shrinking the government "to the size it can be drowned in the bathtub"—is not liberalism.[25] It is anarchy, or risks unbridled power in the hands of the few, and potentially leads back to the state of affairs in Adam Smith's time. Then, the power of the monarch supported by men of title who owned the land and resources might be used arbitrarily to subjugate society, commerce, and individuals to his or her will.

As is commonly quoted: "Power tends to corrupt and absolute power corrupts absolutely. Great men are almost always bad men, even when they exercise influence and not authority."[26] In other words, government can itself become a problem for liberalism (the cause of "freedom from") and "the first defence against arbitrary power, law and government, was itself a power, hence an abiding problem for liberals."[27] Liberals, therefore, hope that resistance to undue power will ultimately come from the people: "The ideal liberal citizen was self-possessed and ready to answer back to authority. Effective resistance had to be collective. Liberalism called accordingly for a shared commitment to laws and institutions that prevented any one interest, faith or class from seizing control of state, economy, or society and turning it to their own domineering purposes."[28]

Personal and Collective Progress

Liberals hope personal and collective progress may allay some of the risks of excessive power and restrain civil conflict. Once again there is a contradiction here: progress depends on conflict (that is, competition) within society but conflict must be "managed" to prevent implosion of social order. Yet, any authority reduces liberty somewhere in society. Nevertheless, liberals have long thought that progress would "make society and its citizens less unruly."[29]

After 1945 progress became defined in terms of the advance of the welfare state. This required universal education, unions to protect workers, and a social safety net that prevented the unemployed or disabled from starving in the streets. Essentially, this provided band-aids to patch some of the worst social impacts of raw capitalism. Until the energy disruptions and "stagflation" of the 1970s, the various interpretations of the welfare state, from the social democratic versions of it in Scandinavian countries to the liberal versions in the Anglo-Saxon ones, worked well. But since the advent of "free-market" ideology, progress has increasingly become defined in terms of "efficiency" and economic growth through reduced corporate oversight (especially in the US and UK) and minimal management of the economy. The result is that welfare states have not so much continued to evolve as they have been under attack to "free up" the market forces necessary for progress defined in terms of economic growth.

Yet, progress is about more than economics. We think of it in terms of development that may be defined as "a complex series of interrelated change processes, abrupt and gradual, by which a population and all its components move away from patterns of life perceived in some significant way as 'less human' toward an alternative pattern of life perceived as 'more human.'"[30] This is how Denis Goulet puts it, but a law professor once questioned one of the authors of this book on the meaning of "human." "What," he asked, "does 'more human' mean?" Liberalism refuses to answer this question and leaves the definition of "more human" to each individual. And society becomes more human as the people are able to explore and expand themselves, their interests, and abilities, which we call wellbeing, as described in more detail in the next chapter. Liberalism only seeks to expand the space within which everyone can pursue their personal interpretation of how to mix the material, social, and spiritual to better fulfill their nature and pursue their goals.

Respect

To reduce conflict and increase trust requires respect for ourselves and for others. The idea is that there have to be "limits to how superior power could treat and above all not mistreat people, or exclude people. . . . [and] restraint from the power of those 'cold monsters': state, wealth and society."[31] This requires respect of employer for employee, of bureaucrat for citizen, and of citizens for each other, whatever their race, religion, or creed. In a liberal society, citizens demand "ample room for public maneuver together with a secure private space" and should have "the self-possession" to stand up for what they want through political involvement.[32] In this sense, instead of order and control being imposed and enforced externally, they are governed internally by individuals responsibly exercising their freedoms. The role of government is then to ensure, as much as possible, that they are allowed to do so.

In our view, however, the post-1945 move to codifying the idea of respect into personal rights that could be legally defended only serves to reduce the import of respect as a useful idea to guide policy. While it may serve to restrain those "cold monsters," and they certainly must be restrained for they impinge on the freedoms of others rather than enhance them, it turns what should be social debate into a judicial contest. It places excessive power in constitutional courts that opine and *rule* on the legality of legislation and liberty. For example, the US Supreme Court has increased the range of actions by which organizations, including corporations, are able to influence voters' choices, thereby damaging democracy by making it appear that the nation's "laws are being bought and sold."[33] It arrived at this anti-liberal end through a long line of precedent-expanding decisions from the initial conception that corporations had to be "persons" under the Constitution in order to be held to contractual obligations. Sometimes it appears to those of us without legal training (and therefore without the distortions of the legal mind) that "the law is a ass—a idiot."[34] From a liberal perspective, it certainly is when it is used primarily to define the outcome of debate rather more than the manner in which it is conducted.

Liberal Capitalism

Liberalism must lead to capitalism for, as Smith argued, capitalism is only the extension of liberal principles into the realm of economics. We opened this chapter with a couple of statements from his *Theory of Moral Sentiments*, and it is appropriate to conclude it with them in their fuller context:

> Nothing is so mortifying as to be obliged to expose our distress to the view of the public, and to feel, that though our situation is open to the eyes of all mankind, no mortal conceives for us the half of what we suffer. Nay, it is chiefly this regard to the sentiments of mankind, that we pursue riches and avoid poverty. For to what purpose is all the toil and bustle of this world? what is the end of avarice and ambition, of the pursuit of wealth, of power and pre-eminence? . . . what are the advantages we propose by that great purpose of human life which we call bettering our condition? To be observed, to be attended to, to be taken notice of with sympathy, complacency, and approbation, are all the advantage which we can propose to derive from it.[35]

It is "natural" to desire to attract the approval of others, and this desire is a social cause of economic activity. Capitalism, therefore, is a "natural" application of liberalism to the production and exchange of goods and services. In other words, Smith expected that capitalism would follow the dictates of liberalism. We might consider this to be an ideal Liberal Capitalism, what capitalism would look like in its "natural state" stripped of more than two hundred years of political tinkering and accumulated market power.

In the next chapter we consider how Liberal Capitalism might combat the social and environmental challenges that have evolved because of two centuries of self-interest and consequent power distortions to Smith's ideals. This gives us a baseline from which we can measure how much and why today's capitalism has been distorted by the self-interested power and ideological conflicts we track through much of the rest of this book. And how we might turn instead to a capitalism based on liberal wellbeing.

Chapter 3

The Present and Future Challenges of Liberalism

Liberalism is famously flexible: it has always adapted to changing conditions. The natural tensions between the four guiding ideas outlined in chapter 2 allow it to emphasize different aspects at different times to rebalance the relationship between them. In doing so it tries to figure out "who shall govern, who shall be governed, and to arrange the actual working of the constituted power" when the critical issue is the "exact sphere to which the government, once constructed, should extend or confine its operations."[1] Just as there is always a tension between capitalism and democracy that must be reconciled, so there is between the rule of the majority and the freedom of the individual. So, when mass democracy threatened homogenization of ethics and culture, the concern was to prevent granting excessive power to the populace and to respect individuality. The alternative extreme is rule by the few over the many.

These tensions can be seen throughout history. The great inequality and mass misery of the working class brought forth by the Industrial Revolution favored progress and economic efficiency but weighed heavily and terribly against respect for the individual. In 1848 and 1870 it also threatened the extreme conflict of revolution in countries across Europe. Later, liberalism favored government power to protect society. Then, in response to the Great Depression, liberalism favored government intervention to support the individual and reignite progress, exemplified by the economics of John Maynard Keynes and the New Deal of Franklin Roosevelt. After World War II such thinking morphed into the welfare state designed around "a comprehensive policy of social progress" with this "social security . . . achieved by co-operation between the state and the individual" designed so as not to stifle "incentive, opportunity, [and] responsibility."[2] Similarly, and more recently, when the Great Recession hit and COVID-19 spread rapidly around the world, governments opened their purses to maintain their nations' economies. In the case of the latter crisis, they notably moved swiftly in many countries to support workers whose jobs would be ended by lockdowns to prevent the spread of the virus.

Liberalism now faces substantial new challenges. First, it must relieve the social suffering from decades of drift toward CorpoCapitalism. In many countries people are less happy than their national wealth suggests they should be. They are prevented from, or not supported in, enjoying wellbeing. But wellbeing may be a casualty of the second challenge, which is the existential threat of climate change. How can power, particularly the power of the state, protect individual autonomy and underwrite progress while ensuring the survival of human life and promoting individual wellbeing? We provide some suggestions in later chapters, but in this one we tease out the relevant issues in more detail. We also consider the other major challenge of ICT, AI, and the automation of production that may radically change power relations and inequality in society and threaten large swathes of the population with unemployment. How can progress respect individual autonomy and project the power of AI for social good? But first, we consider the strong evidence of broad dissatisfaction with the social effects of modern capitalism. This is because the challenges we face must be politically placed in this context; if the existing dissatisfactions are not properly understood from a liberal perspective, then they cannot be properly addressed. And if they are not properly addressed, the other challenges may threaten the destruction of both the natural and social worlds. Therefore, the guiding ideas of liberalism must be the framework for meeting all of these challenges.

Governing Happiness

We have defined liberalism in general terms as providing the space for liberty. In the rich countries today, this becomes *providing the opportunity for each person to pursue his or her wellbeing*. Hence, our definition of Liberal Capitalism. There are two ways to understand and research wellbeing. The most common way is to think of wellbeing as happiness, a goal. For liberalism, it is more appropriate to understand wellbeing as a process of becoming the best version of oneself that one can be and fulfilling one's potential.[3] Happiness, or "hedonic wellbeing," is more accessible for governments but ultimately less satisfying for individuals.

The move toward CorpoCapitalism began in the late 1970s, after the post–World War II economic boom ended in "stagflation." Led by the UK and US, countries began to "free" the market from the presumed "dead hand" of governmental power. The overt objective of this withdrawal of government was to increase the rate of economic growth in the belief that "a rising tide raises all boats." Promoters of "free markets" essentially argued that as long as Gross Domestic Product (GDP) continues to grow, all will be well, and happiness will spread throughout the land. They presumed that income and happiness are directly related. If the national income rose, everyone would be able to enjoy more of the goods and services that capitalism so abundantly produces. In turn this growth in demand would increase employment opportunities and raise incomes for everyone, which then further increases demand in a virtuous circle or "positive feedback loop."

Unfortunately, things have not worked out as promised. Even as the US' GDP per capita nearly doubled between 1972 and 2016, its average happiness changed little. In 2016 it was only slightly above its 1972 level, having declined steadily after 2000.[4] Using official US government data, figure 3.1 shows a similar result. It had long been understood that richer countries usually are happier than poorer ones, but here was one rich country that was not getting much happier as it got richer. In fact, the US is notable for being richer but unhappier than many comparable countries. Figure 3.2 shows that the US has the highest net disposable income of all the larger rich countries (that is, excluding city-states like Luxembourg and Singapore). In other words, Americans on average have more money to spend on the fruits of capitalism than people in other countries, but this is not making them happier. Aside from the US, in general it seems that happiness initially grows at an increasing rate as income increases, but after a certain level of income is reached it grows at a decreasing rate and then levels off.

In sum, being poor does not make you happy, but being as rich as possible does not make you happiest. This is dubbed the Easterlin Paradox, named after Richard Easterlin, who observed that at a point in time happiness varies directly with income both among and within nations, but over time happiness does not trend upward as income continues to

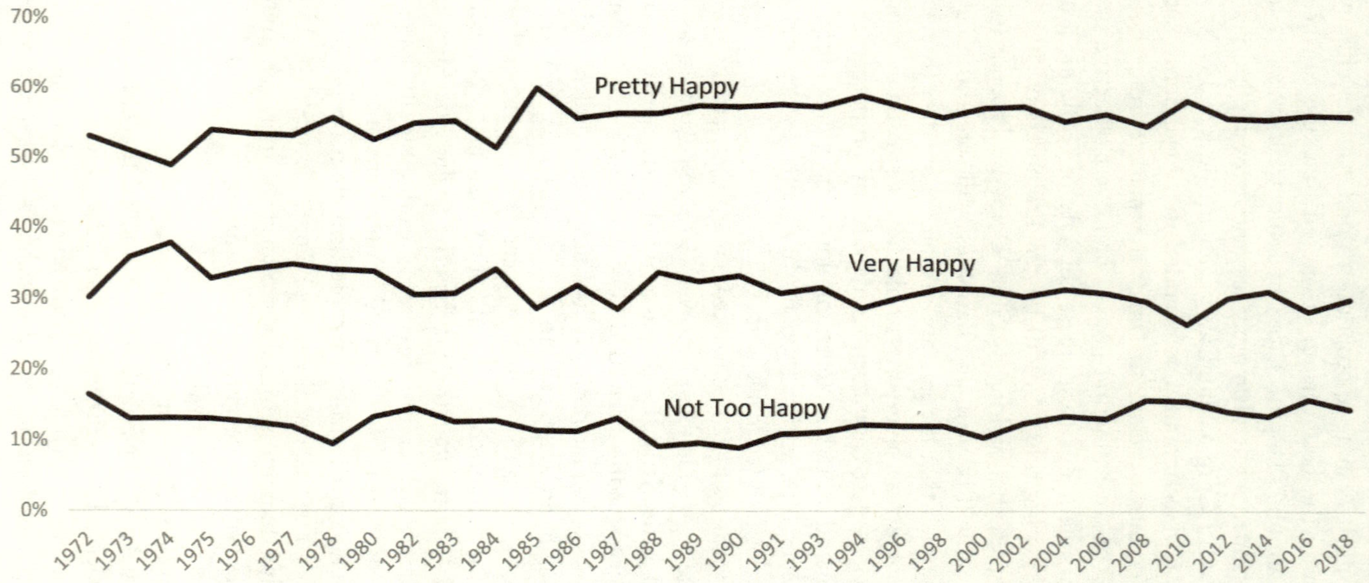

Note: Data from the US General Social Survey accessed at https://gssdataexplorer.norc.org/variables/434/vshow on 14 April 2020. The survey measures subjective happiness with this question: "Taken all together, how would you say things are these days—would you say that you are very happy, pretty happy, or not too happy?

Figure 3.1. Happiness in the US 1972–2018.

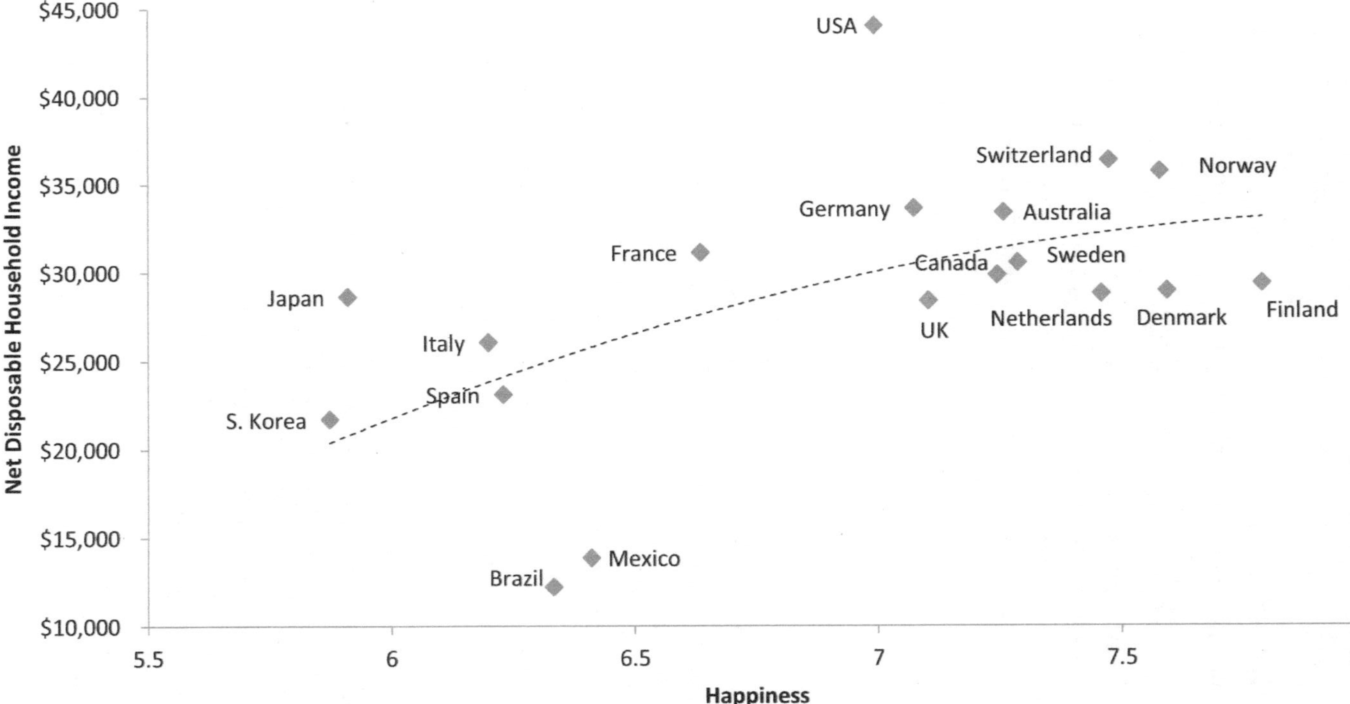

Note: The happiness measure is Cantril Life Ladder Data extracted from online data for chapter 2 of John Helliwell, Richard Layard, and Jeffrey Sachs, eds., *World Happiness Report 2018*, available at http://worldhappiness.report/ed/2018/. Net Disposable Household Income is taken from the OECD Better Life Index accessible at http://www.oecdbetterlifeindex.org/. A polynomial trendline is shown; countries above the line are less happy than their income would suggest.

Figure 3.2. Income and Happiness.

grow.[5] Assuming that "the individual is considered to be the best judge of his own feelings," Easterlin compared levels of happiness as recorded in cross-national surveys.[6] Subsequent research suggests Easterlin's Paradox has remained roughly true, showing that beyond a certain income level an increase in income produces a *decreasing* rate of growth in emotional happiness.[7]

Why might this be? A century ago, Arthur Pigou argued that economic welfare was not necessarily indicative of social welfare or "welfare at large" as he called it. Economic growth may negatively affect society so that "an economic cause may affect non-economic welfare in ways that cancel its effect on economic welfare."[8] In other words, in the rush for economic growth at all costs, the social costs in inequality, unemployment, or harsh working practices, for example, may be such that overall welfare falls. Even with these costs aside, at some point the ability to buy more and more material goods and services that are desired rather than needed becomes unsatisfying.

At the extremes of this argument, one might think that paraplegic accident victims would be much less happy than lottery winners. But research shows that this is not always true.[9] Researchers using open-ended questions to interview lottery winners and victims of accidents that had left them paraplegic have found that, as one might expect, winners rated winning as a highly positive event while the victims rated their accident as highly negative. But interestingly, both winners and victims found ordinary daily events *less pleasurable* than people from the same local area and with comparable demographics who had neither won the lottery nor suffered a crippling accident. In other words, both winning the lottery and being crippled made them less happy with their daily life!

The theory of "hedonic adaptation" might explain the reason why this is the case. Since it was first proposed in the 1970s, it has been tested many times and only slightly modified.[10] Essentially, it explains why buying "stuff" does not improve happiness. With every purchase in excess of basic needs for food, shelter, and clothing we get a "bump" in happiness. But our happiness quickly returns to the same level as it was before the purchase. For example, we buy the latest iPhone (or Manolo Blahnik shoes, Hermès Birkin handbag/purse, etc.) after queuing for hours and we are thrilled. But once we have it in our sticky hand and start to use it, soon it becomes just a phone, shoes to wear, or a handbag. Our happiness, which peaks at the purchase, dissolves back to our normal happiness level. The fleeting act of consuming does not generate lasting happiness. Indeed, psychological research has shown that being materialistic and just *believing* that buying stuff will make us happy, makes us unhappy.[11] CorpoCapitalism's focus on increasing economic growth as a way of increasing welfare can therefore be counterproductive as well as questionable for the strength of the link.

The annual *World Happiness Report*, which we used in preparing figure 3.2, measures "happiness" more broadly than other international surveys. It does not just "measure" self-reported happiness but calculates it based on a range of variables. And interestingly, about three-quarters of the variance between the overall measure of countries' happiness is explained by just six variables, only one of which is directly linked to the economy (GDP per capita).[12] The other variables are healthy years of life expectancy, social support, trust in government and business, perceived freedom to make life decisions, and generosity. Countries that scored highly on these reflect the age-old belief of gurus, mystics, philosophers, and wise old people in general, that there is more to happiness than money. There are many possible reasons for the large differences between countries that we cannot examine here.[13] But these findings support that view that there is more to wellbeing than money and the pleasure it can buy.

Happiness is about more than money, and wellbeing is about more than happiness. Wellbeing comes from the ability to pursue, and potentially realize, the continual, lifelong process of self-improvement that psychologists have dubbed "eudaimonia."[14] Aristotle used this Greek word to mean "living with reason in the pursuit of *arête* or personal excellence."[15] More recently Abraham Maslow described essentially the same process as "self-actualization."[16] Psychology research shows that although there is some overlap between hedonic and eudaimonic wellbeing, they are distinct paths to the "good life" where the latter path is longer and more durable.

The personal nature of eudaimonia by intrinsic motivation and effort rather than in response to external stimuli means that government cannot provide it. Governments and markets can provide hedonic wellbeing up to a point—for example, to raise people out of absolute poverty—but eudaimonia is a bridge too far. Yet, what government can do is prevent or enable the journey individuals make toward crossing that bridge. Because liberalism respects the individual and is focused on the wellbeing of everyone, it among all political *-isms* is uniquely able to avoid preventing eudaimonia and to potentially enable it. Progress need not be defined only in terms of GDP expansion but also through, for example, shorter working hours, greater income equality and social mobility, more opportunities for better social relations (for example, through improved city design), better trust in corporations and governments, affordable childcare services, and health services that lead to longer healthy lives for everyone. Countries like Denmark, whose government already provides many of these benefits, are consistently counted among the happiest because beyond happiness their citizens have the time and energy to improve their wellbeing.[17] Does that make Denmark liberal, when most of the literature counts it as among countries with more socialist motivations? In terms of the outcomes, the answer might be "yes."

Broad enjoyment of opportunities for wellbeing is the essential purpose of government. It can directly give to everyone neither wellbeing nor happiness, but by making the former more possible, it will raise the latter. This is a legitimate use of government power, for by respecting the needs of the people, it will prevent excessive conflict and increase social cohesion. And maybe address the other challenges we face.

Climate Change

"Beware, the end of the world is nigh!" This was the message that a man with a sandwich board once paraded along Oxford Street in central London. Everyone thought he was mad. But perhaps he was prescient, for that also is the message of *The Uninhabitable Earth* by David Wallace-Wells, one of the most recent warnings about a worst-case climate change scenario.[18] As we write this book much of the world is shut down as governments battle the COVID-19 pandemic. A pandemic is a low-probability but dangerous event, or in the immortal words of Donald Rumsfeld an "unknown unknown."[19] We do not know what it is or when it will arrive before it does. Climate change, however, is a known unknown: we know it will happen, its effects are already visible, but we do not quite *know* how and to what extent it will affect our lives. Sophisticated computer simulations employing historical data going back hundreds of thousands of years predict we could potentially see four to five degrees celsius of warming within the lifetime of someone born today, if we do not radically and quickly reduce emissions of greenhouse gases (GHGs). This means, according to Wallace-Wells, that "absent a significant adjustment to how billions of humans conduct their lives, parts of the Earth will likely become close to uninhabitable, and other parts horrifically inhospitable, as soon as the end of this century."[20] Because of the potential for positive feedbacks within the climate system, without action now a runaway vicious cycle of ever-warming interactions could drive an eleven or twelve degrees of warming sometime further in the future. But at just four to five degrees of warming New York would feel like present-day Bahrain, and wildfires would regularly consume Los Angeles while Miami sinks under the ocean. Whole cities, island nations, the White House, and as much as 5 percent of the global population would be flooded. Super-powerful hurricanes would be common, hunger rife, tropical diseases would break out in today's temperate zones and new diseases emerge, perpetual wars would rage, and the world would become half poorer. And capitalism would collapse, as the impact on the world's economy would not be temporary like the COVID-19 pandemic's in 2020. It would be permanent.

Wallace-Wells's message, and predictions like these, are alarmist. Like the man with the sandwich board, he declares, "It is, I promise, worse than you think"! But the message is not necessarily wrong. Through emissions of GHGs (for example, carbon dioxide, methane, and chlorofluorocarbons) since the dawn of the industrial age, humans have already raised the mean global temperature by one degree compared to preindustrial times. In its Fifth Assessment Report, the Intergovernmental Panel on Climate Change (IPCC) states in no uncertain terms that it is clear—in fact "unequivocal"—that human behaviors are influencing the climate system and that widespread impacts are already visible.[21] It warns that without substantial and immediate reductions in GHG emissions it is probable that people and ecosystems will suffer "severe, pervasive, and irreversible" impacts.[22] This is why for nearly thirty years, even as they have argued about how to do so, the nations of the world have agreed that they should cooperate to "stabilize greenhouse gas concentrations in the atmosphere at a level that would prevent dangerous anthropogenic interference with the climate system."[23] Since 2009 dangerous interference has been defined as an increase in average global temperatures of more than two degrees from preindustrial times.[24] In 2015, the world agreed to hold "the increase in the global average temperature to well below 2°C above pre-industrial levels and [pursue] efforts to limit the temperature increase to 1.5°C above pre-industrial levels."[25] But then in 2018 an IPCC report showed that even a 1.5 degree increase that could be reached within little more than a decade could incur substantial changes in local climates that would disorder food supplies, create mass poverty and starvation in some areas, and stimulate mass migrations.[26] Even for rich societies there will be substantial economic and social disruption.

The estimated economic costs of either mitigating climate change or doing nothing are much debated and dependent on a wide range of assumptions.[27] The *Stern Review* in 2006 calculated that climate change would reduce GDP each year forever by 5 percent.[28] Other analyses put the costs lower.[29] However, there is agreement that the economic cost of doing nothing will rise rapidly, and that if action is delayed the costs of mitigation also will rise.[30] This is why the IPCC concludes that avoiding dangerous climate change "will require an urgent and fundamental departure from business as usual" and "the longer we wait to take action, the more it will cost and the greater the technological, economic, social and institutional challenges we will face."[31]

Not everyone has seen the writing on the wall. The former president of the United States, Donald Trump, dismissed the alarming National Climate Assessment published by his own government in November 2018 with the words: "Yeah. I don't believe it."[32] President Trump's views aside, the political obstacles to a global compact are immense. One of the main reasons why is the ideology of CorpoCapitalism that has "infected" many policymakers who believe that economic growth today is essential and can only be delivered by MegaCorps that are unrestrained, and often proactively enabled, by government. A truly liberal government would use its power to transition the economy to secure its people from potentially disastrous changes that would limit their future wellbeing while mitigating as far as possible adverse economic and social effects today. This is merely respecting the people and their needs. But it also would support progress and avert future conflict.

AI, ICT, and Automation

Some rich countries have a declining working-age population and an increase in the old and retired. This is a path along which Japan has already traveled far, with Italy and Germany not far behind. Japan's population is already projected to fall, possibly by more than a quarter by the end of the century.[33] In part this is why Japan is at the forefront of robotics research today for automation is an appropriate response to a declining population. Yet, other rich countries are struggling with endemic unemployment and income inequality, which are often popularly blamed on immigration and globalization. The real target of popular wrath should be automation of production and specifically robots and artificial intelligence.[34] Unfortunately, because we cannot prevent the march of progress, nor as liberals would we suggest that it should be prevented, these challenges to social equanimity are only going to get worse in the short term unless they are addressed.[35]

Robots are already replacing workers. During the Great Recession, the US rate of unemployment jumped by nearly 6 percent.[36] Usually, when growth picks up after a recession, companies hire workers. But not this time. The reason why is that in the midst of the crisis 44 percent of US companies found ways to automate tasks that had previously been performed by people.[37] The result was that investment quickly returned to normal based on a preference by companies to increase production with machines instead of labor, while increased employment came later.

Because it is now easy to automate well-defined procedures and routine or repetitive tasks, lower-skilled occupations that require little social interaction or flexibility are increasingly seeing workers replaced by machines.[38] At the same time, the rapid growth of ICT has reformed business structures and whole markets. The accumulation of data is now the measure of corporations from retail to reinsurance, and from tourism to health care. It also is redesigning work patterns and supply chains. In some countries up to a quarter of all work is now in the "gig" economy of self-employed pieceworkers contracted by corporations in place of permanent employees and without any benefits. With ICT supply chains can now stretch around the world. The Big Five ICT MegaCorps—Alphabet, Amazon, Apple, Facebook, and Microsoft—are creating new industries and controlling (through purchase of innovative start-ups) much of the technological innovation in North America and Europe. China has its own dominant ICT MegaCorps competing for "eyeballs" in much of the developing world. The increasing domination of information sources and flows by ICT MegaCorps is a massive challenge for liberal conflict mitigation and respect of the individual and an aid to authoritarian governments as Orwell foretold.

Unemployment from technological innovation is only going to accelerate, as are its impacts on the workforce. For example, driving in traffic had long been thought to be beyond computers' capabilities and could not be automated.[39] But by the middle of 2018 Alphabet's autonomous cars had already driven more than eight million miles, averaging twenty-five thousand miles a day.[40] This could put anyone who drives a car, truck, or bus for a living out of work. It is not an isolated example. Carl Frey and Michael Osborne estimate that "about 47 percent of total US employment is at risk" from automation.[41] A study by OECD across all the rich countries concluded nearly half of all jobs could be affected by automation and 14 percent of all jobs are highly automatable, allowing employers to discard sixty-six million workers in thirty-two countries.[42] McKinsey, a champion and beneficiary of CorpoCapitalism, projects that by 2030 demand for technological skills (for example, coding), social and emotional skills (as in leadership, management, and caring services), and for higher cognitive skills (for example, creativity) will rise significantly. Demand will decline sharply for basic cognitive skills (data entry) and physical and manual skills.[43] Current trends will accelerate and "displacement will be concentrated mainly on low-skill workers, continuing a trend that has exacerbated income inequality and reduced middle-wage jobs. Automation also will affect sectors and countries differently but portend substantial social dislocation.[44]

In economic terms automation is a sure sign of progress and from a liberal perspective progress is desirable. But measuring it only in economic terms does not equate to the wellbeing of people, any more than increases in GDP are equivalent to increases in happiness. Liberal Capitalism therefore suggests that the introduction of automation should be slowed—for example, through taxation as Bill Gates has suggested—or by subsidizing labor.[45] We will consider some of the options in later chapters, especially chapter 10, but in either case, government intervention is necessary to head off excessive social conflict and suffering.

Preparing for a Liberal Future

Each of these challenges is better fought with Liberal Capitalism than CorpoCapitalism. Wellbeing is a "known known": we know there is a problem and essentially how to overcome it. All we need is the right guiding ideas for governments. Climate change is a "known unknown" that demands government power to preserve progress, secure wellbeing for all, and prevent excess conflict. Automation also is a known unknown but with very different probable consequences. On one hand it may produce much more leisure for all as Bertrand Russell and John Maynard Keynes both predicted nearly a century ago.[46] It also may alleviate the risk for aging countries of declining economic growth and deflation. But without the intelligent intervention of the power of government it easily could increase inequality, unemployment, and conflict.

For liberalism, progress is presumed to reduce conflict by improving the welfare of all. In the most CorpoCapitalist states economic growth is considered equivalent to progress. Yet, it is growth at all costs that has reduced happiness and wellbeing, warmed the climate, and threatens to replace millions of workers with robots. While blind economic growth at any cost promises progress, it actually threatens it through loss of respect for the individual, and social conflict that may overturn stable political systems. The consequences of government negligence may ultimately invite the application of potentially excessive government power. From a liberal perspective, to prevent social conflict and maintain wellbeing the question is not whether to use the power of government, but how much power is needed, what form it should take, and when it should be used.

All three challenges demand liberal governments use their power to mitigate their effects and increase wellbeing. Otto von Bismarck explained the role of modern governments in 1881 by arguing that they

> should cultivate the view also among the propertyless classes of the population, those who are the most numerous and the least educated, that the state is not only an institution of necessity but also one of welfare. By recognizable and direct advantages they must be led to look upon the state not as an agency devised solely for the protection of the better-situated classes of society but also as one serving their needs and interests.[47]

This is a reasonable definition of the purposes of liberal governments. Progress is desirable, but what can progress mean when struggling to avoid a dangerous change in climate while automation remakes economies and societies and changes the meaning of labor? Does an economy that insists everyone work for their living but discards workers on a whim in any sense respect individuals? If most people are mere cogs in the machine of industry, unsatisfied at work, and without meaning in their lives, what wellbeing do they have and what hope is there to contain conflict? The liberal answer is to redefine progress as raising individual happiness and wellbeing rather than solely as growth in GDP. This must mean providing adequate security against known threats to social order and individual wellbeing. In the next part we begin to consider how the dream of Liberal Capitalism has become the nightmare of CorpoCapitalism and accelerated all three of these challenges through the promotion and entrenchment of MegaCorps.

Part II

Losing Liberalism

Liberal Capitalism should be a system of political economy founded on constantly improving individual opportunity, and thereby wellbeing. "Free" markets would seem to be central to this vision, yet today capitalism is increasingly illiberal. "Free" markets grant freedom to whom under what conditions? Why has the pursuit of markets "free" from government oversight neither increased efficiency nor advanced wellbeing for most people? If efficiency grows the wealth of nations, why are so many people in the rich countries so unhappy that they resort to political populists? Do large corporations with international reach grow the wealth of nations yet diminish wellbeing? How can their influence on social outcomes be made more beneficial?

If power aids progress in capitalism, who should wield power over economic activity? Should governments use their power to guide corporations to contribute to addressing pressing problems, like the mitigation of climate change, or should they expect civic mindedness to change business practices and reduce corporate consumption of the Earth? Who should pay for the services government provides and govern its use of power?

Does work make us free or limit our wellbeing? Whose power should determine whether work controls life or contributes to wellbeing? Do social safety nets offset the negative impacts of economic distortions? Should they, or is that solely an individual concern? Does government have the responsibility to provide a job or income for everyone? Who should pay for government services, including the welfare state? Should so-called "liberal" states accept international competition on corporate tax rates or work together to prevent "tax shopping" by MegaCorps?

Chapter 4

MegaCorps

Malefactors of Great Wealth

Chapter 2 laid out the theoretical and ideological foundations for the arguments we seek to make in respect of Liberal Capitalism, and why it is desirable. Yet, as we also explained, the reality for most rich countries, as well as much of the world, is anything but liberal. Here we seek to build on these foundations to make a bold claim: that while great wealth is being produced by modern capitalism, it does not emanate from market forces. To the more revolutionary Marxist reader this will not come as a surprise. Yet to most others, particularly those like us who embrace the ideal of Liberal Capitalism, it will. This is because we are told all the time that we are living in an age of market forces. In fact, global market forces. So claimed Susan Strange at the end of the Cold War. She looked around at this globalized world emerging after the fall of the Eastern bloc and Communism as an alternative to liberal democracies, and pronounced what she said was a well-understood fact by "common people" with "common sense," but which scholars and policymakers were struggling to comprehend. "The impersonal forces of world markets," she wrote, ". . . are now more powerful than the states to whom ultimate political authority over society and economy is supposed to belong."[1] As she observed the seeming powerlessness of what had hitherto been sovereign states, she pronounced them as possessing the mere "façade of statehood."[2] She said that their citizens increasingly recognized the reality that states were impotent against market forces.

Were she still alive today, Strange would likely be unsurprised at the current plethora of surveys showing disenchantment with major parties, and even democracy itself. For "where states were once the masters of markets, now it is the markets . . . which are the masters over the governments of states."[3] The problem is global. As markets have mushroomed "what some have lost, others have not gained. The diffusion of authority away from national governments has left a yawning hole of non-authority, ungovernance it might be called."[4] People want their countries back, they want them to be great again, and they want new leaders who claim that with strong leadership this result can be delivered, even if the so-called experts claim that it is either impossible or undesirable.

But none of this is inevitable. Susan Strange wrote so vividly, and convincingly, that it is tempting to agree with her. Others write in similarly stirring tones, including Jagdish Bhagwati who celebrates the wealth and global development that globalization delivers for everyone on the planet, as well as Marxist critics who claim exactly the opposite is the result, like David Harvey.[5] And everyone in between contemplating the benefits, pitfalls, and policies necessary to govern a world of unbridled market forces whether they arose by political design or technological inevitability. There is no shortage of this literature, and it is not necessarily wrong, but the analysis is far too disembodied. Power does not go away. It is not diffused through the "system." It is not exercised impersonally. It is *possessed.* The actors that possess it are MegaCorps.

The purpose of this chapter is to expand on the nature of these MegaCorps and their power. It has been both taken from, and granted by, their governments that no longer govern states whose economies are underpinned by Liberal Capitalism. Instead, they have been transformed in the image of CorpoCapitalism. As such, MegaCorps are political actors both confronting and supporting states whose CorpoCapitalism they helped to create, and which now supports their interests. After explaining the implications of capitalism driven by MegaCorps, not markets, and a capitalism that is corporate, not liberal or neoliberal, we conclude that the concept of the so-called "free market" is defunct for understanding an economy dominated, at all levels, by MegaCorps. And that, ideologically as well as in reality, the results of this are exactly the opposite of liberalism's four guiding ideas outlined in chapter 2.

MegaCorps, Not Markets

We are accustomed to assuming that corporations are market actors, and therefore must possess market motivations. Rarely, if ever, do critics interrogate their political pathways to power. The critic may write that we live in a globalized world in which policies of privatization and deregulation have undermined the role of the state to the point where all states must don what Thomas Friedman famously dubbed economic "golden straightjackets."[6] In essence, states sacrifice the "clothing" of economic controls they once "wore," in all its variations (whether liberal, statist, socialist, or some other variation), and instead find themselves universally constrained by the disciplines of global, not national, markets. And by global economic institutions that promote globalization, like the World Trade Organization (WTO), International Monetary Fund (IMF), and World Bank. This is not a choice but a structural reality, because unlike the governments of states, multinational corporations (MNCs) are unconstrained by borders. Over time, they slip their territorial bonds and become global rather than national in their orientation as well as operations.

So, if MNCs' interests are not served by one state, they may go to one where they are. Therefore, the conventional wisdom is that politics is now more about markets, market *forces*, market *imperatives*, and market *realities*, than governments. Yet, corporations are not only market actors. As MNCs have grown in size as well as scope they have become so large that they are market controllers. Therefore, we call them MegaCorps. According to Peter Nolan, Dylan Sutherland, and Jin Zhang, by the end of the twentieth century no more than five MegaCorps controlled each of the world's major industries, with around a third of these industries having one corporation accounting for more than 40 percent of global sales.[7] According to Jonathan Tepper and Denise Hearn, this concentration has increased in the years since then.[8]

These authors give many examples of what this means in practice. For example, two MegaCorps make most of the beer consumed by Americans, three MegaCorps make nearly all the world's pesticides, and Apple and Google together account for most of the global app market. Now, this may not necessarily seem like a problem if you like the products and services offered by these MegaCorps. But if you do not, or you would like to exercise your rights in free markets, then it may be. And there is no doubt that your choices are usually extremely limited. They are between iOS or Android, Amazon Prime versus Netflix, Pepsi versus Coca Cola. Sometimes, consumers face an illusion of choice between products that are produced by the same MegaCorp, such as anyone trying to decide whether to choose a Skoda, SEAT, Volkswagen, or an Audi, when they are just four of the twelve brands of automobile produced by Volkswagen Group. Or tossing up the merits of Instagram versus Facebook when the former is owned by the latter. The world has come a long way from the scenario Adam Smith imagined of merchants competing based on the "invisible hand" of markets rather than the visible hand of the state. The contemporary reality is a visible handful of MegaCorps that do so instead.

Their size is astonishing. In 2015, the Fortune Global 500 companies together had sales totaling US$31.2 trillion.[9] Thus, they effectively accounted for nearly half of the global economy.[10] In fact, their sales were greater than the combined gross domestic product (GDP) of the bottom 138 states, and greater than the combined expenditure of the bottom 166 states. And their sales as a percentage of the GDP (or national income) are a good measure to compare the dominance of MegaCorps across countries, rather than that of value added, which economists commonly use. This is because these corporations are best seen as controlling the *networks* in which value is produced. For example, Walmart does not own any manufacturing operations but contracts over one hundred thousand suppliers that produce the products it sells.[11] Other MegaCorps like Apple, Gap, and Nike are also not fundamentally producers of goods themselves. They design them but their core function in the production process is the contracting and logistical management of their supply chains. They sit atop these chains, coordinate them, and therefore embody the value added of the firms that they contract and control within them. Trade within corporate supply chains is estimated to account for up to 80 percent of global trade and the trade statistics reflect intrafirm, more than interstate, patterns of economic interconnectedness.[12] Instead of measuring exports and imports between states, they reflect the strategic decisions of the management of MegaCorps.

The observation that states do not trade is not a new insight. Yet, it is often overlooked in debates about the pros and cons of trade agreements states negotiate. What is new is that trade no longer occurs on the basis of national comparative advantages, which the classical economist David Ricardo claimed should determine what goods are produced in which states.[13] Nor does it happen on the basis of merchants "preferring the support of domestic to that of foreign industry," as Adam Smith envisaged.[14] Instead, trade occurs through competition between the suppliers of intermediate goods and services to MegaCorps as part of the supply chains they control. These MegaCorps make the rules for their suppliers. They make their suppliers' market "forces" through contractual, and indirectly subcontractual, arrangements. In so doing, they also make the rules by which the global economy and trade relations are structured. The implications are considered in more detail in chapter 5, but for now the point is simply this: MegaCorps govern in addition to democratically elected governments.[15]

What then is the point of speaking of market forces, market imperatives, and the many issues associated with market-driven globalization? The vast swathes of analysis written on what these involve in theory and practice, and the complexities of their evolution over time has served to obscure the reality of MegaCorps' power. We know the MegaCorps' names, and their size relative to states and the various intergovernmental organizations that are often so much more the subject of political study. We also know that they dominate the markets for their goods and services. Finally, we know that they control not just how these markets work but how they are globally interconnected.

National CorpoCapitalism, Not Global (Neo)liberalism

This does not necessarily mean that governments are dead, dying, or becoming irrelevant. In fact, that is the last thing that MegaCorps, or rather those running and benefiting from them, would want because as an organizational form they are the legal constructions of states. If it seems as if they *act*, like persons, then this is because states have legally enabled and defined them this way.[16] The reality is that they do not have a separate life of their own, and that they do not have a separate existence apart from, or before, the national laws and regulations that provide the foundations for their operations. It certainly seems that way though, and it is not entirely inaccurate to say that MegaCorps have "taken over" to the extent that all governments serve as merely their "handmaidens."[17] Such a view is similar to the imaginary golden straightjacket noted earlier, in the sense that MegaCorps everywhere are able to get the government support they want regardless of where they operate or have interests. Therefore, they are as global as are the capitalist relations they desire and underpin. But our contention is that in reality these relations are CorpoCapitalist and that responsibility for their genesis as well as their endurance lies with the world's richest states.

Many studies demonstrate that territory still matters to MegaCorps. Alan Rugman and Alain Verbeke show that only nine of the Fortune Global 500 corporations have sales in so many regions of the world that they may be regarded as truly global. Three hundred and twenty of them still derive 80 percent of their sales from their home region, and twenty-five of those that appear to be global are more accurately binational or biregional.[18] The same may often be said of where their productive assets are located, as well as their ownership and control. For example, an analysis done by Clifford Staples of the world's eighty largest MNCs demonstrates that no more than 25 percent of their board members were of a nationality outside the home territory. Only in the case of 10 percent of them were the majority of board members from another nationality.[19] Other studies done on a regional basis say the same. For example, although it is sometimes claimed that over time there is a tendency toward greater multinationality on the part of board members as corporations' operations expand geographically, Kees van Veen and Ilse Marsman's study of European MNCs shows that the main way boards become more globalized is through mergers and acquisitions.[20]

This geographical spread itself is also not as great as often claimed. Despite over sixty years of a supposedly global neoliberal agenda, and claimed sacrifice of states on the altar of global markets, it remains the case that economically powerful states still account for 80 percent of world output, 70 percent of international trade, and up to 90 percent of foreign direct investment (FDI).[21] The FT Global 500 are responsible for at least 80 percent of the world's stock of FDI, around 70 percent of world trade, and 30 percent of the world's GDP,[22] and they are not placeless entities. Just ten states are the headquarters for 84 percent of them. The US alone accounts for 42 percent.[23] With the emergence of Brazil, Russia, India, and China (collectively known as the BRICs) as economic powers it may no longer be as true as it once was that "a statistical profile for the current corporation indicates that it is predominantly Anglo-American."[24] Lately, it is looking a lot more Chinese. But even so, it remains the case that the operational headquarters of MegaCorps are like a map of economic power for the world. The close correlation between national economic and corporate data demonstrates that the richest states house the most dominant MegaCorps.

This suggests that rather than the myth of a radical separation between private and public economic affairs, or a debate around the desirability of free or state-controlled markets—in other words, the old left-right division in politics—the reality is a handful of rich states mutually entangled with their MegaCorps. Now, it is almost impossible to make blanket statements about whether this means the home states of MegaCorps are in charge, or whether MegaCorps are in charge of their home states. It is also impossible to say whether the growth of these states' economic power was caused by the rise of their MegaCorps or vice versa. What can be said is that they got rich and strong together, and that as this has occurred there has been a steady growth in the *size* of government. Contrary to pronouncements about the demise of states and their shrinkage as they become economically straightjacketed in order to let global market forces rip, government expenditure in the G7, the world's richest countries, has actually grown from 37 to over 40 percent of GDP over the last fifteen years. The only countries where it has declined are the world's poorest ones, mostly in sub-Saharan Africa.[25]

If the rich countries' governments have been spending more, this begs the question: What are they spending their money on? In addition to being spent on all sorts of things, like social welfare programs, military investment, and so on, it is being spent on MegaCorps. For example, subsidies to the big players in the fossil fuel industries are worth anywhere between US$544 billion to US$1.9 trillion. That's around 3 percent of global GDP and 8 percent of all government revenues.[26] These are conservative estimates produced by international organizations like the International Energy Agency (IEA) and IMF, but the true amount is probably much more because there is no official global register of government handouts to all the industries involved. In addition, there are a range of tax breaks, preferential treatments (that is, protections), and other payments in-kind that are not included, but which should be, like government support for R&D (as discussed in chapter 9). There are also handouts to MegaCorps at the subnational level. Those by states and local governments in the US are estimated to be around US$45–80 billion every year. Many are in the form of tax breaks that go unreported, or which are not explicitly identified as public subsidies. This means that taxpayers do not know they are the ones paying.[27]

The 2008 Great Recession also showed the lengths that rich states' governments are prepared to go to support their MegaCorps. So big was the bailout that the Bank for International Settlements found that "governments became crucial during the crisis, as traditional sources of funding for financial institutions dried up."[28] The estimated combined expenditures of these eleven states totaled US$7 trillion.[29] This sum represented 19 percent of these states' combined GDP. It is likely that government expenditures to support businesses including MegaCorps during the current COVID-19 pandemic will dwarf those handed out after the Great Recession. An early list of the US companies prospering during the pandemic is dominated by ICT and e-commerce MegaCorps.[30]

For those states most severely affected, the outlays in response to the Great Recession were much larger. For example, the UK spent 44 percent of its GDP.[31] One might contend that the expenditure was necessary to prevent the collapse of the global financial system, but that would miss the point of where the benefits were really conferred. It was not spent on the financial system, nor on the global economy, and often not on those most severely affected by the crisis, for instance, people losing their homes. It was spent on a handful of banks, because on average 70 percent of the banking market in OECD countries is accounted for by their largest three banks, while globally fourteen banks dominate foreign exchange rate markets, and ten dominate global options markets.[32] The handouts to these banking MegaCorps resulted in the concentration of rich states' banking sectors actually *increasing* since the Great Recession.[33] The result is that in 2015 the top three UK and US banks together boasted assets of US$12.5 trillion, while the top ten in the world had combined assets of over US$25.9 trillion.[34] These top ten banks now hold assets equal to around 140 percent of the size of the entire US economy and 35 percent of the global economy.[35]

Governments can always find a reason to spend sums of money in support of their MegaCorps that would normally only be spent during war. What followed in countries like the UK was a politics of austerity as individuals in society picked up the check. It is a sweet deal if you can get away with it, because the crisis was an opportunity for MegaCorps to further ratchet up their market control with the help of their governments. But even absent a crisis, governments are spending handsomely in the service of MegaCorps. It could be argued that in the process they are serving their national interests too. Such is the function of CorpoCapitalism, but as will be shown in chapter 5 it does not necessarily follow that these interests are those of their citizens.

This behavior of governments is not what you would expect if they were stepping back to allow markets to work, free enterprise to flourish, and individuals to be supported in choosing how to meet their potential. Instead, the rich states have lavished spending on MegaCorps.

Changing the Debate

The liberal philosophy that was supposed to underpin capitalism no longer does. For the last four decades the ostensible focus of rich countries' governments has been on economic growth through markets, and the need to heed the "realities" and "laws" of these markets. This has blinded policymakers to the essential requirements of liberal philosophy, which is not about governments doing as little as possible, or supporting and lavishing payments on MegaCorps in order to serve "the market," but instead ensuring their citizens are as free as possible to act and choose in these markets. And not just in markets, but in other ways, though of course markets are a reasonable place to start for understanding what has been lost in respect of the dream of liberalism. For the reality is that many modern expressions of capitalism are not liberal, as in the case of China's variety of it. In the United States, the country that was founded on liberal principles, "liberalism" is now derided as comparable to socialism.

Because of the operations of MegaCorps, global capitalism is certainly no longer liberal. They are not simply market actors. And although they operate globally, or oversee global networks, they are not completely placeless either. In fact, the geopolitical patterns of power revealed as well as produced by MegaCorps mirror those of the rich states where they are headquartered. They reflect these states' power, potentially enhancing it while also being served by it. Putting these observations together suggests a need to change the debate about where political power lies between states and corporations. It suggests three implications.

First, the idea of the free market is contrary to the reality of corporate power. The growth of MegaCorps may have been aided by free-market policies, and the neoliberal ideology underpinning them, but their very nature undermines any vision of them as primarily competing in markets. Markets are neither free nor competitive. Most are controlled by MegaCorps. Far from being market actors, they are actually *anti-market actors* whose interests are served by ensuring markets do not become free and competitive. Heated debates about neoliberalism and neoliberal globalization serve to shroud this reality in a discussion about the pros and cons of competition, privatization, and deregulation. The reality is that CorpoCapitalism is characterized by both big government and big business and their mutually beneficial interactions. As explained in chapter 2, liberal governments are supposed to use their power to prevent any individual, group, or organization from dominating others. Yet, this is in fact exactly what MegaCorps are being permitted to do.

Second, this suggests a need to reembrace the role of rich states in counterbalancing the power of MegaCorps, rather than underpinning it. Liberalism opposes any excesses of power and the most readily available antidote to the growing power of MegaCorps is government. Doing so may seem problematic because it often looks as if national and corporate interests are mutually reinforcing. Yet corporations, whether MegaCorps or otherwise, require the legal support and national institutional structures in the states where they are embedded to function. The governments of these states are responsible for conflict mitigation, which as explained in chapter 2 entails civil power being employed to ensure justice and liberty, not power and control.

Third, if the governments of these states fail to do so, then it is a policy choice. CorpoCapitalism has come about *by design*, facilitated by debates about markets versus states that no longer ring true yet keep being rolled out to hide the reality. The reality is the subjugation of society rather than respect for, and empowerment, of individuals. Rather than enabling personal and collective progress, in a context of respect for ourselves and others, it seems like the interests of MegaCorps must come first or must, inevitably, be *served* regardless of what the people may desire. But rich states' choice of CorpoCapitalism in support of MegaCorps is neither inevitable nor desirable. When this choice is revealed as what it is, and debated for what it produces, then the solutions that could put us on the path to Liberal Capitalism will be more possible. Why it is so difficult to even get on this path is the focus of the next chapter.

Chapter 5

CorpoCapitalism and the Misery of Work

We have long been told that corporations "rule the world."[1] From chapter 4 it should be clear that the potential for this certainly exists, but that it is not inevitable without the help of states. This chapter is about their failures, especially the governments of the rich ones. As they have embraced CorpoCapitalism they have permitted the potential for the rule of the few over the many. As explained in chapter 3, they have done so by espousing the benefits of economic growth at all costs. They have done so in the hope that this will confer social as well as economic benefits. That is how it seems on the surface, and how it is usually ideologically defended. But the economic benefits are not enough.

Politically, CorpoCapitalism is about big government looking after the interests of big business, and it is far from clear that the interests of MegaCorps are equivalent to the needs of most people. They may occasionally coincide, but liberal democratic governments are supposed to enable the people that elect them to individually pursue their needs and wants. Governments are not supposed to be elected to serve MegaCorps in the hope that they will do this for their citizens. It is fundamentally illiberal to claim that this could, let alone should, be the case.

There are many ways we could consider the problematic nature of this state of affairs: of governments practicing CorpoCapitalism to support MegaCorps, and of MegaCorps taking over, or at least potentially fulfilling, the role of governments. But in this chapter, we focus on the most obvious impact of CorpoCapitalism: the misery of work in a world where markets are substantially controlled by MegaCorps. In so doing we build more concretely on the arguments made about happiness and wellbeing in chapter 3. We consider this from the perspective of workers in rich countries, poor countries, and the links between the two. We then look at the pros and cons of self-regulation, driven by MegaCorps' claims of corporate social responsibility (CSR). Increasingly it is argued that CSR can exert, or give rise to, private governance in respect of community concerns, but we explain why it is a fundamentally flawed alternative to government regulation. By its very nature it signals the end of free-market capitalism and democratic processes, and therefore cannot put us on the path to Liberal Capitalism on the basis outlined in chapter 2. We therefore conclude it is time for governments to do what they are meant to do: properly regulate corporate activity to enable the wellbeing of all.

The Misery of Work from Rich to Poor Countries

The mantra of modern working life is that we must all be involved in lifelong learning, so that we build up the skills necessary to embrace a plethora of opportunities in flexible labor markets. The days are gone when anyone can expect to land a steady, full-time job and to hold it for the duration of their working life, or at least a large portion of it. CorpoCapitalism is a principal reason why. Because governments are serving the interests of MegaCorps by cutting taxes, and deregulating the economy, people are meant to thrive through the opportunities that are "naturally" produced for them in the market by MegaCorps and many much smaller businesses.

The rewards are not so great though. Wage stagnation is a problem in most rich countries, but especially in the US. Between 1979 and 2014 there was no change in real wages for the lowest 10 percent of wage earners. This could be dismissed as not a big problem, because it could be contended that there are always boring or menial jobs that pay very low wages. It could also be argued that the workers doing these jobs suffer from a lack of skills. Unlike workers in poor countries, they have the opportunity to retrain, look for a better job, and if this seems difficult then it may be because of issues around labor and social mobility that are not necessarily caused by CorpoCapitalism. Fair enough, but it is also the case that over 2003–2013 there was flat to *negative* wage growth in real terms for the bottom 70 percent of US wage earners.[2] Add to this the growth in temporary workers in the "gig" economy, or those on short-term contracts, plus the role of private employment agencies as allocators of workers to positions, coupled with attacks on organized labor (including the right to strike) and you can see why the results produced are the consequences of government policy, whether by design or by neglect.

Uber is the perennial example of what work for low wages and uncertain conditions means in practice. Uber is a global brand, and a would-be MegaCorp. It is often cast by business commentators as an example of "disruptive innovation," a product of the ICT revolution that is shaking up personal mobility.[3] While the extent to which it is a "game changer" is still being debated, to most of us it is just another way of ordering a taxi. However, to those doing the driving it means bringing their own car, taking their own risks, driving whenever necessary to take care of their own needs, and suffering all the consequences if things go wrong. But while its drivers might be facing the market forces of customers' demands, in the markets where Uber operates it is substantially monopolizing the provision of the service they provide and driving down fares to potentially bankrupt competitors.

The situation is similar if you work for one of the MegaCorps that actually provides a place you go to for work. Without sufficient government regulation of labor practices or the protection of unions—emasculated in several countries, and most especially in the US—increasingly workers labor under the threat of being discarded by their employer. Amazon is emblematic of what this looks like in practice. It is not just a controller of markets, or a dominator of its industry. It is an intersectoral consolidator across industries including content creation, publishing, retail, streaming services, and groceries. It also is a significant provider of less visible services like health care through medical supplies to hospitals and clinics, and cloud computing services with AI for patient care, and most recently by opening its online pharmacy.[4] It then charges prices so low that only other MegaCorps like Walmart in retail or Microsoft in cloud services can compete. So, the MegaCorps carve up industries between them to their shareholders' benefit: Amazon and Microsoft each have a market value of well over US$1 trillion, Apple more than US$2 trillion, and Walmart nearly US$500 billion. Their customers benefit too but for their employees, or their many contract workers, the picture is not so rosy.

A worker in one of Amazon's "fulfilment centers" interviewed for an article by Patrick Hatch described the working environment as a "hellscape." Employees are given a scanner, and as soon as one item is scanned, a solid bar on the bottom of the screen immediately starts to count down, showing how much time they have to reach their next item. It could be anywhere in the twenty-four-thousand-square-meter warehouse. Workers literally jog around about twenty kilometers a shift at "Amazon pace," and they are monitored for every second of their working day. If they do not perform at a certain level, they are sacked. There is not much they can do about it, as employees are hired for Amazon by the Swiss private hiring company Adecco. They could try negotiating with Adecco for better conditions, but then they might not get the job. They are also afraid that if they get a bad name or lose their job, they will not get future contracts. The result is that a MegaCorp is hiring workers for another MegaCorp, and between them they underpin the rules for workplace relations.[5]

Amazon illustrates the situation in rich countries, and it is just the tip of a large iceberg of labor exploitation because the situation is always worse in the poorer ones. The research of Genevieve LeBaron shows that forced labor is a key aspect of most MegaCorps' business models and supply chains. Forced labor involves coercion, compulsion, and deception through practices like debt bondage, manipulation of contracts and credit, and threats of violence. She finds such practices confer at least US$44 billion in profits and affect at least twenty-one million people worldwide.[6] The problem is no doubt more widespread than this, but like the huge handouts of public money to MegaCorps mentioned in chapter 4, there is a lack of formal reporting.

It is surely part of the reason why inequality is a scourge of our modern world. Even if globalization "works" as Martin Wolf says it does to develop the economies of poorer countries, it remains the case that on many measures global inequality has worsened quite dramatically.[7] The distribution of global wealth is so iniquitous that 0.7 percent of the world's population controls 44 percent of the world's wealth, while 70 percent of the world's population has less than US$10,000 to their name.[8] In 2019 the richest 1 percent owned 44 percent of the world's wealth and it is likely that during the COVID-19 pandemic in 2020 the rich gained proportionately more wealth than the poor, thereby increasing wealth inequality.[9] Globalization is not necessarily the problem, or rather it might not be such a problem, if it did not work the way that it actually does: through MegaCorps' control of not just local and national but global labor markets and labor conditions through contracting and subcontracting arrangements. These mean that many of the world's workers are not employed in some postindustrial, disruptively innovative, gig economy. Instead, they inhabit an industrial dystopia where workers compete for small pay against other workers, and not just in the same country but worldwide.

We only notice their suffering when there is a catastrophic accident, like the collapse of the Rana Plaza garment complex in Bangladesh in 2013. This was a substandard eight-story, commercial building that was shoddily built. It eventually collapsed, killing workers making clothes for various brands we all know well, like Benetton, Monsoon, Walmart, Mango, and Primark. Around 1,100 died and 2,500 were injured. Most were women, and many children in nursery facilities while their mothers worked also died.[10]

Whom should we "blame" for the conditions under which workers like these labor and die? Global capitalism seems far too nebulous. Perhaps the Bangladeshi government because much of the building was illegally constructed? Yet, like many governments in poorer countries it does not have the resources to enforce safe working conditions. Certainly, the contractors, and their subcontractors subsequently hired to fill orders, should bear some responsibility. But ultimately it must be the fault of the MegaCorps to whom they supplied the goods. MegaCorps profit from global supply chain networks, of which the Rana Plaza complex was a part. They "sit" atop them, so they surely bear responsibility for knowing and regulating who is making their products and under what conditions.

Workers in both rich countries and poor ones are not enslaved. They are not in irons, and they *do* benefit economically from working for MegaCorps' or for the contractors and subcontractors that supply them. But they have almost no say, let alone control, over their working conditions. Governments underpinning MegaCorps through CorpoCapitalism in rich countries have consciously dealt themselves out of the solutions, while those in poorer ones have trouble dealing with the consequences. This therefore begs the question, should MegaCorps do something about this without the heavy hand of government regulation?

The Potential for Self-Regulation

As we showed in chapter 4, because MegaCorps control their industries, the visible hand of the state has not been replaced by the invisible hand of the market. It has been replaced by the visible hand of these

MegaCorps and their government conspirators. And it is not just the markets for their goods and services that they control, but the markets for the production of them. The result is that there is the growth of what John Braithwaite has dubbed "regulatory capitalism."[11] His argument is that instead of more market forces, more market freedoms, and more competition in them—that is, more Liberal Capitalism—we instead have market control by MegaCorps that results in private, rather than public, governance being necessary as part of the solution to all sorts of problems from the national to global level. It is not enough to say business should be involved in delivering the solutions. Business *must* be, and if it is then it is a source of governance beyond and between the territories of different states.

This is the hopeful flipside of arguments made about powerless states in the face of global market forces. It holds that the desirable social outcomes, in addition to the economic ones, that states can no longer regulate for will have to be taken care of by MegaCorps. And they have been saying that they are delivering these since the 1990s when they started producing reports on their good works and social concerns. They started casting themselves as "citizens," driven by a belief in CSR that sees them as servants of the public good, in addition to mechanisms of profit maximization. Fast forward to 2019 when the CEOs on the Business Roundtable, a group representing MegaCorps, actually declared that their primary purpose is no longer to maximize profits in order to serve shareholders' interests, as the influential economist Milton Friedman declared in 1970. Instead, it is to deliver benefits to stakeholders, very broadly defined. In fact, anyone affected, or potentially affected, by their MegaCorp's business. In other words, to serve the interests of society.[12]

Now, it may seem naïve to uncritically believe these rich and powerful corporate leaders, just as it is to put faith in the pronouncements of politicians. Yet, there are two solid material (that is, financial) reasons why you might: strengthening brand value to serve the interests of shareholders by attracting the best staff, being able to extract a price premium, and engendering customer loyalty; and preventing unwanted regulatory intervention. MegaCorps can embrace CSR for strategic advantage, increasing their profitability while claiming they require no regulations imposed in how they do so.

That is a little less naïve, and if there are beneficial outcomes for society then this would be a good thing. But as we have been at some pains to point out, it is surely doubtful that the interests of MegaCorps and the public at large are usually synonymous. In fact, surveys of business leaders themselves give the lie to their own pronouncements. For example, the Fortune 500 World's Most Admired Companies list is compiled annually based on questionnaires provided to corporate leaders. What is striking about the top five most admired companies is that *none* of them are ranked as such for the criterion of "community responsibility." These firms' rankings are derived mostly from other attributes, particularly management quality, quality of products/services offered, innovativeness, and soundness of financial position. They are admired for focusing on more traditional financial measures of success.[13]

In respect of regulatory intervention, it also takes no great leap of logic to conclude that the intention behind CSR commitments is to ensure that CSR does not stand for "Crisis Scandal Response" when things go wrong and to hide what they do as opposed to what they say.[14] For example, a study by Angela Davis, David Guenther, and Linda Krull demonstrates that companies with the most extensive CSR programs are also those with the most aggressive tax minimization activities. They conclude not only that "the payment of taxes is not viewed as an important socially responsible activity" but also that "CSR and taxes act as substitutes rather than complements."[15] In other words, CSR primarily serves the function of "window dressing."

It might be contended that this is true for paying taxes, but not necessarily in general, because the reason why MegaCorps do not want to pay taxes might be that they are already fulfilling their social responsibilities. They care so much that they want to look after social concerns in the way that governments used to do. This is what Apple says. It has accepted well-documented exploitative practices in its global supply chain, particularly scandals surrounding employment conditions in Chinese factories manufacturing its products. The conditions at Foxconn Technology, which manufactures its iPhones, received a lot of attention a few years ago. Workers were reported to be living in cramped, unhygienic dormitories and suffering from sleep deprivation because they work up to one hundred hours per month of overtime for very low pay.[16] In 2010, thirteen workers died from seventeen suicide attempts between January and November. The company responded by installing safety nets at some of its dormitories to catch the falling bodies. The bad publicity resulted in "ritual burnings" of pictures of iPhones in Hong Kong demonstrations and a university study of the abusive practices endured by workers at twelve Foxconn factories that characterized them as "labor camps."[17]

Apple's CEO Tim Cook was so appalled that he visited China in person. Independent observers were also sent to the factories, audits were conducted, and demands made by Apple that conditions be improved.[18]

Maybe Apple's response explains why it did not suffer much of a backlash in terms of its financial performance for what might be regarded as its Rana Plaza moment. But we think Susan Adams is more correct when she noted at the time that "Apple is such a hugely popular company and the buzz around the new iPhone is so great, reports of continued worker abuse will not dampen the public's enthusiasm for Apple products or affect the company stock price."[19] Far from suffering negative impacts, in the years following revelations of the suicides, Apple was the world's most profitable phone manufacturer.[20] Therein lies the rub. The problem with CSR is that you do not have a lot of choice if you are an Apple phone user, embedded in the Apple world. Just as you do not have much, or sometimes no, choice of which airline to fly on many routes, or buy all your products and services from Amazon online, or need a ride and book an Uber. The problem is a lack of choice, a lack of free markets, which is why CSR is antithetical to the market drivers that are supposed to underpin it.

Who Governs?

CSR and the potential for self-regulation should not just be debated for the extent to which they can solve problems that were once thought by the likes of Milton Friedman to be the responsibility of government. They represent nothing less than a struggle over the central question in politics: Who governs? As Doris Fuchs notes in *Business Power in Global Governance*, corporations can seek to influence governments through lobbying and personal connections. The result is a "revolving door" rather than a separation between business and government. They also tend to get what they want because of their economic dominance. The result is that big business occupies a "privileged position" by comparison to other voices in society. But the political prize MegaCorps seek is to be in a position where their concerns do not just have to be taken into account, but where they are entitled to make the rules rather than influence how the rules are made: to self-govern.[21]

We should be under no illusions. The concentration of wealth and ownership—in market and geographical terms—outlined in chapter 4 means that MegaCorps *can* dictate the rules of global production, given weak(ened) national and even weaker international governance, which means that labor exploitation is both viable and profitable. And they *do*. But it does not mean they *should*, and it certainly does not mean that they *must*. The reason that they are now in this position is the massive political, economic, and ideological project of global sweep and reach designed to free up market forces that rich states embarked on from the 1970s to the 1980s—that is, what, as we noted in chapter 1, is often called neoliberalism, though as we have shown quickly morphed into CorpoCapitalism. What it ensured instead is the control and manipulation of markets for private, as opposed to the public, good.

If MegaCorps are to provide the solutions, the results can only be less than what is required. For example, MegaCorps' audits of their operations, like Apple's annual *Supplier Responsibility Progress Report*, seem like a way of identifying why work is miserable and what can be done about it.[22] But audits such as these are voluntary, and not mandated by legislation. Also, there is no legal requirement that any identified failures be corrected. They are done by private professional services firms, often one of the Big Four, which are PricewaterhouseCoopers (PwC), Ernst and Young (EY), Deloitte, and KPMG. These are MegaCorps themselves, and together they audit 99 percent of the corporations on the FTSE 100 Index. They also offer a variety of consulting services (including on tax minimization) to the world's largest global corporations—for example, PwC provides services to 429 of those listed in the Fortune Global 500.[23] So, there is reason to suspect that they may not be sufficiently independent (and therefore critical) of the MegaCorps that are their source of income. Like MegaCorps hiring workers for other MegaCorps (as with Adecco for Amazon), in this case MegaCorps are auditing other MegaCorps. Thinking about where their interests lie, it is easy to reach the view that the vast majority of social or ethical retail audits are "not trying to find things out, they're trying to prove that something is not there."[24]

The results need to be debated not just in terms of efficacy, but in terms of democratic legitimacy: who governs and who *should* govern. Whether it is desirable that MegaCorps do what democratically elected governments are meant to do. We say that they should not, because we agree with Adam Smith that "the mean rapacity, the monopolizing spirit of merchants and manufacturers, who neither are, nor ought to be, the rulers of mankind, though it cannot perhaps be corrected may very easily be prevented from disturbing the tranquility of anybody but themselves."[25] However, the reality is that this is exactly what is happening. Markets have been *allowed* to become ever more concentrated not because of market forces but, as Colin Crouch points out, through government-approved mergers and acquisitions that were held to increase efficiency or initially reduce consumer prices.[26] Maybe they sometimes do, and maybe they sometimes do not, but what we know is that they always limit choice and keep out competitors. Eventually they allow prices to be raised. As wages stagnate and workers' conditions deteriorate, MegaCorps have done so to the extent that a study by Jan de Loecker and Jan Eeckhout estimates corporate markups in the US were relatively steady at around 18 percent up to 1980, but that the market power produced by corporate mergers is correlated with markups increasing thereafter to 67 percent by 2014.[27] In sum, MegaCorps have been enabled by governments to disturb the tranquility of everybody but themselves and their shareholders.

Get Back in the Regulatory Ring

Chapter 4 concluded with the need for states to reembrace their role in counterbalancing, rather than underpinning, the power of MegaCorps. This would be the first step in getting on the path to Liberal Capitalism. It is hardly a radical suggestion, because free-market economists in the vein of Milton Friedman would surely blanche at the idea of corporations possessing the right, let alone the obligation, to act in the interests of society as opposed to shareholders. He would turn over in his grave at the notion that they bear responsibility for the happiness and wellbeing of society as a whole! In fact, the other side of the coin to his declaration that "the social responsibility of business is to increase profits" was that it was the social responsibility of governments to regulate in the public interest. Business has a responsibility to obey the resulting laws.[28] If those laws are about enabling and protecting business, especially big business, while reducing civic protections, then it is anything but clear this is what Friedman had in mind, even if it may be correct to point out that it was the result of his argument. No true liberal who believes in markets and market forces would ever want this.

The liberal thought that was supposed to underpin such a view no longer does so. The focus of rich countries' governments on economic growth through markets has blinded policymakers to the liberal obligation to ensure their citizens are as free as possible to act and choose in these markets and in their lives in other ways.

As explained in chapter 3, governments therefore need to act. This is because broad enjoyment of opportunities for wellbeing is the essential liberal purpose of government. To reduce the misery of work, rich countries' governments must ensure that the exploitation of workers is not going on within their borders. They should also act to ensure, as far as possible, that MegaCorps headquartered in their territories are not behind the modern miseries of work in poorer ones. Poor countries' governments do not have as much leverage against MegaCorps, which is why global governance underpinned by rich countries is required to ensure living wages and conditions, especially in factories that are part of big brands' supply chains. Trade based on comparative advantage is problematic enough given MegaCorps' strategic control of these supply chains, rather than the market forces created by free trade between states. But at the very least it should not be based on either forced or unfree labor. If a global agreement can be reached, along with requirements and restrictions on subcontracting, with penalties on corporations for noncompliance, as is the case for trade distortions in the WTO, then we might yet be able to build a liberal, rather than CorpoCapitalist, world order. But let us not get too ahead of ourselves. Before such possibilities can be considered, in chapter 6 we first look at the national institutional changes that are necessary.

Chapter 6

Providing for Individual Wellbeing

Everyone in a democratic country would probably agree that it is desirable for individuals to be free to make well-informed choices. Yet, as we know from chapters 4 and 5, markets are neither free nor competitive. In markets and beyond them, individuals are unable to make all the choices they might like to make, let alone those that are desirable for addressing the world's present and future challenges. CorpoCapitalism ensures this is the case as governments protect and subsidize MegaCorps. These in turn limit and define the choices individuals can make in both their consumption and employment. Although this is the reality of the world in which we live, it is not inevitable. It has been a political choice, and other choices are possible. As they are made, they should address the central dilemma for every rich country, which is how to maintain or improve wellbeing for everyone.

This is hardly a new idea. Nor is it a new observation that for capitalist democracies it is a tricky one, because as we have shown capitalism and democracy have an uneasy relationship. Too much of one tends to limit the other. Their goals are fundamentally at odds, and therefore must be reconciled. Liberals believe that this is done through the construction of institutions. Institutions are not simply formal organizations, like parliaments and government departments, nor formal laws and regulations. They are also the culturally based informal "rules of the game," or what may be thought of as "standard operating procedures"—what might be expressed as "how we do things here"—that give rise to the laws and legislation by which organizations operate. The definition of institutions used by Peter Hall and David Soskice in the introduction to their seminal book on *Varieties of Capitalism: The Institutional Foundations of Comparative Advantage* is probably the most useful. They say that institutions are "a set of rules, formal or informal, that actors generally follow, whether for normative, cognitive, or material reasons."[1] So, institutions are the rules that societies make because they believe them to be right, because they think about the issues they face in a certain away, and because they believe that acting in a certain way produces beneficial results.

The reason why liberals in particular like institutions is that unlike authoritarian regimes—for example, China, or historically South Korea—they do not embrace the notion of strong leaders and strong governments that "get things done" regardless of their citizens' concerns, desires, and rights. Instead, they want formal institutions (such as laws and regulations) and informal institutions (including culturally based, implicitly agreed procedures) to ensure the rule of law, open debate, transparency in decision-making, and accountability for the decisions made, in the hope that these will promote the guiding ideas of liberalism: conflict mitigation, power prevention, personal and collective progress, and respect for every individual.

CorpoCapitalism does not do this because it is not liberal. Yet, it has sprung from countries that espoused a belief in liberal principles and has become deeply institutionally embedded in them. That is a huge problem, because the institutions that successive governments design are implemented and embedded in social, economic, and political systems over a long historical period. They become the conventional wisdom. They have a "taken-for-grantedness" about them. They are resistant to change. So, therefore, now is CorpoCapitalism. If radical changes in a country's policies are difficult, then radical changes in their institutions that inform these policy choices are harder still.

With the difficulties of institutional change in mind, this chapter looks at the ways governments normally protect and expand individual wellbeing. Such efforts are not always flexible enough and sufficiently resilient to meet large challenges as they have appeared, like the 2008 Great Recession. Nor those that we must now face, like those identified in chapter 3. Any inability further harms individual wellbeing for many, and as in the past economic growth driven by consumption alone will not alleviate them. But crucially, in this chapter we show that given the defects in their current abilities to deliver opportunities for wellbeing, the conventional wisdom on social welfare that worked in the past in what are regarded as liberal states, are now inadequate. Therefore, we outline the paths of institutional changes that will be necessary in countries that once practiced Liberal Capitalism but now are CorpoCapitalist.

Social Welfare

Liberalism proposes progress as a way to reduce conflict and increase liberty. However, following Margaret Thatcher and Ronald Reagan this idea of progress has been widely interpreted, and narrowly defined, to mean that countries should increase economic growth. Like saying the best form of welfare is getting a job, it is claimed that the best way to increase social welfare is through growing the economy. Neither of these views is completely wrong. It is true that working is better than being on the dole (because apart from the monetary rewards, work provides structure to life and social connections), and life is generally better in an economy that satisfies more needs and wants than one that struggles to do so. Yet, it is also clear that economic growth on its own does not easily equate to happiness and wellbeing, as shown in chapter 3. And that it does not easily equate with the liberal idea of *progress* without the intervention of government power to distribute the benefits and inevitable costs fairly. Indeed, if we measure progress at the micro level of the individual, or even the municipality, economic growth for the country as a whole is often associated with a *decline* in wellbeing for large segments of the population if growth's benefits are not equally distributed. For example, America's former acceptance of open trade with China under WTO rules increased economic growth but has decimated some industries and towns in the US.[2]

The social impacts of growth-obsessed capitalism are not the same in every rich country either. Figures 6.1 and 6.2 compare income and wealth inequality for selected countries.[3] Few countries have collected class income data for long enough to be useful and only the US and France collected data before 1980 for the share of the lowest 50 percent of income earners. From the countries for which we have data we have selected Anglo-Saxon "market economies" such as the UK, US, Canada, and Australia as well as several European countries (and Japan for the top 1 percent) that have long been avowedly more egalitarian. Figure 6.1 shows that in nearly every country the top 1 percent increased their share of the national income after about 1979. The only outlier has

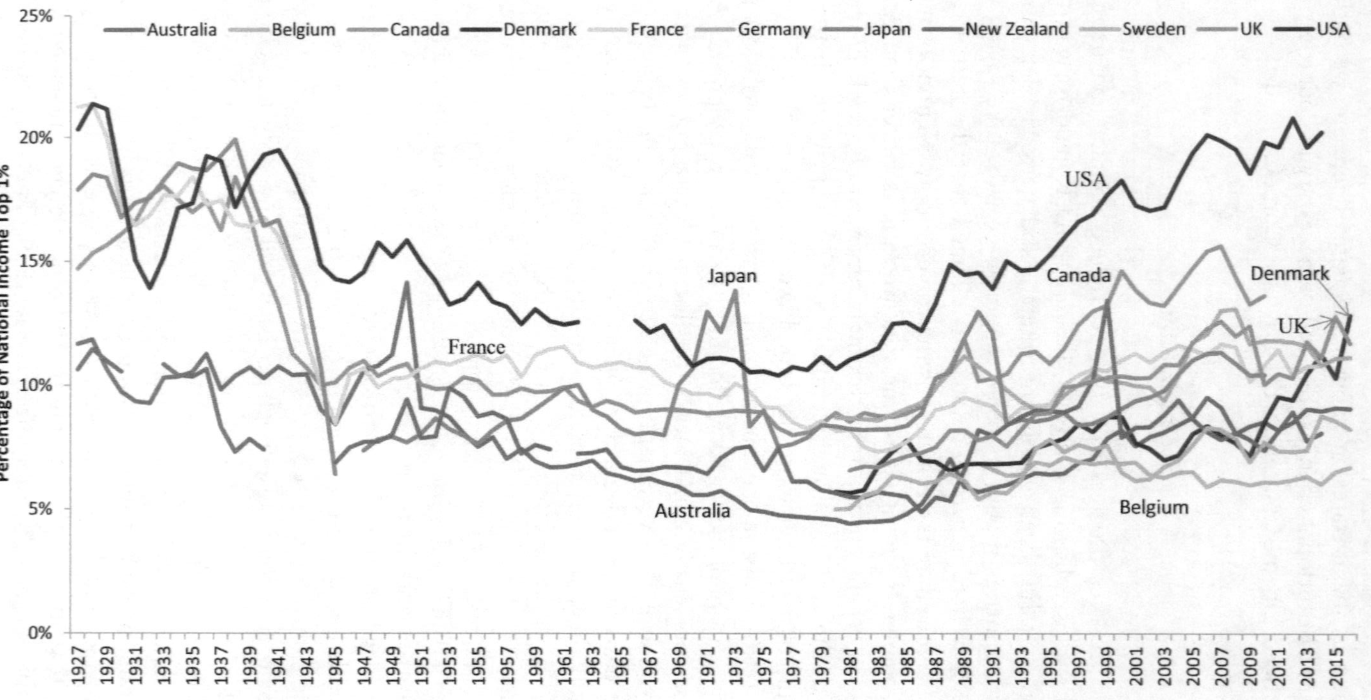

Figure 6.1. Top One Percent's Share of National Income.

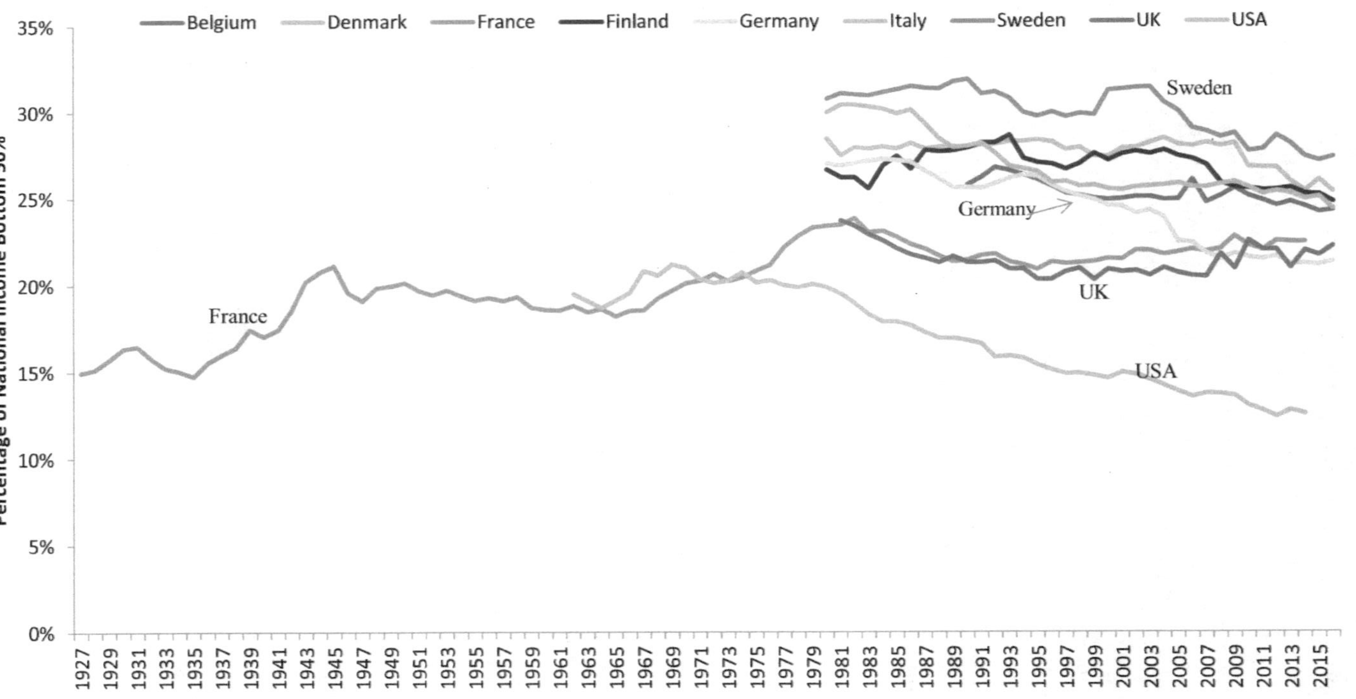

Figure 6.2. Bottom 50 Percent's Share of National Income.

been Belgium where their share has remained level. In 1927 the highest income earners in France and the US garnered nearly one-quarter of national earnings and in both countries their share declined to a low point in the early 1970s. After 1977 in the US and 1984 in France the rich increased their share, but much more rapidly in the US than in France, returning the richest Americans to about the same level as their grandparents earned in 1927. Although Margaret Thatcher moved rapidly toward a market-friendly version of capitalism in the UK by denationalizing several major industries and reducing the power of the unions, by 2016 the share of the richest in Britain was about the same proportion of the country's income as that of Danes and Germans.

The rise in income inequality is about more than just the growth of the earnings of the rich. In many countries the poor have also become poorer, as figure 6.2 shows. Even in Sweden the poor have lost share, though from a higher initial level than in any other country. France steadily increased the share going to the poorest 50 percent until about 1982, yet after a small decline by 2015 it had increased back to the level in the late 1970s. The UK followed an almost identical trend between 1981 and 2015, while the poorest Germans lost share slowly from 1985 and then more quickly after 1994 to a level below the UK by 2016. The real outlier has been the US. After 1979 the poorest Americans saw their share fall rapidly from 20 percent of national income to 13 percent in 2014. Simply put, the distribution of pretax incomes in the US has become rapidly *more unequal* after 1979, a period that coincides with the most radical turn to growth-obsessed, market-led economic policy. Even after taxes and social welfare transfers are considered, the US income inequality is significantly higher, and rising faster, than the OECD average.[4]

It is the withdrawal of government, or to be more accurate the reorientation of its role to serve MegaCorps rather than citizens, that has caused these changes. Especially in what are supposed to be the liberal countries. In the US, government has withdrawn the farthest and fastest. For example, the wage stagnation in the US noted in the previous chapter should be seen in historical and comparative perspective. In 2001, the US had a minimum wage that was higher than that in the UK, New Zealand, Canada, Ireland, Israel, Japan, Slovenia, and South Korea.[5] By 2018, a dozen countries including each of these previous laggards had a higher real minimum wage. It could be contended that income inequality doesn't matter if economic growth is robust, because "a rising tide lifts all boats." As we show in more detail in chapter 8, that is true to some extent, but despite a rising tide of economic growth, countries with higher inequality are less healthy, their societies less robust, and their economies less productive.[6]

To put it technically, they have lower levels of social capital: relationships among people that allow society to function successfully without some authority needing to step in with regulations, controls, and punishments. To put it more simply, the choice is between governments that are tough on law and order, and public control, versus those that underpin individual freedom and empowerment. Robert Putnam is a leading light in the field, and his landmark book *Bowling Alone: The Collapse and Revival of American Community* pointed out that societies with high levels of trust, with individuals engaged in all types of intercourse with each other and therefore willing to be engaged in public meetings, committees, political parties, and other social groups, are more productive. As we saw in chapter 3, national surveys show that these are also the benefits that make people happy and add to their wellbeing. When individuals are more civically engaged, this produces virtuous cycles in which good deeds are done without the need for regulation, and social norms are observed without the need for authoritarian control. Society is more cohesive and less riven by political or social differences. By contrast, societies with low levels of social capital in which individuals only look after themselves and care little about the societies in which they live, face a breakdown of trust and an erosion of social cohesion. Individuals compete in a vicious cycle to look after only their own desires, believing that nobody else will ever help them and likewise being disinclined to help others. This is not because they are intrinsically "selfish" or "bad" people, but because it seems like the rational thing to do. They see others looking after themselves, getting wealthier; they expect nothing from them, and so decide to become like them.[7] They do so because of the lack of a properly functioning *welfare state*.

Varieties of Welfare States

The word "welfare" conjures images of government handouts or charity. But as we saw in chapter 3 welfare is much more than this. Understood as "welfare at large" it is essentially synonymous with wellbeing. As we have already explained, governments need to perform a balancing act to reconcile the benefits of capitalism with the inequalities and challenges for social cohesion it potentially produces. Indeed, as Gøsta Esping-Andersen puts it, every state "must bear responsibility for securing some basic modicum of welfare for its citizens."[8] If they do this, then there are at least the foundations on which their citizens may build for outcomes that are beyond basic. If they do not do so, they tend to fall apart, because a country that allows social capital to plummet can only endure the results produced if it becomes increasingly repressive, and repression cannot last for long. Thankfully, in a democracy what tends to happen before things become too cataclysmic is that a government that abrogates responsibility for the welfare of its citizens gets voted out. It must respond to the concerns of its electorate whose welfare must be addressed, or it will lose power. Therefore, a democratic state must *be*, as well as have, a welfare state.

But what does a welfare state look like? For John Rawls, "social and economic inequalities are only justifiable" if there is a benefit for all, and especially the "least advantaged."[9] This suggests that a welfare state should redistribute the opportunity to acquire the income and wealth to reduce inequality. It sounds like the state ensuring equality of outcomes, but although it may result in something approaching this result, he goes on to explain that this primarily requires "fair equality of opportunity."[10] Liberals who argue for equality of outcomes are misrepresenting the true nature of liberalism. The role of the government and the state's raison d'être is not to guarantee high income and wealth to all, but to govern social and economic processes to better equalize the opportunities to achieve those outcomes. So, there is a tension between whether the role of the state in respect of citizens' welfare is to either ensure outcomes or opportunities for individuals. This tension produces varieties of welfare states, and it also results in capitalism being expressed in different ways in different countries.

Modern capitalism is institutionally diverse. Some countries' economies have been highly coordinated by their governments, and some even controlled. Others have been relatively "free" in the sense that the state is believed to perform a minimal regulatory function by only refereeing market interactions, being somewhat at "arm's length" from the market and firms operating in it. The result is that the extent to which countries have moved in the direction of CorpoCapitalism, and the different speeds and ways they have done so, reflects their prior institutional arrangements. It is important to keep these differences in mind otherwise we may not see the possible trees from the overall wood of capitalism. We risk asserting an "institutional monoculture" that produces a capitalist world of markets that are "inevitably" free of any regulation before launching into grand critiques of the results produced on the basis of these inevitabilities.[11] This is what is often done, and when it is done the assumption seems to be made that, for better or for worse, there must only be one form of the state: small, privatized, and marketized.

As we have shown, because of CorpoCapitalism and MegaCorps this is actually a bit of a "fairy tale," which is how John Braithwaite and Stephen Wilks characterize so much of the debate around neoliberalism.[12] The reality is that governments are not small and powerless, but that they can and should make choices about how they organize their economies. Each choice will have different social impacts. Does government favor individual labor mobility versus unionization to protect long-term employment? Does government strategically coordinate business or does it stand back and lightly regulate to provide business with the freedom to make choices based on market signals? Does business itself coordinate its activity or does it prefer competition? Does government govern through MegaCorps or more directly to enable the wellbeing of individuals? In asking questions like these we are asking about informal and formal institutions. For example, there might be an informal widely held belief that nonunionized, highly mobile labor is good for the economy, with this giving rise to formal laws favoring business rather than organized labor, whatever the social effects of requiring labor to be geographically mobile. Or that it is self-evident that the government should be responsible for making long-term plans about industry policy, resulting in the creation of formal ministries and legal controls to ensure it can do so. Or that business investment is ensured by allowing monopoly control over intellectual property, with formal laws to ensure that competition is on the basis of this and not products resulting from the open sharing of technical know-how. The point is simply this: only ideological zealots would say capitalism is simply bad, good, or *must* be one form or another.

Reality is more complicated. For example, *corporatist* states focus less on markets and market efficiency as a means of providing welfare, instead acting to uphold more traditional class relations underpinned by such institutions as organized religion and family, with rights assigned and legally ensured by the state on the basis of class and social status. Examples include Western European countries such as Austria, France,

Germany, and Italy. *Social democracies*, like the Scandinavian countries, have an agenda in which high equality and high social standards are stressed, with services and benefits guaranteed approximately equally to all members of society by the state. Often welfare is extended to the point that the government substantially takes over the role of family support.

In contrast to both these varieties of welfare states, a so-called liberal state is one where the government primarily has responsibility for the protection of individuals from the worst effects of economic change. Currently, this is interpreted to mean that it provides social assistance on the basis of means testing, with modest transfers and social insurance programs predominantly designed to cater to those members of society on low incomes or who have suffered unemployment or some injury that makes them unable to work. Meanwhile, a market *mentality* (as opposed to the actual reality of CorpoCapitalism) and a belief in the importance of market relations predominates and is supported and underpinned by the government. Welfare is therefore designed to support the minority in need, primarily temporarily, so that the majority can be free to look after themselves. Examples of such governments are to be found primarily in Anglo-Saxon states such as the US, UK, Ireland, New Zealand, Canada, and Australia.

This is an admittedly brief outline of the three welfare state types used today, but there are many studies that show that these different types of states have emerged, and that as they do so they retain an institutional commitment to their types.[13] But note what we said in the previous paragraph on liberal states underpinning a market mentality. The problem with this is that such a mentality now undermines markets. It does so because a belief in free markets, and a "hands-off" approach to them, translates as more freedom for MegaCorps. This is the case even before the protections and subsidies lavished on them, examples of which were given in chapter 4. In fact, such welfare handouts for big business can even be "spun" as market-enabling policies, because they are supporting supposedly competitive market actors! The result is that MegaCorps are given "liberal" freedoms, while due to growing social inequality and the loss of social mobility individuals in society are denied theirs. As the erosion of social capital occurs, the state must then play more of an enforcement than enabling role for the opportunities of its citizens, and so is no longer liberal in its orientation.

In general, if institutions do not adapt to changing conditions, they may lose influence and effectiveness and lead to economic, social, and ultimately political disaster. In respect of formerly liberal states specifically, David Harvey notes that where "entrepreneurial and corporate activities were surrounded by a web of social and political constraints . . . the neoliberal project is to disembed capital from these constraints."[14] We would substitute the word "neoliberal" with CorpoCapitalist, and the word "capital" with MegaCorps, because otherwise the impression given is that there is something liberal going on. It is not, because the result is those institutional configurations that once favored the free market have produced MegaCorps. Nor is all capital enabled, because small business owners are at the mercy of these MegaCorps and their market control. As such, an enduring focus on liberal institutions now serves to ensure that the free market is undermined as it supports freedoms just for MegaCorps. The moderating role of the state in ensuring a modicum of welfare for citizens has been replaced by a state that acts to embed CorpoCapitalism. Both are then passed off as a liberal or neoliberal commitment to individual freedoms when the opposite is the case.

The result is that discontentment has grown to the point that the prolific German economic sociologist Wolfgang Streeck claims the rise of the Trump administration in the US, Brexit in the UK, and resurgent nationalism across Europe are symptoms of an *interregnum*: "a period of uncertain duration in which an old order is dying but a new one cannot yet be born. The old order that was destroyed by the onslaught of the populist barbarians in 2016 was the state system of global capitalism." While it lasts "a great variety of morbid symptoms will appear," as indeed they have.[15]

The Future of the Liberal Welfare State

Institutional inertia means that change is often slow, and path dependent. In other words, institutions once in place tend to endure and linger, and they follow well-worn paths as they resist change. That is why they are ascribed to long after they have ceased to perform their ostensible functions. But there now is much pressure for change, as well as the need for it. Hence our key contention, which is that none of the so-called "liberal" states are truly liberal as we define liberalism in chapter 2. We think that the type of welfare state a liberal government produces should be one that balances power between all economic actors by encouraging conflict between producers—that is, preventing any firm from gaining excessive, let alone monopoly, power—and gives workers the right to choose their own paths to wellbeing while organizing for their economic collective security. That would be a good starting point, and it is the kind of starting point that does not define what individuals should get, nor what firms should do. It is not about outputs and outcomes, so much as inputs and opportunities, and therefore is a liberal conception of the role played by institutions.

If that all sounds too abstract, some simple questions may help to make things more concretely clear. Who has power in the so-called liberal democracies today? It would be heroic to say individuals. It would be more reasonable to say MegaCorps. What is the point of the welfare state in liberal states today? The official answer is that it remains the support of individuals who cannot look after themselves, ideally until they can get back on their own two feet and do so. Also, to help them in doing so. But with growing inequality and declining social mobility (which we discuss in more detail in chapter 8), the reality of political support for free markets and individual self-determination is less the purpose of the state than support for MegaCorps. With the reality of support for them through subsidies and laws that ensure their interests are served, the idea of individuals responsible for their success or failure in increasingly unequal societies is ridiculous.

What is the role of the state in ensuring individuals can provide for their needs? The truly liberal answer would be that the state should provide an enabling role rather than taking over the provision of these needs, as is more the case in other varieties of welfare state like social democracies, nor should it allow that class structures dictate this as in corporatist states. The more realistic answer, though, is that individuals' fortunes in states currently considered liberal are in the hands of economic and political forces that are no longer supporting or serving their own interests. This is because Liberal Capitalism is now CorpoCapitalism.

So, what is to be done? Changes to tackle these problems must start with taxation and representation, which are the focus of chapter 7.

Chapter 7

Taxation and Representation

In a liberal society everyone is primarily responsible for their own well-being. Meanwhile, through their government they pay for medical or health insurance to cover the costs of treating illness and disease, and public education that gives all the opportunity, but not the guarantee, to thrive. They also contribute to a welfare system that helps the needy, supports the unemployed, and responds to crises. Similarly, roads and public transport are socially beneficial and should be equally available to everyone. So should the regulation of industrial activity to prevent environmental harms like climate change, as this benefits everyone as well as life on the planet. In each case, everyone should contribute in some measure so that there are benefits that are available to all that could not be provided entirely privately through the market.

Liberal Capitalism therefore needs the active intervention of government in addition to the freedom of the market. It seems odd though, that what many governments managed to do in the past with economies that were smaller, and in times that were often at least as challenging, if not more so, now seems such a great challenge. For example, the New Deal program of public works projects and reforms was implemented not at a time when it was easy to do so, but during and in response to the Great Depression in the US. Likewise, London's Tube was built in Victorian times, and the National Health Service implemented in the aftermath of World War II when the UK was broke. Somehow, there seems to be a lack of money now to embark on such endeavors, which is a real concern because the challenges we now face are much bigger than building train lines or hospitals.

A lack of money is not really the problem. As explained in the previous chapter, MegaCorps and CorpoCapitalism have undermined the institutional basis for the liberal ideal of a welfare state. The welfare state is meant primarily to support those in need, ideally until they can look after themselves. Today, such an idea actually seems radical in what are supposed to be liberal states, because they no longer are. For example, when Senator Bernie Sanders proposed "Medicare for All" as part of his platform for seeking the Democratic 2020 presidential candidate nomination, he was attacked for being a socialist. But he was proposing something fundamentally liberal: universal health *insurance*, not universal health *care*. When such a proposal is seen as contentious, then it is clear that the institutional "rules of the game" are not liberal ones.

In this chapter, we consider some concrete solutions to where the money can come from in a liberal context to pay for the investment necessary to address the challenges we face now, and in the future. We examine the way in which many corporations, especially MegaCorps, are avoiding paying their "fair share" of tax while making huge profits. We make the case for why corporate taxation should not so much be increased as simply collected, from MegaCorps in particular, as a way of funding the initiatives necessary to ensure that the benefits of Liberal Capitalism can be recaptured. This is because in a liberal economy the business of business should be business, while safeguarding individuals' ability to provide for their own wellbeing is the responsibility of a liberal state. But first, we consider the roles of government versus business in the world in which we live, rather than as we might ideally imagine it.

The Business of Business

For Ronald Reagan "government" was the problem, while "business" was the solution.[1] Since then this idea has percolated to policymakers across the world through the fairy tale of neoliberalism. As noted in the previous chapter, according to this fairy tale governments must become small and do as little as possible, while markets and market actors are free to do whatever they like. They also potentially perform the functions normally associated with government through proactively embracing opportunities for CSR and private governance. If not this, then they more passively promote economic growth, through which social wellbeing is supposed to be an inadvertent outcome. From a liberal perspective, the government should not attempt to solve all problems, decide what is good for society, and then deliver what it knows is best for its citizens. But, as noted in chapter 5, Milton Friedman famously said that the social responsibility of business should be the maximization of profits, while the role of government is to make rules that business adheres to in so doing.[2] The problem is that MegaCorps are relatively freed from government regulation as a result of a belief that they are market actors, and that free markets are a good thing, while the role of government is looking after them. Hence the reality not of Liberal Capitalism but CorpoCapitalism in the service of MegaCorps, as we have shown in the last three chapters.

Say you are not a purist, as Milton Friedman was, and you pragmatically are willing to entertain the notion that it might be a good thing that MegaCorps perform roles that government traditionally performed. The problem is that MegaCorps are not in a position to do so. Because they serve the interests of their shareholders, they are spending most of their profits on paying dividends, and buying back their stocks in order to drive up their share price to give the impression of strong performance and enrich executives with stock options and "performance" bonuses. William Lazonick demonstrates this to be the case in an extraordinary piece of research published in the *Harvard Business Review* with the title "Profits without Prosperity." He shows that between 2003 and 2012, 54 percent of the earnings of S&P 500 companies were used to buy back their own stock in an effort to increase their share price. A further 37 percent was used for the payment of dividends, including to board members. On average, there was only 9 percent left for productive investment. Some companies had much less than this, as the data for some well-known MegaCorps presented in table 7.1 demonstrates. Household names like Microsoft, IBM, Cisco Systems, Procter and Gamble, Hewlett-Packard, Intel, and Pfizer spent over 100 percent of their profits on stock repurchases and dividends. In the case of Hewlett-Packard, a whopping 177 percent! In other words, these MegaCorps had not just nothing whatsoever left for productive investment but actually were going well into the red to manipulate their share price and enrich their shareholders, boards, and executives.[3]

What this means is that value *extraction* instead of value *creation* is these MegaCorps' main goal. As Lazonick notes, "trillions of dollars that could have been spent on innovation and job creation . . . over the past three decades have instead been used to buy back shares for what

Table 7.1. Top 10 Stock Repurchasers, 2003–2012

	Exxon Mobil (US$ billion)	**Microsoft (US$ billion)**	**IBM (US$ billion)**	**Cisco Systems (US$ billion)**	**Procter and Gamble (US$ billion)**	**Hewlett-Packard (US$ billion)**	**Walmart (US$ billion)**	**Intel (US$ billion)**	**Pfizer (US$ billion)**	**General Electric (US$ billion)**
Net Income	347	148	117	64	93	41	134	79	84	165
Stock Repurchases	207	114	107	75	66	64	62	60	59	45
Dividends	80	71	23	2	42	9	35	27	63	87
TOTAL	**287**	**185**	**130**	**77**	**108**	**73**	**97**	**87**	**122**	**132**
% Net Income	**83%**	**125%**	**111%**	**121%**	**116%**	**177%**	**73%**	**109%**	**146%**	**81%**

Source: Data from William Lazonick, "Profits without Prosperity," *Harvard Business Review* 92, no. 9 (September 2014): 54–55.

is effectively stock-price manipulation."[4] The scale of the misallocation of resources is staggering. If you study business, or first-year economics, you will be told that what business does is maximize profits, some of which are rightly paid to shareholders whose interests they serve. The rest is withheld for investment in productive capacity, and developing new products and processes, in order to ensure and increase future profitability. This is not what happens anymore, or at least not as much as anyone who believes in free markets and entrepreneurial spirit might hope. Because MegaCorps control their markets, they do not have to focus on investing to defend against competitive pressures, leaving them free to distribute more of their profits to bid up their share price for the benefit of owners and managers. They can pay dividends and buy back shares instead of investing and innovating and in the process reduce the taxes they or their shareholders must pay.[5]

While this is not sustainable, it is understandable. MegaCorps are mostly publicly listed companies, and to some extent their boards cannot be blamed for focusing on maximizing the share price in the short term as their "dominant touchstone objective," because if they fail to do so they risk becoming the target of a hostile takeover.[6] A high share price also allows MegaCorps to acquire innovative potential competitors to cement their dominant position in the market, as for example Facebook did in paying $21.8 billion to buy loss-making WhatsApp.[7] Adam Smith well understood where this would lead though, and it is why he explained his distaste for the "joint stock corporation" in the following terms:

> The directors of such companies . . . being the managers rather of other people's money than their own, it cannot well be expected that they should watch over it with the same anxious vigilance. . . . Negligence and profusion, therefore, must always prevail, more or less, in the management of the affairs of such a company.[8]

This is why there are huge profits without prosperity as corporate leaders and wealthy shareholders get big returns, while workers and communities—in fact pretty much everyone else—are told to pick up the check through paying higher taxes or higher prices for services off-loaded by government. It is also the motivator for closing plants, laying off workers, and offshoring jobs. These are the social costs that any Trump supporter will tell you are among the reasons why he gets their vote, or why a Brexit voter wants more British jobs for British people.

The Business of Government Is Business

Lazonick also notes that "as risk bearers, taxpayers, whose dollars support business enterprises, and workers, whose efforts generate productivity improvements, have claims on profits that are at least as strong as shareholders."[9] As can be seen in table 7.1, there is certainly no shortage of money to fund a Liberal Capitalism welfare state in the US, and no doubt the other rich, capitalist countries should their governments choose to do so. The problem must be that governments no longer see this as their role. At least, that is what the data suggest, because it shows that the size of government in rich countries has grown steadily over time, not fallen. As noted in chapter 4, government expenditure in the G7 group of rich countries has grown from 37 to over 40 percent of GDP in the last fifteen years.[10] So has tax as a percentage of GDP across all OECD countries, from an average of around 30 percent in 1980 to around 34 percent by 2016. So, rich countries are taxing and spending more, and figure 7.1 shows that the share of tax on corporate profits in total tax revenue has actually increased across OECD states since the early 1990s. Despite falling after the Great Recession, it is currently on average around 9 percent. This is higher than in the 1980s, despite most rich countries having reduced corporate tax *rates* since then.[11] In addition, many corporations engage in various tax minimization opportunities offered them by states, as well as shifting the jurisdiction in which they report profits in order to minimize the tax they pay overall. This therefore suggests that corporate profits must have grown a lot for the share of corporate tax paid to have increased, despite the opportunities for reducing the rate at which it is paid. By comparison, other sources of tax revenue have remained relatively stable, although the share of personal income taxes in total tax revenue have fallen while social security contributions have increased, so that the two have converged to have a similar share of the total.[12]

The data show that there is no lack of government expenditure, nor a lack of ability on the part of governments to decide where taxes are levied (for example, on social security contributions rather than income), nor a lack of capacity to levy taxes on corporations per se. It should also be noted that great variation between states may be noted if one digs down into the data. Such digging reveals some surprises. For example, figure 7.2 indicates that since the turn of the century, the share of corporate tax in total tax revenue has always been *higher* in what we

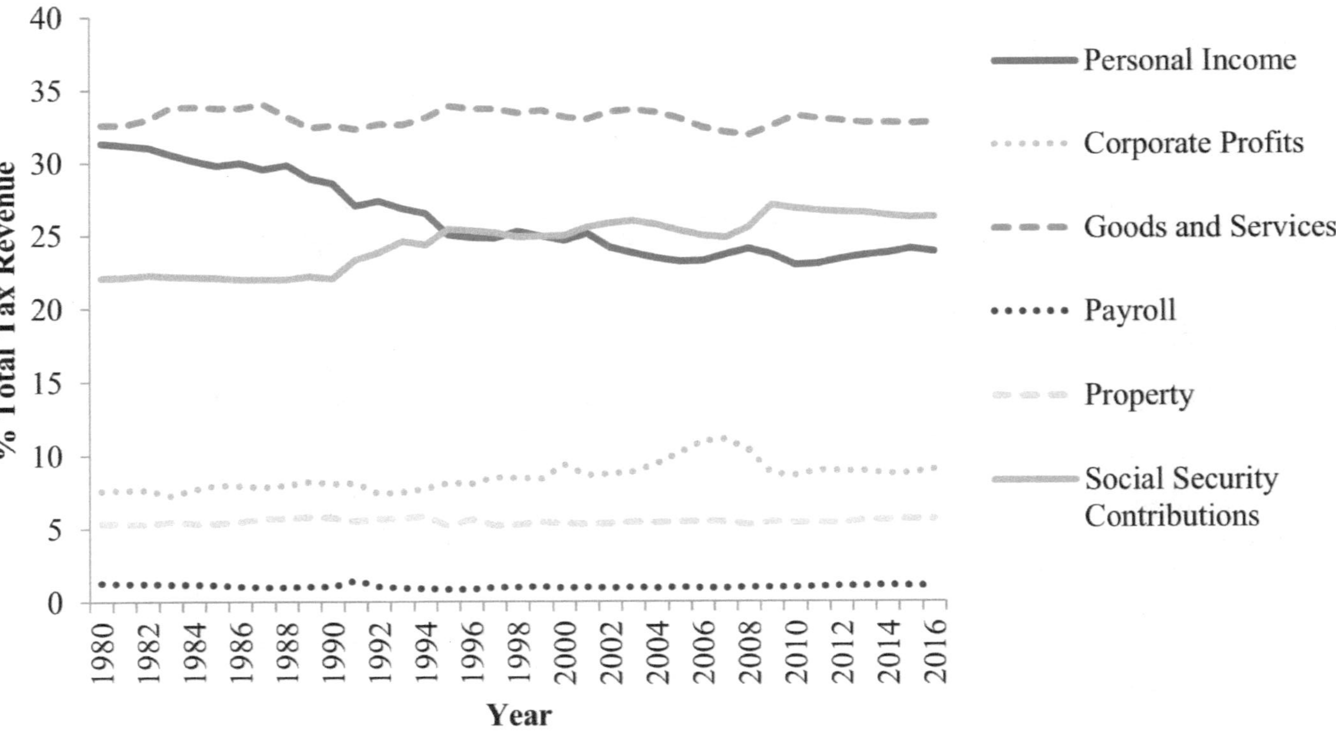

Figure 7.1. OECD Average Share of Taxes in Total Tax Revenue.

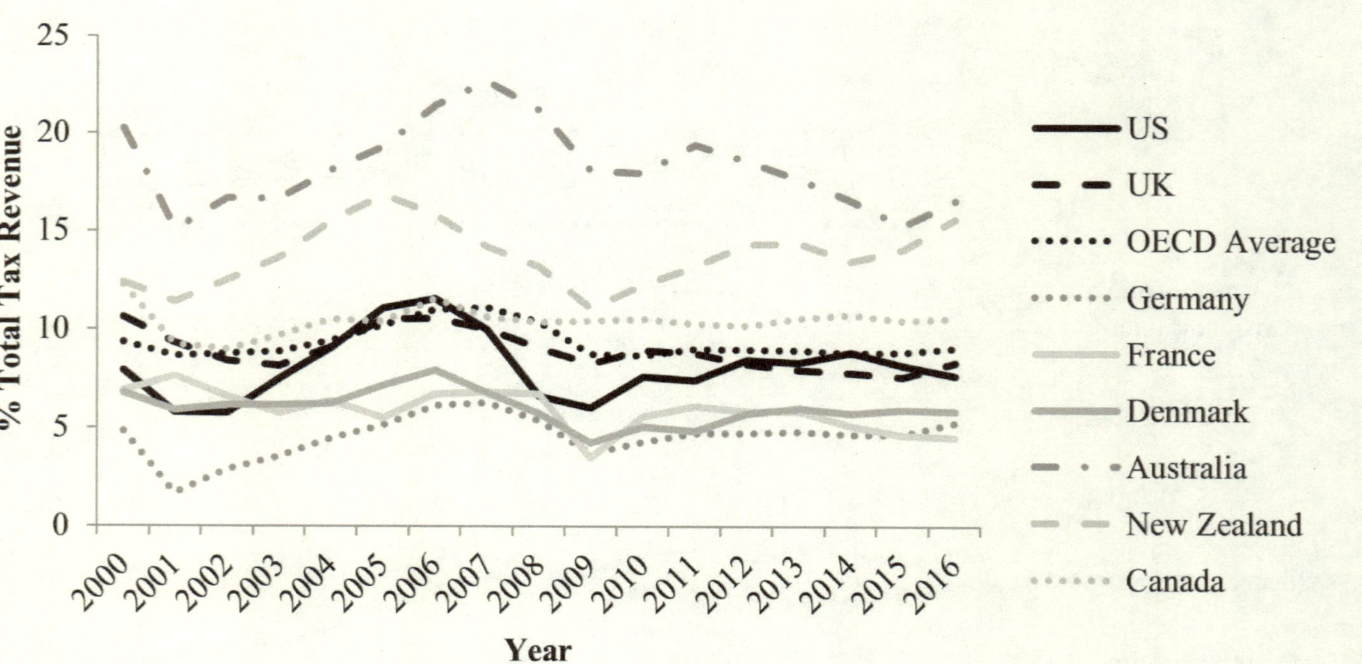

Source: Data from OECD, "Tax Revenue," 2018, https://data.oecd.org/tax/tax-revenue.htm.

Figure 7.2. Tax on Corporate Profits in Total Tax Revenue.

noted in chapter 6 are usually regarded as the so-called "liberal" capitalist states of the US and UK, than in corporatist or social democratic capitalist states like Germany, France, and Denmark yet much lower than in Australia and New Zealand. This may seem counterintuitive, but it stands to reason as citizens in the latter countries pay very high personal taxes to fund their extensive (nonliberal) welfare states. In other words, those who receive the benefits of enhanced state welfare systems that contribute heavily to individuals' security of incomes and lifestyle (and which enables their wellbeing) pay the check, not corporations. Governments can tax corporations if they want to, or tax their citizens instead, but states that are regarded as liberal have usually opted to do more of the former than the latter. Indeed, truly liberal states would prefer to tax corporations, especially MegaCorps, rather than individuals.

In general, a great deal of discretion is possible on the part of governments in how they structure their tax systems. Whom they tax and at what level is not dictated to them by undeniable market forces or inevitabilities of other descriptions, but political *choices*. Yet, even if governments decide to properly fund a liberal welfare state, they may have trouble taxing the profits of MegaCorps specifically, as opposed to corporations in general. Because MegaCorps are fundamentally multinational in their operations, an argument that has been doing the rounds since the 1980s and the end of the Cold War is that governments can no longer tax them as much as in the past. MegaCorps want lower taxes, and if they do not get the policies and incentives that they desire in one country they will move their operations to another country where they can. Just how globally "footloose" MegaCorps actually are in reality is debatable—for example, see the data presented in chapter 4, which suggest that their nationality still matters—but even so, just the threat to move their operations is usually seen as a key reason for competitive corporate tax rate reductions among rich countries. However, tech MegaCorps like Apple locate their most valuable and frequently used intangible assets (such as patents, custom software, or other technical know-how) at subsidiaries in low- or no-tax jurisdictions (such as Ireland or Bermuda). They then charge operating units elsewhere for using these essential assets. In this way they can separate taxable profits from operations and minimize their taxes globally.

This is therefore another fairy tale, with MegaCorps behaving like Big Bad Wolves. They threaten to huff and puff and blow down states' houses if they are not allowed to enter on their own terms. The effects produced are real, though. For example, Philip Cerny has analyzed the way that states believing this to be the case have become "competition states" with the policy objectives of "the promotion of free enterprise, innovation and profitability in both the private and public sectors."[13] But the real story is that MegaCorps do not need to move their locations because, as noted in chapters 4 and 5, they sit atop networks of contractors and subcontractors. They make decisions about which ones to hire and fire in different countries in order to supply their products and services. This means that they do not have to be footloose themselves in search of the policies and conditions they desire. They place that burden on others. They particularly do not have to be footloose in the pursuit of lower taxes. They can remain headquartered in their home countries, shift where they report their profits, and in so doing often *pay no tax at all*. The result is that global corporate tax avoidance denies governments around the world US$240–650 billion per annum. Revenue losses to governments from tax avoidance by US-based MegaCorps alone have been estimated to be at least US$100 billion.[14]

These are actually extremely conservative figures because there are debates about what constitutes tax avoidance. MegaCorps can legitimately report their profits in different jurisdictions due to having operations in multiple countries, and their strategies to aggressively reduce the tax they pay are largely legal. This is due to them taking advantage of serious flaws in the global taxation system. These flaws date back to the development of legal mechanisms to avoid double taxation in the 1920s, prior to MegaCorps rising to prominence.[15] They have been used as loopholes to allow MNCs to shift profits from high-tax jurisdictions to low-tax jurisdictions, or what are known as "tax havens." MegaCorps take advantage of these loopholes through accounting methods that allow profit to be moved artificially, to minimize taxable profits. The OECD refers to much of this behavior as Base Erosion and Profit Shifting (BEPS) because it erodes the tax bases of states where economic activity occurs to other locations where profits are reported. Instead of preventing double taxation, these antiquated regulations now provide plenty of opportunity for what Pascal Saint-Amans, director of the Center for Tax Policy and Administration at the OECD, labels "double non-taxation."[16]

The problem then is not a liberal one; it is a regulatory one. International competition in corporate tax rates is not liberal because the power of MegaCorps tends to raise personal tax rates or reduce government services. So, it is not a consequence of neoliberal globalization, but of the interests of MegaCorps supported by CorpoCapitalism, particularly as practiced by the US government, which has long hampered international cooperation to prevent BEPS. When the OECD published its seminal report *Harmful Tax Competition: An Emerging Global Issue*, the first attempt by an intergovernmental agency to name and shame tax havens, the attitude of the Bush administration was telling. It was actively anti-reform, as it worked to undermine OECD efforts to reduce the opportunities for tax avoidance. The excuse for this position revolved around a probusiness ideology coupled with arguments regarding sovereignty.[17] Ultimately, US Treasury Secretary at the time, Paul O'Neill, stated that the US "does not support efforts to dictate to any country what its own tax rates or tax system should be, and will not participate in any initiative to harmonize world tax systems."[18] At the time the US was the home base for 41 percent of the world's five hundred largest MNCs listed in the FT Global 500.[19] In essence, this position meant that the world's most economically powerful state, where most of the world's potentially major tax avoidance culprits are headquartered, was unwilling to curtail the abilities of their MegaCorps to engage in tax-avoidance strategies. Meanwhile, the US aggressively pursues individuals who use tax havens to reduce their personal income taxes.

Efforts at an international agreement have moved at a glacial pace ever since, hampered by the US at every step.[20] Then in 2017 the US "Tax Cuts and Jobs Act" significantly reduced corporate tax rates, substantially reduced the tax on repatriation of profits earned overseas, and greatly reduced taxation on certain company tax structures. As a result, while a company like Amazon could record more than $11 billion in profit it was able to *pay no US federal corporate tax*.[21] Instead, it received a tax rebate of $129 million. Indeed, fifty-nine other US MegaCorps paid no US federal corporate tax in 2018.[22] Now the US has become a tax haven for MegaCorps, again undermining the OECD's efforts.

The Role of Government Is Representing Its Citizens

It should be obvious that the role of government under Liberal Capitalism is to represent the interests of the citizens that democratically elected it. Also, that it does not impose measures upon its citizens that do not serve their interests. Ideally, the government of a Liberal Capitalist state would act not so much as a governor of society, as it should be a *balancer* of the competing interests of different societal stakeholders: individuals, the organizations to which they belong, the functions the organizations perform, and the interests they pursue. It is the referee not a player. Following the arguments in chapter 6, different answers are possible in every country because of their unique institutional configurations. But the reality seems to be that in CorpoCapitalist states the interests of MegaCorps are being served by the government. From a liberal perspective that might be a reasonable standpoint if business were accepting responsibility for the social and environmental costs of their operations. But MegaCorps do not have sufficient incentive to do so. Their main incentive is to look after their shareholders.

What is required first is that an international agreement be reached to crack down on MegaCorps' ability to avoid tax through BEPS. Next, states should reconfigure what they do with the money they already collect, as well as the billions more that they should collect. In this regard, it cannot be stressed enough that at the moment, instead of focusing on competing in markets, MegaCorps go looking for government subsidies and state protection to carry on with business as usual. Welfare, which under Liberal Capitalism should be directed at poor and needy individuals, or those down on their luck, too often is directed instead toward MegaCorps as direct subsidies or through tax breaks. As a student of one of the authors put it, what this demonstrates is that in rich countries MegaCorps seek handouts in what is a case of "socialism for business and the rich, and capitalism for the poor."

That may sound harsh, but there is an abundance of evidence in support of this statement. In *The Establishment and How They Get Away with It*, Owen Jones points out some of the many ways in which big business is supported politically and financially by the British government. For example, between 2003/4 and 2010/11 £177 billion in tax credits were paid to poor workers. Not the unemployed, but *workers*. As he rightly points out, these are not a handout to the poor so much as "a subsidy to bosses for low pay." In effect, "employers hire workers without paying them a sum of money that allows them to live adequately, leaving the state to provide for their under-paid workforce."[23] It's the tip of a very large iceberg of billions of pounds in handouts to big business that he catalogues, the potential extent of which was revealed in 2008/9 when, as noted in chapter 4, US$7 trillion was spent by eleven rich countries on bailing out big banks and stimulating their economies. Or, as again noted in chapter 4, the US$1.9 trillion spent on subsidizing and protecting the fossil fuel industries. The trillions of dollars of public money spent on handouts to MegaCorps could surely be put to better use than the government-backed subsidization of their oligopoly or monopoly power that ensures they are too big to fail.

Instead, it could be spent on supporting workers whose wages have been stagnating for decades, as we showed in chapter 4. Or those in the gig economy who are exposed to employment uncertainty. Or those who are losing their jobs to automation. Automation is beneficial for MegaCorps because it is more efficient to produce more with less labor, and at a lower price. Also, robots do not call in sick, form unions, or demand benefits. But it is not clear that it is beneficial to society at large without some redistribution of the benefits, and it certainly is not for the workers who lose their jobs because of it. Because workers are also consumers, it also tends to depress demand on which capitalist economies subsist. Likewise, the flexibility inherent in the gig economy is surely desirable for corporations and potentially for some workers. For example, it may be a useful source of additional income for self-funded retirees, or young people desiring work flexibility while studying at university. But there are surely costs that come with the benefits for some that need to be addressed in respect of the many who are forced to live with irregular income. Unknown unknowns like the present global COVID-19 pandemic, or an environmental crisis, show the precariousness of such casual labor.

Ensuring the security of all from environmental disaster is another primary responsibility of any government. So, under Liberal Capitalism government has a leadership role in driving new technologies, products, and processes to mitigate and adapt to climate change, as will be discussed in more detail in chapter 9. For now, it suffices to say that in the absence of greater government intervention there is little incentive for corporations, mega or otherwise, to invest in mitigating climate change *specifically*. They may have an incentive to reduce costs in the interests of their shareholders by using technologies that mitigate climate change while satisfying consumers' demand for goods and services that are cheaper, faster, and smarter. This may marginally reduce GHG emissions. But they would be severely punished by investors for focusing on emission reductions as an overriding priority, if these came at the expense of lower profits, reduced dividends, or falling share price. If products and services embodying the most advanced technological innovations designed to produce the lowest GHG emissions are not demanded by consumers or embraced by shareholders, corporations cannot be blamed for failing to invest in them. Therefore, the government must.

Making Government and Business Work for Society

In general, it is always tempting to throw your hands in the air and declare that things are too complicated, or that in a more globally interconnected world they are inevitable, or that governments are either powerless or part of the problem. But if we step back and think in terms of preferred goals as opposed to historical actions, then the possibilities open up. What is the point of taxation? Who do our democratically elected representatives represent, and who should they represent? Who do they enable, and who should they enable? From a liberal perspective the answer is clear: the people, individuals, every one of us, as equally as practical. The enormous amounts of money already available to the governments of rich countries, and the money that should be available if they could prevent global corporate tax avoidance, should likewise be directed toward enabling and supporting individuals' opportunities, as opposed to dictating their options. Now, this is not the case. With trillions of dollars going to MegaCorps, and an ideology of CorpoCapitalism to underpin it, taxation is increasingly levied in the service of MegaCorps, while they manage to avoid paying it themselves.

As this book was written, the world was celebrating the fiftieth anniversary of the moon landing. Many opinion pieces echoed that of John Schwartz in the *New York Times* who posed the question "we went to the moon, why can't we solve climate change?"[24] The amount that was spent on putting a man on the moon at a time when the global and American economies were smaller was truly staggering. But the desire was greater and US taxes were higher. If the vast sums of money available today were spent on challenges like reducing inequality and mitigating climate change, then real progress could be made. Instead they are being spent on shoring up the status quo that is neither liberal nor presages a liberal future.

Another parallel may be drawn. The photographs of the Earth from the moon changed the way people saw our planet: a blue oasis of life in the black, lifeless void of space. It is time to see our world again not as it is so often portrayed but as it really is: capitalism that is no longer liberal, with governments that profess a belief in liberalism focusing their efforts on MegaCorps and the wealthy. Therefore, it is time also to realize the potential for promoting a Liberal Capitalist future. In the next five chapters, we look at strategies for achieving this.

Part III

A Liberal Correction

A populism tinged with nationalism and autocracy is rising in many rich countries. Many people seem unsatisfied with their lives under modern capitalism managed at the behest of MegaCorps. Or are Brexit, the election of Donald Trump in America, and right-wing populists in Turkey, Hungary, and Poland a rebellion against overweening government?

What is the disease in capitalism that contributes to this discontent? Is economic inequality, that is commonly blamed a natural consequence of capitalism, or a conscious choice? If it is a conscious choice, who made that choice and how can it be reversed to better equalize individual economic opportunity? How does economic inequality affect society and act on individual wellbeing? Does it encourage striving and upward mobility or build barriers to personal advance?

Innovation is necessary to address the challenges we face, but it can also cause them. The replacement of labor by automation is a product of technological innovation, and the impact of this needs to be moderated in some way. But can innovation help to prevent dangerous climate change? What can states do to make innovation prevent this existential crisis? Ultimately a discussion of questions like these leads to deeper ones, like what is the purpose of the economy? What is it for? Is it economic growth, national prosperity, or enabling individual joy? What principles should guide the governance of the economy or should it be left free and society adapt accordingly? Can the normal levers of governance such as taxation provide sufficient remedy? How should politics determine who decides the purpose of the economy? What are liberal values and how can they be accepted and applied?

These are all questions that lead us to consider resilience not just in respect of ongoing challenges but the crises to which they give rise as the effects become more acute. How this happens is not universal. Climate change is an expected crisis (science has long predicted its outlines), but as we write the COVID-19 pandemic is raging that has blindsided governments. What is the role of governments in planning for low-probability, high-impact crises? Should governments forego efficiency and economic growth to provide a resilient context within which individuals can optimize their wellbeing? And does resilience only mean returning to the patterns of life before an unexpected crisis? In the end, is it possible for social and economic systems to dynamically adapt to changing conditions while retaining the stability institutions provide? Do existing institutions prevent Liberal Capitalism, yet hold hope for it?

Chapter 8

Capitalism and Its Discontents

According to Thomas Piketty, the natural law of capitalism is that the rich get richer faster than the rest.[1] Without external restraint, income and wealth inequality grow naturally and incessantly, until inevitably as a consequence of history "wealth is more unequally distributed than income."[2] In the last century the rise of labor unions, two devastating World Wars, and a Depression helped to restrain this "natural" growth of inequality. After 1945 governments expanded social welfare systems, further slowing, and sometimes reversing, this natural effect of capitalism.

Since around 1980 an ill wind of change has blown through political institutions and economic growth has overwhelmingly benefited corporations, their owners, and managers. As shown in chapters 4 and 5, four decades of CorpoCapitalism has allowed MegaCorps to run rampant and inequality to accelerate. The resulting unparalleled freedom for MegaCorps is a derangement of Adam Smith's vision. He had hoped to free all the people, not just giant corporations. Supported by governments, and now with power over them, these new "sovereigns" have moved well-paid work to cheaper countries, battered unions, forced reductions in taxes on their exorbitant incomes, ever more rapidly consumed the Earth's resources, warmed the climate, and weakened the institutions that could restrain the destruction they are wreaking. Chapters 6 and 7 explained how in most rich countries during that period social safety nets have begun to fray while income tax rates have declined and contributions to social welfare programs decreased, again benefiting the wealthy and high income earners and costing the poor some shelter from the challenges of life under capitalism. In short, the progress of CorpoCapitalism dismantled state defenses against inequality and accelerated capitalism's natural tendency to increase inequality.

Unsurprisingly, this has had devastating effects. As inequality has risen it has slowed economic growth, reduced government investment, diminished social mobility, and for most people shrunk opportunities for wellbeing. As we show in this chapter, there is nothing good about increasing inequality. We focus on the US, because as the exemplar of a rich country practicing CorpoCapitalism, it has most reaped the whirlwind of greater inequality—in both incomes and wealth—with resulting underwhelming economic growth, reduced social mobility, cramped wellbeing, and disrupted democracy. While this state of affairs is unfortunate for many, it must be remembered that this is a political decision that can be reversed. It is not an inevitable consequence of capitalism that cannot be restrained.

Inequality and Slow Growth

It is no coincidence that economic growth has slowed as inequality has risen. As the figures in chapter 6 showed, inequality has risen in most rich countries in the last four decades. In the same period, the average rate of economic growth in the US (the most unequal large rich economy) has been 2.7 percent. Yet, in the prior thirty-five years the average growth rate was more than a third higher at 3.7 percent annually.[3] Other rich countries have suffered a similar slowing in economic growth while inequality has risen. While these data do not prove that inequality reduces growth rates, there is reason to suppose it does. So how might the lower growth rates in rich countries be caused by inequality? There are several ways in which this might play out.

First, as MegaCorps consume more of the national income, they leave less for small corporations and workers. Figure 8.1 suggests that, freed from government strictures and operating globally, rich country MegaCorps are a primary cause of profits' growing share of national incomes. That means that labor's share declined. At the same time rising inequality drew income from the poor and middle class to a small group of high earners. Now, the poor spend all their income while the rich save most of theirs. This means that as inequality rises, consumer demand, which is the lifeblood of rich countries' economies, grows more slowly

Note: This graph is from Era Dabla-Norris et al., *Causes and Consequences of Income Inequality: A Global Perspective* (Paris: IMF, 2015), 13, is based on data from Bloomberg L.P. and IMF staff calculations, and is used with permission. Emerging markets include Brazil, Chile, China, India, Indonesia, Korea, Mexico, Philippines, Russia, South Africa, Thailand, and Turkey.

Figure 8.1. Index of Estimated Corporate Profits.

than GDP. This is because GDP includes all economic activity including consumption and investment, whether or not productive or useful, and values polluting activity at the economic cost of its remediation and treatment of its effects. If consumption growth is slow, investment in productive assets to satisfy future demand falls, and overall economic activity slows. However, to maintain their lifestyle and status as their income fails to keep up, lower income earners have resorted to borrowing. These trends have been exacerbated, not caused, by the recurring recessions and economic crises we have experienced in recent decades.[4]

Secondly, technology, globalization, and government policies have tended to shift the distribution of labor's shrinking share toward higher-skilled work. Because of the growth of global supply chains enabled by ICT, rich countries have seen demand for skilled workers rise much faster than for unskilled employees. This bids up wages for the already skilled and well-paid and suppresses wages for less-skilled workers. And where production has returned to rich countries, as we saw in chapter 3, automation has replaced—and will continue to replace—many manufacturing jobs that once were filled by well-paid semi-skilled workers.[5] Even as unemployment has fallen in most countries since the Great Recession, most of the jobs newly created have been in the low-paid service industries, often on a casual or contract basis.

There is no doubt that private investment spurs economic activity. With the rise of a belief by many rich countries' governments that economic growth is best spurred by reducing tax rates on corporate profits, high personal incomes, and capital gains, one result is that the average corporate tax rate across them fell from 32.5 percent in 2000 to 23.9 percent by 2018.[6] Another result is that while average personal income tax rates on average wages also declined between 2 and 6 percent, the marginal tax rates for the top earners declined an average 7 percent, and the income at which the marginal top rates applies has risen 22 percent.[7] Some might equate such policies with an embrace of neoliberalism, but as we have shown such policies are aimed at supporting MegaCorps rather than freeing up markets. In fact, they have distorted markets because they have increased the funds available for MegaCorps and the mega-wealthy, and have done so in a fashion that does not enhance market efficiency. What they have resulted in is growth in "excess savings" beyond that required for productive investment—in technological innovation, factories, or machinery and equipment. As a result, the rate of economic growth has slowed but asset prices have risen, primarily benefiting the wealthy and increasing inequality, which again feeds into a vicious circle of declining consumption, decreased investment, and rising asset prices.[8]

For example, as we saw in chapter 7, many MegaCorps have used the windfall from tax reductions to buy back their shares or acquire competitors to increase their market dominance rather than to innovate. Similarly, wealthy individuals have "invested" in nonproductive assets such as rare art and antiques, vintage cars, debt instruments, or even the stock market. Such "investments" have driven up asset prices much faster than the rate of inflation without increasing the rate of productive investment. As a result, since 2009 stock markets and house prices have increased rapidly in many countries. The former benefits the rich, while the latter increases middle-class debt and prices many younger workers out of the housing market. As Joseph Stiglitz notes, despite the "savings glut" produced by tax reductions and the increasing proportion of GDP earned by capital, the global financial system has failed to support real global investment needs, including in climate change mitigation and better enabling personal wellbeing.[9] Meanwhile, automation of production is accelerating, which further benefits corporations and their wealthy shareholders at the cost of well-paid jobs.

Slower economic growth and lower tax rates cut into the state's services. A primary purpose of government power is the provision of *public goods*—things that are equally available to all. These include national security and much public infrastructure such as roads and air traffic control that protects and supports private productive investment. Similarly, in many countries a system of national health insurance helps to protect people when they get sick, and to also ensure they remain productive. Thus, high government revenues can support strong social *and* economic benefits, in the process enabling wellbeing for all. In contrast to the modern move to lower taxes to spur growth, as growth weakens and tax revenues decline, policymakers are tempted to reduce spending on public goods. This stymies private investment and economic growth. It also cuts social welfare programs that support those losing out from shifts in the demand for labor. At the same time that welfare payments and other government services are reduced, increasing inequality increases the demand for them, and the vicious circle tightens yet further.

Richard Wilkinson and Kate Pickett show that countries with higher inequality are less healthy and their societies less robust.[10] They have higher rates of homicide, low birth weight, obesity, teenage birth, mental illness, drug overdose mortality, violent crime, incarceration, hostility, and racism. They also have lower levels of trust, educational performance, child wellbeing, social capital, and social mobility. These problems are not all caused by inequality, but they are related to and exacerbated by it. This is why in a comparison of income inequality to an "Index of Health and Social Problems," the US is both the wealthiest and most unequal country but its "inequality trumps average income" in explaining its social ills.

Inequality and Wellbeing

Because humans are social beings, they measure themselves against others.[11] Wellbeing is strongly impacted by how we feel we are valued by others, by the "status" we enjoy. In *The Broken Ladder* Keith Payne describes and explains much of the research surrounding social comparison, social status, and social health.[12] The subtitle of his book is revealing: "how inequality affects the way we think, live, and die." As Payne writes, "Inequality makes people feel poor and act poor, even when they are not."[13] It is human nature to seek status and to use material things to demonstrate it. Psychologists tell us that we can gain high status in two ways: through achievement or dominance. The rich countries are materialist societies and it is common to signal achievements (and thereby status) to neighbors, friends, and the world at large by the things we possess, the size of our house, the make of car we drive, the clothes we wear. Modern capitalism aids and abets this behavior by offering more opportunities for such displays and thereby encourages excessive consumption that, as we saw in chapter 3, contributes little to wellbeing. Or as Payne comments:

> If our response to inequality is shaped by our need for status, then inequality is not simply a matter of how much money we have; it's about where we stand compared with other people. Money, from that perspective, is simply one way of keeping score. *Feeling* poor matters, not just *being* poor.[14]

Poverty is therefore not just about wealth. A lack of money causes it, yet it is experienced as an absence of the "normal" possessions that most people have. As Adam Smith observed more than two centuries ago, people are poor if they do not have the things most of us would consider normal accoutrements of life, which includes more than food, water, and shelter. For him, "necessities" include "not only the commodities which are indispensably necessary for the support of life, but whatever the custom of the country renders it indecent for creditable people, even of the lowest order, to be without."[15] And being without such normal possessions denotes a "disgraceful degree of poverty, which, it is presumed, no body [*sic*] can well fall into without extreme bad conduct." The relationship between inequality and status also is recursive. As Payne notes, "inequality affects our behavior, and difference in behavior can magnify inequality."[16] Always and everywhere the effect of *perceived* poverty is corrosive.

Poverty is a "disease" of the mind that is not easily eradicated. Beyond actual poverty, the feeling of (relative) poverty in an unequal society can scar a child for life and prevent success in school and later in the job market.[17] One highly educated American who now earns more than $700,000 a year still bears the scars of growing up poor.[18] As one of eight children, Christian H. Cooper says he felt panic "at the prospect of a perpetual uncertainty about everything in life, from food to clothes to education." Such sensations can actually change human biology, "reduce the surface area of the brain, shorten telomeres and lifespan, increase your chances of obesity, and make you more likely to take outsized risks." With his high income he still feels he does not have a "safety net" and suffers from "stress, self-doubt, anxiety, and depression."[19] He may have escaped material poverty, but in the process, he has lost family connections without finding a purpose beyond himself. In short, money alone has not bought him wellbeing.

Inequality and Social Mobility

Social ills become ingrained because in highly unequal societies children are less likely to better their parents' income and status. For example, in America a child born in 1945 had a 90 percent chance of earning more than his or her parents. By 1985 inequality had risen and that kid's chance of bettering his or her parents had fallen to less than 50 percent.[20] It has declined further since then.

Figure 8.2 shows that the higher the inequality of incomes, the more earnings persist between generations. This means that children of poor parents will struggle to do better than their parents while rich kids have a small risk of falling below their parents. In this way a vicious circle can develop between economic inequality and society, as between those demanding welfare payments and the government's ability to provide them. If the economy is a ladder, high income inequality means that the steps on the ladder are further apart, and the ladder harder to climb. So, as inequality increases, the space between the steps grows and social mobility falls, which thus "cements" existing inequality.

CorpoCapitalism increases inequality because it grants greatest advantage to the "luckiest" individuals and corporations—that is, those "holding all the cards." Neuroscience tells us that none of us has completely free will and our accomplishments (or lack of them) are often largely the result of our circumstances.[21] If we are born rich, there is no skill in being rich. If great wealth is down to intelligence, then we

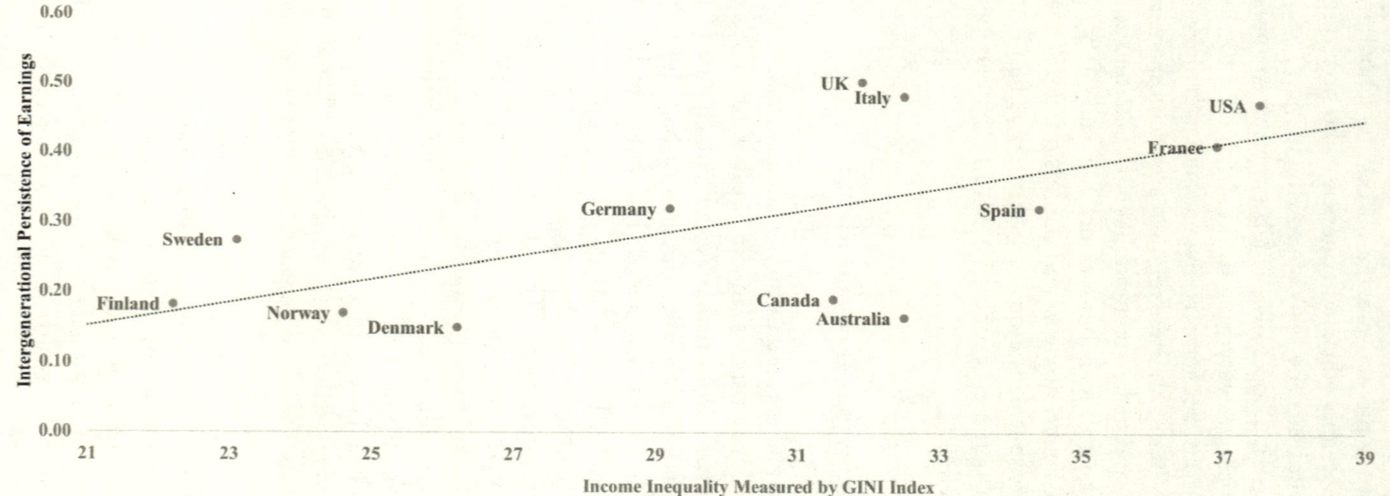

Note: Data from OECD, "A Family Affair: Intergenerational Social Mobility across OECD Countries," in *Economic Policy Reforms: Going for Growth* (Paris: OECD, 2010), 183–200; StatLink http://dx.doi.org/10.1787/784787325068; and the World Bank at https://data.worldbank.org/indicator/SI.POV.GINI. GINI values are for years between 1984 and 1987 except for Unified Germany for 1991.

Figure 8.2. Income Inequality and Persistence of Earnings.

are just lucky to be born intelligent, but if intelligence is learned not inherited, we are lucky to have had the parents and teachers we did. What about character? It too is from nature and nurture, not just from personal volition. Perhaps success is a matter of opportunities? Yet, the ability to grab opportunities usually depends on education, connections, character, wealth, and so on, that can put us in the right place at the right time. In Liberal Capitalism governments do not guarantee outcomes but build institutions and governance processes, as John Rawls proposes, to distribute more opportunities to the least fortunate—that is, to even out luck or reduce the effect of luck alone.[22] Although Jean-Paul Sartre wrote that "existence precedes essence," meaning that we create ourselves through our actions, this freedom means nothing in the economy without resources and opportunity. Therefore, governments should actively raise up the least fortunate and potentially tax great wealth, as will be discussed in chapter 10. Also, in Liberal Capitalism institutions would as far as possible prevent a "winner-take-all society" that has emerged in many countries today so that the benefits of growth are more widely shared.[23] For individuals, governments would support greater social mobility for *both* the poor and the rich, while for corporations they would increase competition to restrain MegaCorps.

There are many ways to increase opportunity, resources, and social mobility, but the most important is to prioritize investment in education. It is no accident that countries with the best performing public educational systems, like the Nordic countries, also enjoy lower income inequality and, as we saw in chapter 3, a happier population. According to the OECD, their workers are also more economically productive than those in the UK and US.[24] There are two principal explanations for how education benefits individuals in rich countries.[25] First, well-paid work increasingly demands advanced levels of reading comprehension, math, and good cognitive skills, because globalization exports to poorer countries the drudgery of production while retaining product design and supply chain management at home. Second, as production demands more skills, education is increasingly a "positional good" that gives job preference to those with higher educational qualifications.[26] They are assumed to be able to think critically, learn, and adapt more readily while less educated workers are increasingly sidelined to poorly paid low-skill jobs that, because of automation, are disappearing. However, highly unequal societies reduce the effectiveness of education as a "luck leveler." Poor children are less prepared for school and richer kids "start and probably finish further and further ahead."[27] Without massive investment in reversing this disadvantage, social mobility declines further, and inequality hardens. Of course, wealth or a high income can always buy a better education (and connections to the elite) in a private school or university.

So, in a CorpoCapitalist state where big business, big government, and elite connections between them are favored, money can buy luck. Casting this as a matter of liberal freedoms allows those who benefit to pull the wool over people's eyes. It is indeed surprising the extent to which many living under CorpoCapitalism have no idea how much opportunity for advancement their state denies them. Although European countries have greater social mobility than the US, it is the Americans who are optimistic about their ability to climb the ladder while Europeans are less much less optimistic.[28] The American Dream, a tantalizing phantasm of liberal personal hopes, motivates many Americans to strive for an imagined better future. Even though for most their dreams are thwarted by great and growing inequality, dreaming means that they do not recognize how difficult it is for them to join the ranks of the rich, just as it is hard for the rich to join the ranks of the poor.

Damaged Democracy and the Role of Government

The same economic shifts that have increased inequality are a primary culprit for the rise across the rich countries of a nativist and authoritarian right-wing populism. The definition of populism is slippery but is generally understood as an ideology that rejects elites, including "experts," in favor of the "general will" of the people.[29] Authoritarian populism sells the idea that a powerful individual or group can correct the errors of experts but harbors within it the threat of dictatorship, which can ignore the needs and will of the people. While inequality in the US is higher than in Europe and social mobility less, European right-wing parties have captured an ever-increasing share of the national vote in 33 countries (see figure 8.3). From almost nothing in 1980 populists on average claimed more than 22 percent of the popular national vote by 2018 with a range from 0.5 percent in Malta to 68.9 percent in Hungary. And while they were initially more inclined to be left-wing in orientation, they are now predominantly right-wing, being often led by a charismatic leader who can put widely held fears into words that defy critical analysis by their believers, while drawing on nationalist sentiment.[30]

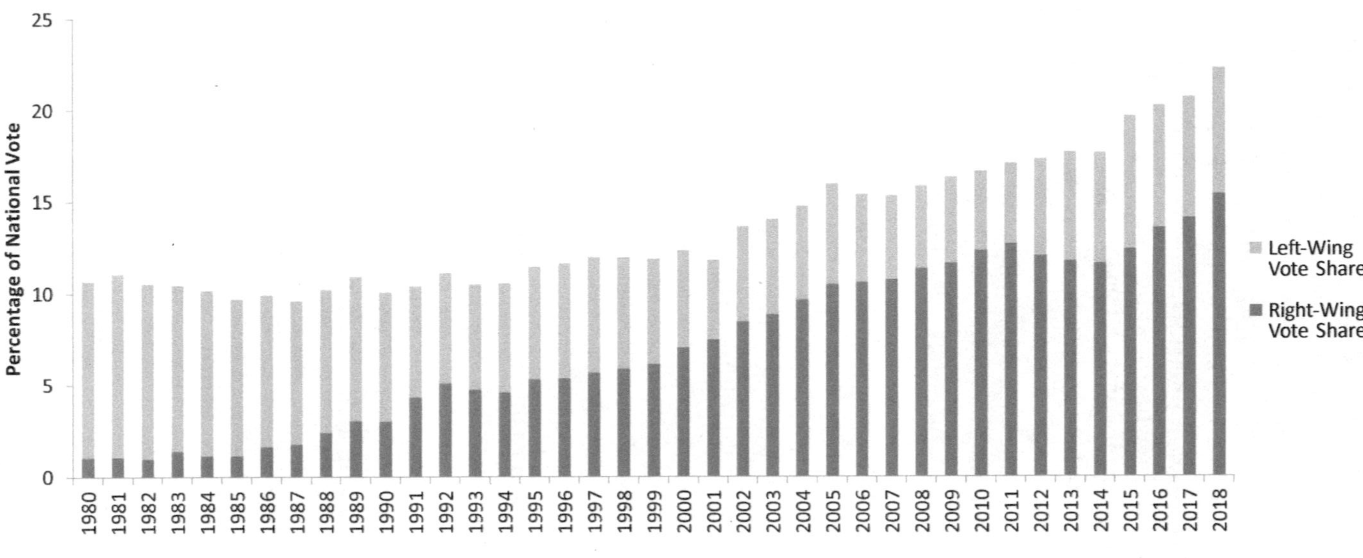

Note: Data from the *TIMBRO Authoritarian Populism Index*, accessed at https://populismindex.com/ on 10 July 2019. For each year, the average percentage of the populist vote is that for the most recent year in which national elections were held.

Figure 8.3. Average Percentage of Populist Vote in 33 European Countries.

Based on our previous discussion, it should be clear why this is the case. The surge in right-wing populism appears to be the result of a loss of social status for a significant portion of the population. Ronald Inglehart and Pippa Norris, for example, conclude that right-wing populism emanates from cultural backlash from a loss of status as a result of emergent economic changes.[31] Globalization and automation favored by MegaCorps hollow out rural towns and cripple long-established industrial centers; the CorpoCapitalist withdrawal of governments from their social duties cuts into people's trust, and wellbeing; and labor mobility in search of work breaks social and family ties. So does a lack of social mobility. This breeds an almost subconscious dissatisfaction with the state that populists can feed off. They can tell people who to blame—perhaps immigrants, minorities, or China—and claim that they alone can return their lost status.

Research by Noam Gidron and Peter Hall shows that changes in subjective social status—where each of us believes we sit in the social hierarchy—are more keenly felt than abstract ideas like inequality. In eleven of twelve countries with very different political histories and cultures the "relative social status of men without a college degree is lower today than 25–30 years ago" and in most of these countries the social status of men relative to women fell between 1985 and 2015.[32] The economic cause of men's loss of social status is CorpoCapitalist destruction of many well-paid jobs in industries like mining and manufacturing. This may be why right-wing populism tends to draw its energy from older, usually male voters, as well as those who are less well educated. A similar effect in the US upper Midwest appears to have elected Donald Trump.[33] For decades most less-skilled workers had reliably voted to the left, with the Democratic Party, but by 2016 many had lost well-paid jobs and suffered a decline in status. So, they voted with the grandiose populist.

If we are not careful, that which replaces CorpoCapitalism will be considerably worse than the problems it has caused. As we have explained, this is most evident in the US where inequality has grown rapidly over the last four decades because of decidedly *illiberal* CorpoCapitalist economic policies. Other countries that have adopted some of the same policies have also reaped the ill rewards of governments interfering in markets to both *increase* inequality and *reduce* economic growth with devastating social consequences. In the US CorpoCapitalism has emphasized "trickle-down" economics, which favors capital over workers (thus the continual fall in tax rates) and cozy relationships with

MegaCorps as we have described. The idea was to raise living standards by freeing corporations from taxes and regulations on the assumption that they would then invest their gains in job-producing economic activity, which would then reward workers with higher pay. This approach requires policies that allow the strong to consume the weak, encourage executive innovation, and loosen up the labor market. The argument for corporate acquisitions has been that consolidation and the resultant oligopoly in most industries (see chapter 4) is acceptable as long as consumer prices do not rise in the short term. Considerations of local market power are cast aside with arguments that MegaCorps are more efficient and more competitive. The former criterion is based on the rising tide lifting all boats argument we dismissed in chapter 6. The latter we showed to be redundant in chapter 4. But it has directly increased inequality.[34]

The introduction of tax-favored, equity-based compensation, and a relaxation of rules on corporate governance has caused a nearly nine-fold increase in average compensation for CEOs of US public company executives since 1981.[35] Other executives have similarly benefited from the creation of "incentive stock options." Usually based on increases in annual profit per share, or a related metric, executives can now engineer their own pay in several ways that have nothing to do with improvements in productivity or innovation. Indeed, the rising wealth of senior executives is the result of incentive-based pay that primarily rewards financial engineering, like the stock buybacks explained in the previous chapter, and "brute luck."[36] As a result, CEOs' pay in the US is higher than any other country (with the UK in second place) when controlled for firm size and industry.

It has also increased inequality by allowing MegaCorps to acquire greater control of workers, as was shown in chapter 5. Unless government legislates protections for workers' pay, benefits, and working conditions, emergent global economic changes empower corporations and weaken unions and the worker protections they have long delivered.[37] Figure 8.4 shows that wages have not kept pace with productivity (as economic theory presumes) in most rich countries. In addition, US federal law requires no paid vacations and average paid vacations granted by corporations are less than one-third the legally mandated vacation days in much of Europe. The US also is the only rich country that does not mandate paid parental leave (on a par with New Guinea and Suriname) or require paid sick leave. Indeed, the US comes last in nine of twelve employee benefit categories.[38]

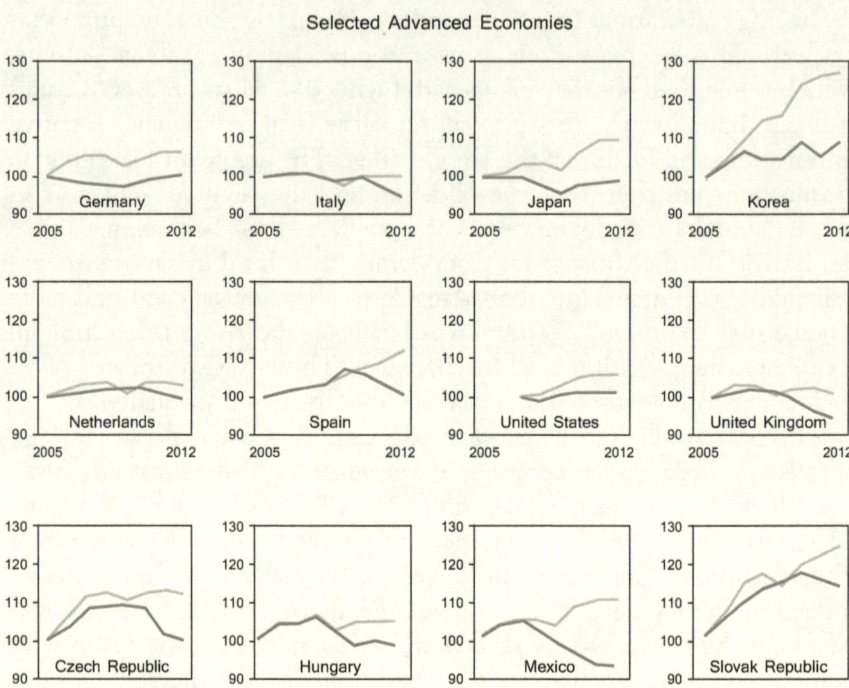

Note: Era Dabla-Norris et al., *Causes and Consequences of Income Inequality: A Global Perspective* (Paris: International Monetary Fund, 2015), 14. Used with permission.

Figure 8.4. Real Average Wage and Productivity.

If great inequality is endemic to capitalism and socially corrosive, for the sake of social harmony and political stability it should be prevented or mitigated. Adam Smith recognized the risk when he advocated that "the acquisition of valuable and extensive property, therefore, necessarily requires the establishment of civil government."[39] That same year the American Declaration of Independence argued that governments organize their powers to effect the safety and happiness of the people. It made no mention of giant corporations. If great inequality undermines the safety and security of the people, governments should act to rectify the situation, if only to prevent populists from rising from the ashes of civic harmony.

The liberal response is to optimize opportunities and spread access to them more evenly. All rich governments offer free primary and secondary school education to teach what is needed to "succeed in life" and some offer free college education as well. And as we noted earlier, education is one of the keys to providing individuals with opportunities and the potential for social mobility. But truly "free" markets and good schools alone will not fix inequality. Economic orthodoxy holds that policies that redistribute resources and even opportunities reduce economic growth. Many researchers disagree. Robert Putnam, for example, concludes that "America today has plenty of scope for simultaneously enhancing equality of opportunity and economic growth" through investing in better schools.[40] Similarly, governments congratulate themselves on any fall in unemployment, but it has not lessened inequality: the majority of new jobs are for low-skill, low-paid service work. As shown in chapter 3, this trend is expected to continue as automation advances. States need to do more. Yet, reducing inequality is a massive task. As Anthony Atkinson has commented, "to get back to where we were when the Beatles were playing" the UK would have to reduce its inequality by nearly 30 percent from its current level to the level of inequality now enjoyed in the Netherlands.[41]

Yet, inequality reduction has been achieved before. After World War II, inequality levels in the Netherlands fell by 8.5 percent, in France and Italy by 9 percent, and in Finland by 11 percent.[42] In most cases governments strengthened the social safety net and raised tax rates on incomes. Today, however, rich governments are not attacking the underlying structural causes of inequality. As Atkinson argues, the rate of reduction in inequality needed today may not be possible by just using the same tools that worked in the past. Under CorpoCapitalism, tweaking the welfare state is playing with parameters and barely a band-aid. New solutions are needed, as we discuss in chapter 10. But first, in chapter 9 we consider how governments can combat the existential crisis of climate change with technological innovation.

Chapter 9

Technological Innovation for the People

Almost all industries and people are either implicated in, or impacted by, climate change. Obvious contributors to GHG emissions are the production and use of fossil fuels in industries like energy generation, cement, construction, and transportation. Changes in land use through intensive agriculture and deforestation also contribute to emissions. Often overlooked is unsatisfying overconsumption built on competitive status-seeking and lazy habits, like the online delivery of goods from the other side of the world. The changing climate that results will generate novel challenges in the form of new diseases, old diseases in new places, deadly heat waves, floods, droughts, and violent storms. As the IPCC has succinctly noted, the anticipated changes in the climate system will increase "the likelihood of severe, pervasive, and irreversible impacts for people and ecosystems."[1]

Broadly there are two ways to prevent a dangerous increase in the accumulation of GHGs in the atmosphere. First, governments can use their power to change the behavior of people and organizations. But while liberalism accepts the use of government power, it should be used sparingly, and primarily to manage excess conflict as well as prevent alternative concentrations of power. Ideally, it should only sparingly control how individuals pursue their wellbeing or corporations their profits. Second, states can generate and disseminate technological innovations that are specifically designed to reduce GHG emissions so that people can live their lives unmolested by authority. To prevent the impacts of climate change manifesting as multiple crises experienced all at once demands innovations in products, processes, and materials that are so radical they reorganize whole energy and production systems. We call this type of technological innovation for the people "climate innovation" and it is our focus in this chapter.

In our earlier book titled *Climate Innovation: Liberal Capitalism and Climate Change* we showed how MegaCorps reject researching or adopting climate innovation unless there is a "business case" or government regulation requiring it.[2] That is why today many rich countries use economic incentives in an attempt to improve the business case for climate innovation. For example, their governments subsidize wind power and solar photovoltaics because they produce carbon-free energy, and they regulate some activities that are excessively polluting, like coal-fired power stations. Yet, such small selected positive and negative incentives are wholly inadequate to the task at hand: to prevent dangerous climate change or protect humanity from it. Much more is needed.

As it appears unlikely that dangerous levels of GHG in the atmosphere can be avoided, states also must plan to adapt to a changing climate. No single government policy, nor a focus by governments on individual problems as if they were stand-alone issues, will be enough to address the many impacts, including risks to public health through hotter heat waves, longer droughts, more violent storms, new diseases, the spread of tropical diseases and disease vectors to temperate zones, and continuing bacterial and viral mutations. As health is the foundation of wellbeing, protecting public health in a warming world is a primary requirement of liberal states. But this is not just a philosophical question. Preventing the impacts in advance must be the state's responsibility because there is insufficient profit to attract innovation from the MegaCorps that have the necessary capabilities. And when they hit, it may be too late for MegaCorps to profit from rolling out the necessary products and services. The current COVID-19 pandemic has brought forth the fastest ever production of a vaccine, but this speedy success has been heavily lubricated with billions of dollars in financial incentives from governments and philanthropic organizations.

Climate innovation is central to both mitigation of, and adaptation to, climate change. But our premise in this chapter is that markets have trouble producing the innovations needed, except possibly accidentally, and that MegaCorps backed by states as they are at present likely will not. Therefore, governments must accept responsibility for climate innovation. They must use their powers to make it happen. Because technological innovation can change work patterns, social structures, and human lives, states also have the responsibility to ensure that individual wellbeing is not harmed by the innovations needed to corral climate change. In other words, their governments must safeguard Liberal Capitalism from climate change *and* climate innovation. As we will show, climate innovation to protect the planet is more complex than most policymakers presume.

The Market Innovation Process

In popular imagination new technologies come from a lone inventor or a couple of buddy entrepreneurs in a garage. For example, Apple was "created" by two "visionaries": Steve Jobs and Steve Wozniak. Or at least that is the creation myth of the MegaCorp, but in truth innovations usually emerge from a complex process: *the iterative interaction of science possibilities with market demands*. This means that most innovations that reach the consumer are the result of choices by profit-seeking firms.[3] A simple way to think about this process is to imagine scientific discovery ("invention") as a spark. But a spark will not start a fire without fuel. The fuel is an appropriate infrastructure of laws, finance, and engineering and technical skills, plus a culture to support further research and development (R&D) and organizations that do it in order to turn scientific knowledge into something useful. Finally, to turn that small fire into a conflagration, consumers must demand the products of this development process.

The last part of the process is where profit-seeking corporations excel. If they operate in competitive markets, they are seeking a competitive edge. If they are MegaCorps and dominate their markets, they look for new ideas, concepts, designs, and scientific knowledge that they can control and turn into something from which they can further monopolize profits. This can be a new production process that reduces costs, or a product that better meets consumers' needs. So, information constantly surges in both directions between science and market until it produces something deemed profitable to a corporation. Figure 9.1 is a simplified representation of what we call "market innovation," which in reality is much less linear and more iterative (especially between applied science and niche markets as ideas are tested) with entrepreneurs, policy advocates, and research and educational organizations playing important roles. But it shows that financial inputs during the process normally move from public money for the higher-risk scientific research to corporate investment for the lower-risk final stages of product design and marketing.

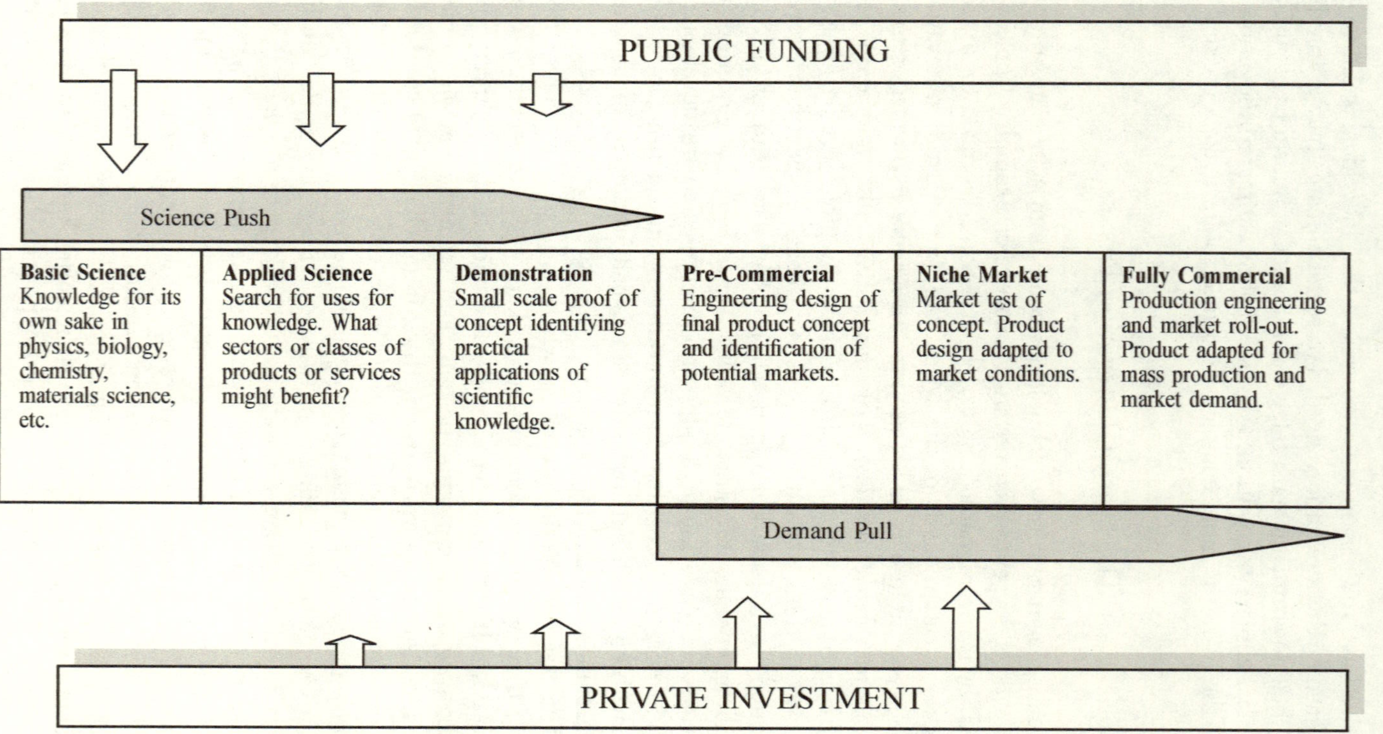

Figure 9.1. The "Market Innovation" Process.

Governments commonly participate in this process in several ways. They provide much of the scientific R&D funding with grants and contracts to universities or corporations, and sometimes conduct the R&D in government-owned labs. Through patents they then protect the resulting innovations for several years, usually as a corporate monopoly, because the private sector acquires the rights to the resulting technologies. But sometimes governments themselves directly purchase the resulting products. For example, the US government has designed and purchased innovative military and aerospace equipment, much of which has had spin-off civilian applications. Governments also subsidize corporate R&D by allowing a broadly defined set of costs and expenses to be deducted from taxable income. In every rich country, including those espousing mythical "free markets," the invisible hand of the state supports innovation by corporations. Table 9.1 shows the magnitude of government support for R&D through direct expenditure and tax allowances, in a selection of countries. Even excluding the substantial value of patent protection, in total their governments provided between 21 and 52 percent of all national R&D expenditures.

Because the market innovation process is organized around the interests of corporations, it is designed with the primary aim of producing innovations likely to be profitable. This is another example of Corpo-Capitalism, as when the market innovation process involves MegaCorps, governments support, fund, and often *do* the basic R&D necessary for their interests to be served. Sometimes game-changing radical innovations will emerge, but more often market opportunities induce MegaCorps to make merely *incremental* improvements in product design or production processes that increase the quality, or reduce the cost, of products. The needs of society are not the primary aim.

So, it is generally accepted that current technologies together with expected market-induced innovations will be insufficient to mitigate GHG emissions, and why more radical technologies will be needed to prevent dangerous climate change.[4] Although many governments lavish subsidies on alternative energy systems like wind and solar, and this may increase consumer demand and encourage corporations to expand production, it will not be enough. This is true whether the corporations are MegaCorps or not, because their aim is not mitigating climate change. Their motivation in broadly diffusing the new technologies is not even primarily environmental. It is profit. So, even with indirect government support through subsidies and regulation of more polluting technologies,

Table 9.1. Government Support of Business R&D

	US	UK	Japan	China
Tax Allowances (% GDP)	6.8	15.0	11.0	6.6
Direct Government Expenditure (% GDP)	12.8	8.8	13.7	6.0
Government Share of All R&D Expenditures (% Total)	26.5	51.3	21.7	23.5

Note: Data from OECD.stat. The four countries were selected at random but other rich countries provided similar levels of support.

the market innovation process will only *unintentionally* produce the radical climate innovations required to prevent dangerous climate change.

National Innovation Systems

Effective climate innovation is likely to be more uncertain, and with longer lead times, than market innovation. The radical innovations needed typically emerge from deep, long-term research and the integration of innovations across several disciplines. This was once the preserve of MegaCorps, like Bell Telephone in the US. Its Laboratories ("Bell Labs") produced the transistor, data networking, cellular telephone technology, solar photovoltaic cells, digital cameras, lasers, and communication satellites.[5] Dozens of its scientists have won Nobel Prizes, Turing Awards, and other major scientific prizes. This ability to integrate technologies to create world-changing innovations once was the strength of capitalism. With CorpoCapitalism that era is long past.

As we showed in *Climate Innovation*, capitalism in general is not well adapted to producing the radical climate innovations needed. But CorpoCapitalism is particularly ill-suited to this role because, as we discussed in chapter 7, the data show that MegaCorps now primarily focus on paying shareholders dividends, remunerating their executives and board members, and manipulating their share prices. In 2014, for example, US MegaCorps distributed more to shareholders than their net income, boosting their share price and executives' rewards.[6] Freed of the need to compete in their industries, and instead being able to focus on control over them, they spend much more on these activities than they invest in R&D.

Public corporations of *any* size are less likely than private corporations to make long-term investments. Andy Haldane, the recently retired governor of the Bank of England, estimates that eliminating short termism and investing more long term would raise UK national income by 20 percent.[7] Public corporations with a dominant or controlling shareholder, as occurs more frequently outside the US or UK, appear to invest with longer-term horizons but are risk averse.[8] In contrast, private UK corporations are much more likely to hoard capital and invest it in longer-term innovations than public corporations. They also invest their profits at four to eight times the rate of quoted companies and have investment stocks that are four to five times larger. However, most private corporations usually are not large enough or risk-embracing enough to invest in the science needed for radical climate innovations. The problem is that *all* corporations are motivated by profit, but only incidentally by environmental imperatives like climate change. If they focus on radical climate innovation, it is best if they are large in order to have the resources to do so, yet the data show that when they are large public corporations—in other words, MegaCorps—they don't. With the help of government they can protect their position of market supremacy, or use this position to knock out or purchase potential competitors that may have developed climate innovations that threaten it.

The investment choices of all corporations are influenced by the legal and cultural context in which they operate, which is the domain of governments. States, therefore, clearly have a role in organizing the legal framework within which corporations choose their strategies. But the laws and regulations made by their governments on such matters as patents, corporate governance, executive compensation, corporate taxation, and R&D allowances are imperfect tools for directing market-based national innovation systems toward effective climate innovations. Their direct participation in such matters is an essential component of climate innovation, and of Liberal Capitalism.

A Mission for Climate Change

Today, only governments can match the innovative heft of a Bell Labs. A few private organizations like the Bill and Melinda Gates Foundation actively support climate innovation, among other innovations, but none of them have the deep pockets and technological range of governments. Nor the ability to make the necessary economy-wide transformations. This is not to suggest that governments should themselves fund and manage all innovation. Not only would this be illiberal, but it would be ineffective as history has demonstrated many times that they are ill-equipped for the tasks. When they pick and choose technologies, they tend to get it wrong, like the Anglo-French supersonic Concorde: a technical triumph that was years late, ran over its budget 20,000 percent, and was a commercial failure. However, they can stimulate and organize R&D for climate innovation throughout the economy.

Governments must have a clear goal and appropriate mechanisms. As Mariana Mazzucato argues, " 'wicked' challenges [like climate change] in the sense that they are complex, systemic, interconnected, and urgent requiring insights from many perspectives" demand a "mission-oriented" and closely coordinated set of policies.[9] A mission uses "systemic public policies that draw on frontier knowledge to attain specific goals."[10] They imply a new "direction of change" through "tilting (rather than leveling) the playing field to favor certain types of change more than others."[11] This has to go beyond the limited government intervention of "market-fixing" with a few positive or negative incentives. Missions are complex because they are "less clearly defined and indeed must be co-defined by many stakeholders."[12] A mission to mitigate climate change with technological innovation demands cohesive policy across many institutions for a portfolio of carefully defined, risk-accepting, innovation projects by a variety of private and public actors investing in multiple industrial sectors.

Mission governance requires a well-defined purpose. For climate change this might mean setting a "net zero" target date. Several countries have set themselves the target of reducing net GHG emissions to zero by 2050 or earlier. As noted in chapter 3, if copied by every country, even this target will probably be insufficient to avoid dangerous, unpredictably catastrophic impacts. Yet, even a target such as this is a "big ask" because fossil fuels, urban sprawl, the car culture, and a whole range of corporate and individual habits are deeply embedded in a fossil-fueled consumer culture in the rich countries. So, if an earlier target can be set it would be better. Then once it is, the technological challenges must be clearly defined. For climate change these might include energy storage systems, fusion energy, small nuclear power cells for use by municipalities, "faux-meat" products from vegetables, materials research to increase solar energy efficiency and reduce energy loss across the electric grid, carbon capture and storage, increased agricultural efficiency in water use, disease- and drought-resistant crops, and so on. Prior industrial revolutions happened largely by accident. But with the existential threat of climate change, serendipity is not a plan. A Green Industrial Revolution is required.

From Mission to Innovation

Governments can use three principal mechanisms to implement missions and make them effective: research coordination, appropriate financing, and market shaping.

Research coordination has a well-proven model to follow. For more than six decades the US Defense Advanced Research Projects Agency (DARPA) has been successfully defining specific technology needs and managing the coordination across government research centers, universities, and corporations in many industries to create the integrated innovations needed for science-fiction-like solutions to the most challenging technical problems. Established in 1957 in response to the Soviet launch of Sputnik, DARPA has contributed basic research to many commercial technologies despite a small $3 billion annual budget and only two hundred staff. These include computer communications protocols and the Internet, the World Wide Web, Windows, videoconferencing, Google Maps, personal computing and the mouse, voice recognition, UNIX, basic cloud technology, the learning personal assistant, the global positioning system, the Urban Photonic Sandtable Display using 3D holography, stronger and lighter materials, body armor, microelectromechanical systems, turbofan engines used in large commercial aircraft, computer security, Internet anonymity, satellite technology, and supersonic and stealth aircraft technology.[13] Once a target technology is chosen, DARPA program managers coordinate research activities across multiple scientific and engineering disciplines and between research institutions and potential users (primarily in the military). Because program managers have a systems-level perspective and are highly regarded in the scientific community, they can bring together disconnected researchers and organize "disparate research activities spread throughout [the US] national innovation ecosystem" and build networks among researchers that directly influence the development trajectory of new technologies.[14]

The Advanced Research Products Agency for Energy (ARPA-E) in the US Department of Energy adapts the lesson of DARPA to the problems of energy production and use. According to its website it advances early-stage "high-potential, high-impact energy technologies that are too early for private-sector investment" to generate innovations with "the potential to radically improve U.S. economic prosperity, national security, and environmental well being [*sic*]" through novel energy source and storage technologies.[15] However, ARPA-E is no DARPA. It has an operating budget of only US$300 million annually, program managers rotate in from other government departments and do not have the systems perspective and close relations with researchers of DARPA program managers, and all further development is left to corporations. In addition, the former

Trump administration tried to substantially reduce ARPA-E's budget or shut it down, though Congress maintained its funding.[16]

Appropriate finance recognizes that the source of funding dictates the direction of research. In market economies, governments financially support innovation in general solely to increase economic growth. However, to implement a climate change mission demands a directed and coordinated financing of a large number of research activities and innovations across the whole economy.[17] Because the science-based corporate research centers like Bell Labs are long gone, "if policies favor a subset of financial actors [for example, banks, venture capitalists, etc.], these actors will come with their particular priorities of financing" and drive overall innovation in their preferred direction. In other words, whoever pays the piper calls the tune. To meet the exigencies of climate change nothing less than a series of radical technological innovations is required, and this means that new and interdisciplinary science will be needed that governments alone can fund. In accordance with Liberal Capitalism, they should abjure directing and managing; they should rather set targets and timetables, and in the manner of DARPA organize cooperation among corporations, universities, and government research organizations to meet them. A stable and equable climate like the one enjoyed for the last several centuries is a *global* public good "whose influences are felt around the world rather than affecting one nation, town, or family."[18] It is in the interest of every state to financially back the economy-wide radical transformations to ensure this is damaged as little as possible.

Market shaping means using institutions and policy to draw innovations through from demonstration of the technology to commercialization. The best way to do this is for governments to *become* the market and directly purchase novel technologies. DARPA has been effective in part because the US military is its sole customer. Other commonly used ways to get consumer demand to "pull" innovations through to the market include government purchases, outright banning competing high-emissions products, and subsidizing lower emission alternatives. For example, several countries ban the sale of energy-inefficient incandescent light bulbs, regulate the fuel efficiency of gasoline vehicles, and subsidize the consumer price of more efficient technologies. While accepting the need to guide consumers to reduce their GHG emissions, liberalism prefers "positive incentives" such as subsidies over "negative incentives" that regulate what may be produced and sold. Negative incentives imply a restriction, however small, of choice and personal wellbeing. Subsidies, however, reinforce and enlarge consumer preferences so that corporations take notice and bring innovations to the market.

But if consumer subsidies are not large enough to drive the energy-inefficient products out of business, then regulation of production processes could be considered as it does not directly impact individuals' wellbeing and is acceptably liberal. In Liberal Capitalism corporations, especially MegaCorps, do not deserve the same consideration as individuals, very much the obverse of today's reality as described in chapters 4 and 5. Yet, in time technological innovation to reduce the costs of more climate-efficient products may perform the same function. Rather than regulating production, removing subsidies of highly polluting products would be more economically efficient. As noted in chapter 4, many countries subsidize the extraction and production of fossil fuels by contributing to corporations' production costs. It is a straightforward step in the right direction and merely reforming fossil fuel subsidies could lead to direct reductions in carbon emissions of 6 to 26 percent in addition to making less emissions-intensive energy sources more competitive.[19] While removing them is politically poisonous in many countries, Liberal Capitalism would approve of the removal of such poorly directed, market-undermining incentives.

Market-enhancing measures like carbon taxes are designed to increase the final price of products in proportion to their contribution to GHG emissions, reduce the consumption of more polluting products, and increase sales of less polluting products. Therefore, they have the same negative incentive effect as regulation. An alternative economy-wide form of regulation is called cap and trade. Successfully implemented in the US through the 1990 Clean Air Act, it puts a national cap on polluting emissions and then allocates an allowance of emissions to producers in proportion to their historical production. In other words, if the national cap would amount to a reduction of 30 percent in national emissions, every producer would be required to reduce their emissions in the same proportion. Periodically the cap is reduced, forcing producers to continually reduce the pollution that they emit and dump on others, frequently by installing innovative technologies. It is a liberal policy because it does not directly impact individual consumer freedom and wellbeing, although it may do so indirectly by increasing the cost of production for some producers who then pass these costs on. One observed effect of cap and trade policies has been to increase the demand for innovations that reduce the regulated pollutants. But there are other, more pervasive costs and benefits across society as a whole that must be considered.

Innovation and Society

Technology has always affected society and individual lives for both good and ill. If radical technological innovation becomes central to mitigation of, or adaptation to, climate change, it has the potential to be as socially disruptive as automation and AI. How might Liberal Capitalism address this challenge? In the popular mind radical technological innovation *determines* how society develops. For example, many Hollywood science fiction blockbusters, such as the *Terminator* franchise, sell the idea that technology will begin developing itself and will come to dominate society. This notion of "technological determinism" encompasses two separate ideas. First, that technology develops "autonomously" following scientific advances or the internal logic of scientific processes, and second, that such innovations have significant power to shape society.[20] The two ideas are often joined so that "autonomous technology (in both its development and use)" is said to shape social relations.[21] In a sense, technology has always made society in its image, as Lewis Mumford argued in his classic text on *Technics and Civilization*.[22]

Today, however, the unregulated social impact of most technologies is not so straightforward. For example, the internal combustion engine gave us cars spewing pollution, harming health, and changing the climate; roads that destroy neighborhoods and create urban sprawl; and a massive fossil fuel infrastructure. It also engendered romantic notions of geographical freedom for the people, a way of life for some, and an expansion of the American Dream.[23] Yet, differences between countries mean that the institutions and culture of society impact not just the development and selection of technologies, but also how they are implemented and used.[24] So, although the advent of the affordable automobile permitted suburbs and urban sprawl in the US, it did not do so to the same extent in more compact European cities because governments heavily taxed personal transportation while providing inexpensive public transportation and protected bike lanes. Natural conditions also may affect how innovation is used, such as the extent of geographical space in some larger countries like the US, versus smaller ones like the Netherlands.

In reality, neither society nor technology dominates. For example, the First Industrial Revolution (in England) in the late eighteenth century emerged from new technologies like the mechanization of spinning and weaving, steam power, and improved animal husbandry. But these were enabled by effective financial institutions and improved transportation that allowed the new joint-stock companies to build factories, which undercut individual spinners and weavers and drove them to cities and factories. This history of joint developments in technology and society is encapsulated in the concept of the "Techno-Economic Paradigm" (TEP). A shift in the TEP, such as the First Industrial Revolution, is a "major upheaval of the wealth-creating potential, and fabric, of the economy" enabled by a combination of technologies and political and social institutions that then reverberates through the economy and society.[25]

The social impacts of a TEP may be large, yet subtle, and often unpredictable. For example, the vacuum cleaner, piped water, and the washing machine (all products of the Second Industrial Revolution of the late nineteenth century) eventually freed women to leave the home and enter the workforce.[26] The most recent one is the ICT revolution, which is now producing AI and automation that increase efficiency and free workers from drudgery but put them out of work or "enslave" them in new ways. Yet, AI also promises to enable huge advances in many other technologies, including climate innovation.

Only a new "Climate" TEP (CTEP) can combat climate change. As in previous TEPs, this must combine institutions designed to outline and support a national mission and set ambitious technological goals. A DARPA-like agency (a CARPA?) will be needed to coordinate R&D among disparate participants including corporations, private foundations, universities, and state labs and regulate the flows of funds. A CTEP would displace old technologies, create new institutions both formal and informal, reorder social structures, and change peoples' lives.

As we lean on innovation to save us from extinction, liberalism demands a human face on the technologies developed and commercialized. If the business of business is to be business, then only the state can ensure that defending an equable climate does not unnecessarily reduce individuals' freedom to enjoy wellbeing. So, while a CARPA could set technological goals, it would also have to anticipate as much as possible their social effects so that the state can develop the institutions to mitigate expected harms.

Government Governing

According to some economists, as the challenges of climate change are increasingly felt and recognized, social pressure and market demand will "induce" innovations. This assumes that consumers know what they want and demand, for instance, more expensive and smaller electric cars rather than the affordable, comfortable, traditional ones they know and love. It also assumes that the technologies required to meet this demand are lying in wait and will be "discovered" as needed. CorpoCapitalist institutions and the governments that underpin them cannot be relied on to produce this result. What is most likely is that MegaCorps will continue to profit from GHG polluting technologies, perhaps reducing emissions with cost-effective incremental innovation, until we reap the whirlwind of the climate change disaster.

Government must perform its essential role of governing for the people, not for MegaCorps, and back technology for the people to develop and adopt radical climate innovations. Because there is no certainty that the climate innovations created will suffice to mitigate climate change, early development of the institutions of a CTEP is advisable as well as development of institutions and technologies to aid adaptation to a changing climate. Like all previous TEPs, this one will set economic systems on a new trajectory and stimulate economic growth, but liberal governments will also have to anticipate and mitigate the inevitable social impacts. As liberal governments organize the creation of radical climate innovations, whether aimed at technical challenges or the health effects of a changing climate, they will plan to mitigate any social externalities of selected technological pathways. For example, they might give priority in climate innovation to technologies that employ less-skilled workers at good wages. For the same reasons, they should abstain from most research into automation technologies that are *only* designed to replace labor but that have minimal or no climate benefit.

Climate change is an existential challenge for humanity. Yet, while mitigating or adapting to it, states also must tackle the many negative social impacts of CorpoCapitalism, from governance by MegaCorps to inequality and low wellbeing, as well as the automation MegaCorps seek. As we show in the next two chapters, Liberal Capitalism can address both the economic and political aspects of the institutional changes needed.

Chapter 10

The Purpose of the Economy

Liberal Capitalism was supposed to free the economic system of production, consumption, and exchange from the dead hand of a feudal monarch. So, the essence of Liberal Capitalism was to be the freedom of individuals to own and trade their property and labor. Yet, as states in recent years were persuaded that supporting the interests, and fulfilling the desires, of MegaCorps would increase the rate of economic growth, they moved toward CorpoCapitalism. For several reasons, in the 1970s economic growth had stalled. By removing regulations and restrictions on corporations thereafter, they hoped growth would return. While at first growth rates did rise, as we showed in chapters 3 and 8 it is clear that this liberation of MegaCorps did not similarly liberate people's wellbeing.

The reason why people's welfare and wellbeing did not climb even as GDP rose is primarily because CorpoCapitalism enabled a rapid increase in inequality. The great majority of the gains in GDP went to MegaCorps and a small sliver of high-income earners and the wealthy. In some countries most people saw little or no increase in their real incomes for decades. As we noted in chapter 8, Thomas Piketty has shown that in capitalism the wealthy always win because, except for wars and revolutions, they generally enjoy a return on their investments that is higher than the economy's growth rate.[1] Putting it simply, the wealthy always do better economically than average, even during pandemics when government support of financial markets has driven many asset prices higher. Thus, inequality inevitably increases. But capitalism per se was not the cause of the increase in inequality since the 1970s. It was the result of a political choice to actively support MegaCorps in the expectation that it would increase economic growth while ignoring most of the social and environmental consequences of that choice. In other words, CorpoCapitalism.

This tale of political manipulation of economic outcomes raises the question of what the economy is for. Is it just to grow or should it grow in a certain way? Who should benefit from economic growth? MegaCorps or most people? Liberal Capitalism is clear that the purpose of the economy is to provide the means by which *everyone* can live autonomously with opportunities to choose their lives.

States should therefore not "promote a particular view of the good life," but instead should support an institutional framework that "enables people to form and pursue their own conception of the good life."[2] A primary pillar of this good life would be the promotion of a stable, equable climate and adequate opportunities to meet basic needs and enjoy wellbeing. States should also ensure that employment pays enough to support workers, or that they receive a basic income to support them when work is unavailable, as may be the case as automation becomes more intelligent yet affordable. If the rich countries are to move from the deficiencies of CorpoCapitalism and its insufficient welfare state to a Liberal Capitalist state—to which with their wealth they should aspire—while combating climate change and adjusting to automation's discarding of human labor, the role and methods of governance must change. No longer can states patch the problems They must meet them head-on for people to be able to take responsibility for their own wellbeing, broadly understood. Giving them the ability to do so has been ignored for too long.

Democracy by MegaCorps or for the People

As noted in chapter 5, the CEOs of nearly two hundred major MegaCorps have declared that their primary purpose is no longer to maximize profits. In August 2019, these members of the exclusive Business Roundtable signed on to a Statement on the Purpose of a Corporation saying that they "share a fundamental commitment to all stakeholders including customers, employees, suppliers, and the communities in which they work, as well as generating "long-term value for shareholders."[3] The signatories and their MegaCorps have yet to put these words into practice, but merely the fact that they made this proclamation suggests to some that they may believe that rather than the "dead hand" of government being a problem, the reality is that its touch is too light! This would seem to be why the CEOs would promise to take increased responsibility for curing the ills of society and environment despite the conventional wisdom of recent decades that profit-maximization should be their main objective. Another explanation might be that like CSR it is a ploy to dissuade government from better regulating their activities. But even if they mean what they say, it is unclear how they will implement their novel beliefs.

In any event, governance by CEOs and their MegaCorps is undemocratic and illiberal. It does not respect the individual and her or his wellbeing, it solidifies the power of MegaCorps, and suffocates healthy conflict and competition with monopolies. If these MegaCorps are now to collude on what is good for society and act together based on what they decide, rather than focusing on competing in markets, the potential for cartels increases. It therefore disrespects not only the preferences of the populace but even the choices of people more narrowly defined as simply consumers. Governance by CEOs and their MegaCorps therefore cements a completely inappropriate social and political leadership role for an elite of wealthy individuals and the MegaCorps they run.

Rather than more of a role for MegaCorps in directing social as well as economic activity, some scholars propose more of a role for governments. The Nobel Prize–winning economist Joseph Stiglitz argues for a "progressive capitalism" based on a new social contract that better balances the roles of government, market, and civil society and, therefore, rewrites the rules of the economy.[4] He says that government must do more to aid the transition to a twenty-first-century economy with better retraining programs and industrial policies, and place-based policies that recognize the value of social relations and family integrity. Then he adds the need to strengthen the social safety net. In reading his entertaining book, it is difficult to ignore his preference for European ways over American ones. We do not believe that the European countries he so admires have delivered an economic and social nirvana, but we do believe that more needs to be done to transition the *notionally* liberal capitalist states to *truly* Liberal Capitalist states—that is, so that they are not liberal in name only. To do so means implementing the four guiding ideas of liberalism presented in chapter 2, because these *are* the purpose of the economy: accepting some *conflict*, encouraging *progress*, *respecting* individual life choices, and proscribing the use of excessive *power*.

Economic Efficiency or Fairness

A small book published in 1975 is widely misunderstood and as a result of its title has become an important lodestar of policy to many conservative policymakers. Arthur Okun's *Equality and Efficiency: The Big Tradeoff* could, at face value, seem to claim that equality is the enemy of efficiency and growth, and if so to justify the end of the welfare state that had sustained postwar capitalism for thirty years. Over that period, the distribution of income had been fairly static in the rich countries and had even become more equal in some. But like other economists at the time, Okun thought that this state of affairs was a feature of capitalism alone. Therefore, he thought middle-class incomes would increase roughly in line with the overall growth rate of the economy, and that policy should be directed at increasing the national rate of economic growth. Yet, he also cautioned:

> The domain of rights is part of the checks and balances on the market designed to preserve *values that are not denominated in dollars*. For the same reasons that an investor holds many different stocks and bonds in his portfolio, society diversifies its mechanisms for distribution and allocation. It won't put all of its eggs in the market's basket.[5]

He further noted that for this reason "real gross national product should not and cannot measure social welfare." Okun believed that everyone who participates in economic life should earn no less than half of the *average* income, that access to luxuries may be allocated unequally but access to essentials such as education be allocated equally, and that there should be no "contrasts between the civilization of different classes."[6] These values are fully consonant with Liberal Capitalism because they involve equality of opportunity as opposed to equality of outcomes.

To deliver true wellbeing for all, classical liberals in the vein of Adam Smith have always advised that government must continually balance the demands of society with economic efficiency to maintain progress and suppress excessive conflict within society. Indeed, Smith foresaw the need for governments to manage the social and political impacts of short-term economic shocks as well as the long-term adjustments necessary as a result of putting markets in charge. So too did Keynes 150 years later. Today, governments faced with potential climate catastrophe, high and rising inequality, and labor-less automation must consider the long-term viability of the state while respecting the private purposes of the people. This means that governments must reserve to themselves the power to effect social change yet use that power judiciously to keep the economic goose of capitalism laying the golden eggs of material plenty.

Governments and MegaCorps around the world have (or it may be more accurate to say had) taken to heart Milton Friedman's dictum that "the social responsibility of business is to increase its profits," but as we noted in chapter 5 Friedman never advocated the withdrawal of government or the withering of regulating institutions.[7] He expected government to make laws in the interests of society that business would follow because they were effectively enforced. As such, the role of government was to ensure fairness, safety, and all other manner of desirable social outcomes, while the role of corporations was to make money. Although his followers might not like to admit it, this view actually dovetails with, rather than opposes, those held by critics of liberalism who generally say that it fails to bind people to the group, community, or nation and encourages them to go their own way. Liberalism, they say, cannot transport us to the mythical land where collective morality and the desire to live in accord with others overrules the naked self-interest so evident today.[8] Milton Friedman would agree.

Let us step back and start from the position that what is central to healthy societies is fairness. Evidence from history and anthropology shows that self-interest is actually not a principal characteristic of humanity.[9] Humans, like most primates, harbor an innate sense of fairness and want to punish those who have more.[10] The free market is blind to such values, yet it too is important because humans are also possessed of an innate and very social "disposition to truck, barter and exchange," which Smith and other liberals celebrate.[11] They also recognize that the lack of ability to do so, or an inability to benefit from so doing, destroys happiness and then destroys society. As such, liberals accept that gross inequality increases conflict and retards progress, in addition to disrespecting those who suffer from it. They therefore accept that something must be done about it.

The many perceived defects of liberalism are the consequence of treating liberalism and capitalism as one and the same. Today, they are not. But people expect fairness as well as economic freedoms. We therefore *naturally* expect the rules of the game to be fair, not rigged for the benefit of a tiny minority, so that anyone with brains and effort (and some luck) might advance. Liberals understand that this expectation of fairness that glues individuals into groups and holds societies together leads to conflict when it is obviously overridden. So it is with the economic aspects of the challenges we face. As we will show in the following sections, a liberal response to them must seek to apply the government's power only where and when necessary, and in such a way as to preserve personal autonomy, in order to balance economic efficiency with fairness. We start with climate change.

Preventing Climate Catastrophe

Climate change will impact, and already is impacting, every industry in every country. So will policies to prevent a climate catastrophe. If actions are taken early enough, there may be the opportunity for economic growth as a result of them, but the later they are taken the greater will be the costs of dramatically reducing emissions—in rich countries by up to 80 percent. So, doing less now will have greater economic as well as social costs later.

Action must be taken, and market mechanisms like carbon taxes or cap and trade systems are popular among mainstream economists. We showed in the previous chapter that carbon taxes are more invasive of personal autonomy and consumer liberty (and, therefore, less liberal) than cap and trade. And while liberalism rejects command-and-control approaches if directed at individuals' behavior, as a regulatory approach to MegaCorps' production methods it is more acceptable. However, any national strategies to limit producer emissions will only generate marginally innovative technologies and therefore contribute less to both climate mitigation and economic growth than a government-led mission for climate innovation.

More fundamentally, nonmainstream economists like Yanis Varoufakis question why market solutions to climate change like cap and trade or taxes are considered "best." As he writes:

> The only reason to adopt a market solution such as this is because government can't be trusted, and yet this solution depends entirely on the government for it to work. Who decides what the original quota of pollution will be? Who monitors each farmer, fisherman, train or car's emissions?[12]

The same criticism applies to the rate to set carbon taxes and how to vary them to allow for behavioral changes. But Varoufakis has a larger point to make, which is that arguments revolving purely around calculations of costs and benefits using economic values risk missing the point that a balance needs to be struck between efficiency and fairness. Those who lose their life to climate change or a pandemic (as we are experiencing in 2020–2021) do not make economically rational bargains with God. They would give almost any economic asset not to die. Even more so, if enjoying wellbeing living under Liberal Capitalism. Which they do not if they live in grossly unequal societies.

The secret of capitalism is that it accumulates wealth throughout society to be reallocated to increase production and productivity. The secret of CorpoCapitalism is its accumulation of wealth and power by a self-interested elite. Jeffrey Sachs suggests that one billion dollars is enough for anyone. Four large houses, a private jet, what else does one need?[13] It is not for government to set the answer to this question. However, because wealth is substantially a matter of good fortune—the country, the time, and the family into which one is born, the education one receives, the people one meets, and so on—there are valid reasons for governments to limit the accumulation of vast wealth in an elite.

Countries have grown rich that have used institutions to prevent an elite from cornering wealth and power.[14] It is a catastrophic irony that those same countries now glory in a new elite that is decimating the beneficial strength of Liberal Capitalism in the name of raising the nation. Too many governments have abdicated too much of their role as provider of public goods. Often, they are happy to delegate that function to wealthy individuals. As a letter to the editor of *The Economist* eloquently explains:

> The real problem is that so many public goods, such as education, the arts and philanthropy [and we might add, climate change], are already dependent on private billionaires and their sometimes benign but sometimes sleazy foundations. But why should we invite corporate billionaires to control which social and economic problems deserve attention, to say nothing about how those problems might be treated?[15]

This echoes the idea that responsibility for social concerns cannot be left to the whims of unelected CEOs and the MegaCorps they run and that preserving the public good of a clement climate cannot be left to plutocrats. They can protect themselves, but it is a central responsibility of elected governments to protect *all* their people and especially those with fewer resources or opportunities. This requires new institutions and modifications of old ones not only to incite climate innovation but to mitigate its impacts. In creating the institutions to do so governments must—as we advocated for climate innovation in the previous chapter—seek to anticipate and alleviate the impacts they are likely to have throughout society and economy. And not just on climate change but on inequality, economic growth, and wellbeing.

Wealth and Capital

At the heart of addressing such concerns is the regulation of how wealth is accumulated and used. For our current purposes, "wealth" is equivalent to net assets (total assets less total liabilities). For individuals it may include a person's home and personal assets, as well as financial assets, for corporations their net assets. Capital, however, is wealth that is directly invested in a productive enterprise. Capital is how wealth is put to productive use and is the lifeblood of productive enterprises. It finances productive capacity, necessary business operations, and technological innovation. Its source may be private wealth (for example, investing in start-up enterprises before listing on public markets) or the accumulated (retained) profits of a productive enterprise.

Wealth is what is accumulated; capital is how it is used. And its use may be productive, unproductive, or even destructive, depending on the institutions that enable and regulate it.[16] Entrepreneurs like Jeff Bezos or Mark Zuckerberg are lauded for accumulating massive wealth. Whatever the faults of Amazon and Facebook, it must be acknowledged that they built businesses and employed workers. However, profits from many financial activities such as share trading, financial engineering, and real estate development are more extractive than productive. Similarly, purchasing shares on a stock exchange (after the original listing) simply represents an *allocation* of wealth. It does not provide capital to enterprises as they only benefit from an increase in the value of their shares, which may just enable acquisitions of other firms or increased executive bonuses rather than the creation of new products or processes. Therefore, to enable progress and so reduce conflict, Liberal Capitalism would want to optimize the overall capital in the economy for productive investment.

Thomas Piketty, Emmanuel Saez, and Gabriel Zucman argue that because it is nearly impossible to measure the income and consumption of the wealthy, the best way to prevent excessive wealth accumulation is to tax it.[17] The primary way to achieve this is through wealth and inheritance taxes. To counter wealth inequality, several rich countries levy an annual tax on personal wealth. Historically, tax rates have been low, revenues minimal, and administration cumbersome. However, through improved fiscal technology, including cross-border wealth declarations, an efficient and effective progressive taxation of wealth should now be practical. Each country would have to determine the appropriate tax rate, but generally an annual tax on wealth of around 5 percent could at least stabilize the net holdings of the wealthy in order to prevent the wealth gap from widening.[18] Higher marginal tax rates on the largest fortunes would begin to reverse wealth inequality. And in determining the tax *base*, wealth that has been invested as capital in productive enterprise that employs a minimum number of workers, or that is invested in basic research for climate innovation, could be exempt. A range of options could thus be considered in order to reduce wealth inequality to either the historical level of the post–World War II period, or whatever level most people consider fair while preserving the accumulation of wealth that supports capital investment.

Most countries impose taxes either on estates or inheritances to reduce the intergenerational advantages of wealth. And why not? From a liberal point of view, it is legitimate to question why future generations should feel a sense of entitlement to be born into great wealth that is due to no effort on their part. In other words, to be born into an elite that can earn income or gain education without effort due to the ownership of previous generations' accumulated assets. Tax rates on inherited wealth that optimally balance efficiency and equity might be as high as 50 to 60 percent or more. A political argument for even higher rates might be hard, but a moral argument could certainly be made for them.[19] For example, the "Gilded Age" industrialist Andrew Carnegie claimed that amassing wealth was idolatry, though he did it very effectively. However, he also wrote that "the man who dies rich dies disgraced." Giving away wealth as Carnegie did cements his memory in thousands of libraries across America and a university. Modeled after his sentiments and actions, The

Giving Pledge hopes to make the world's richest people address society's most pressing problems.[20] Politics in some countries has ensured that estate taxes generate little revenue, do nothing to raise opportunities for the poor, and little to restrain the rich.

Yet, why the choice of social improvements should be left to a few hugely rich people is hard to justify over a more democratic redistribution of wealth on death. Increasing the wealth of the poor would also help close the wealth gap. Anthony Atkinson proposes a distribution to every child at birth, a birthright of citizenship that could be paid out of wealth tax revenues.[21] The state may also aid poorer savers by guaranteeing a rate of interest higher than inflation to match the investment advantage of the rich. And likewise, it may implement a range of initiatives to balance incomes.

Balancing Incomes

Most rich countries use progressive tax rates on labor income to reduce the disposable income of the highest paid. Canada and the US also use a negative income tax to raise the disposable income of low-wage earners to help combat income inequality. Yet, in most countries it is clear that income inequality before tax has risen and, in some countries, (for example, the US) income inequality after taxes and transfers has not fallen. If the wages of the majority of workers are stagnating or failing to increase by as much as those of a small minority of high-income earners, as noted in chapter 5, then a progressive tax system is not so much a solution to the problem as a band-aid on it. A more direct way to increase the earning of low-skilled workers is to require employers to pay at least a minimum wage that is indexed to an appropriate measure of the inflation in the costs of basic needs. A higher minimum wage would decrease the number of working poor, potentially increase demand, and thereby drive economic growth. This certainly seems like a better, and more liberal, approach than supporting and subsidizing MegaCorps to do so.

Opponents of a more livable minimum wage argue that it risks pricing low-skilled labor so high that it encourages work to be automated away, or that it reduces youth employment.[22] However, the overall rate of unemployment is affected by many other factors including the structure of the economy, labor laws, available and demanded skills, and global competition. For example, minimum wages vary widely between countries as do unemployment rates. In 2018 Australia had the highest at US$23,976 while in the US it was US$15,080, and most EU countries had minimum wages between these two extremes.[23] While unemployment (especially among the young) is higher in most EU countries than in the US, unemployment in Australia was only slightly above that in the US. And even if a higher minimum wage threatens employment of low-skilled workers or the young, governments can mitigate the effects by adjusting other policies, including retraining and employment subsidies.

Even more than this could be considered. Universal basic income (UBI) is a simple idea with big implications. Much has been written on it recently, though it is a concept that has been around since at least the sixteenth century in the writings of Thomas More and Johannes Vives and in the eighteenth century by Thomas Paine, a liberal philosopher responsible for much of the thinking behind the US Constitution.[24] Today, UBI is understood as a periodic payment to every citizen, a basic endowment supported by the natural or physical wealth of the nation.[25] The broadest definition of UBI is that it is unconditional, automatic, not means tested, individual, and a right of citizenship.[26] It is "the provision of basic levels of economic security to reduce inequality and promote solidarity, in the face of technological and environmental change" and an antidote to the place CorpoCapitalism has taken the world.[27]

It looks on the surface like a radical, maybe even socialist alternative to CorpoCapitalism. But it is not. It is nothing less than the basis for the Liberal Capitalist state of the twenty-first century. The government does not tell people what to spend the money on, does not dictate how the funds might be spent in general, and does not prevent anyone from earning more because of their individual endeavors. Instead, it enables individuals to make choices that may improve their wellbeing. It differs in nature and social impact from the welfare state, which ekes out minimum support through a Kafkaesque bureaucracy pedantically applying myriad rules. In principle, it is not essentially different from public education, public health services, or state provision of basic health care, each of which are the basis for the opportunity to increase personal wellbeing and autonomy. While it is provided through the government, it frees everyone from its bureaucracy and control.

It also allows those sidelined by automation to support themselves while looking for alternative work or reskilling. Lower-skilled workers still in employment have a little more power when negotiating conditions, or when applying for a job with an employer. In short, it begins to relieve many workers from the inevitability of wage slavery. Echoing many of the reasons against a livable minimum wage, opponents of UBI argue that it will starve the economy of labor. While much research is speculative at this point, some of it shows that receiving unearned income has little or no effect on labor supply.[28] In fact, to believe that it does suggests that the only way to get people to work is to punish them for failing to do so, rather than encouraging them through the obvious rewards. But first, the rewards must be there.

If they are not, then UBI also encourages creativity, perhaps giving individuals time and space to better develop their abilities and to understand what brings them wellbeing. It supports "the power of the people to reach their creative potential," through entrepreneurialism and risk-taking.[29] It also would support volunteering among the working age population, which would enhance social capital. Today, much volunteer labor is provided by retirees supported by a state pension. A UBI may operate similarly, encouraging younger people to build a society as well as an economy.

UBI is not a fairy tale. It is being tested in many rich countries and has attracted interest, for divergent reasons, across the political spectrum. It is being considered or trialed in the UK, Hawaii, France, Ontario, and Finland. The Finnish trial found that UBI participants were happier but were not more likely to get a job, which the trial designers had hoped would happen.[30] But even if it doesn't do this, UBI may perform other important social functions. In 2020, the government-imposed lockdown to prevent the spread of the deadly COVID-19 virus prevented most Spaniards from supporting themselves through work. This prompted the Spanish government to plan the biggest test yet of UBI. It aimed to supplement the incomes of up to three million of its poorest citizens.[31] The minister of economic affairs was quoted as saying: "We're going to do it as soon as possible. So, it can be useful, not just for this extraordinary situation." In fact, as the minister commented, the government hopes it becomes a "permanent safety net for the most vulnerable." Recently, however, the economic costs of the current pandemic have overwhelmed Spain's small wealth tax and forced a substantial modification. Now it is to be more targeted at poverty as a "permanent" minimum income for those earning less than 40 percent of the median monthly income, in which case it becomes an indirect subsidy to employers who do not pay a living wage.[32]

UBI is no panacea. By itself it will not protect economic security against a changing climate or diminish the economic control and power of MegaCorps. It also needs more research and testing. But it is a legitimate first step in addressing the problem of income inequality.

Government to the Rescue

Governments should govern. That means reducing the power of MegaCorps and eliminating corrosive CorpoCapitalism. It has happened before. In the US in the early twentieth century, President Theodore Roosevelt actively broke up anticompetitive monopolies and cartels ("trusts"). As he kick-started his Progressive Era reforms, Roosevelt declared:

> When I say that I am for the square deal, I mean not merely that I stand for fair play under the present rules of the game, but that I stand for having those rules changed so as to work for a more substantial equality of opportunity and of reward for equally good service.[33]

His administration was classic Liberal Capitalist in its objectives. For example, he also said:

> The State cannot prosper unless the average man can take care of himself; and neither can it prosper unless the average man realizes that, in addition to taking care of himself, he must work with his fellows, with good sense and honesty and practical acknowledgement of obligation to the community as a whole.[34]

The common presumption is that everyone will support themselves through work if they are able. Liberal Capitalism agrees that liberty implies personal responsibility to support oneself, if one is able, and contribute to the community. However, logically, that is only possible if the central purpose of the economy is to provide the means by which everyone may potentially support themselves. For this to be a legitimate purpose, the economy must be organized to provide jobs at the right wages—to people with the right skills within a changing climate—and rapid automation. It also means addressing, rather than supporting, the power of MegaCorps. In the next chapter we consider how judicious application of government power can do that.

Chapter 11

The Purpose of the Politics

Liberal Capitalism is not simply a set of policies. It is rather a set of policy *orientations* informed by political *values*. These produce ideologies that affect how, what, and whose interests are served. That sounds a bit complicated, because it is, but we explain later how they do. Just as it is simplistic to say poverty will be made history when we do X, Y, and Z, so it is simplistic to say that capitalism's liberal promise will be realized when all states do A, B, and C. What is required are the institutional settings that make this promise more likely to be realized, based on the belief that it should be. That is an easy thing to say in theory, but it is harder to say what it means in practice because the world does not work like the models presented in textbooks. For example, students of politics learn that there are nationalist and Marxist perspectives in addition to liberal ones. Adherents to these other traditions have different visions of the way the world *should* work. Nationalists stress the role of "the state" in controlling and transforming the economy, and in *making* "the market" rather than enabling it. Marxists are drawn to revolution as a way of overturning the class relations produced by capitalism that they believe ensure a small and powerful elite dominate and exploit a growing mass of alienated workers. They desire a postcapitalist world. Others still may be drawn to the power of ideas, of culture and identity as determinants of political processes, as stressed by more sociological and postmodern approaches. But if all they do is try to work out whether the world "is" liberal, nationalist, or Marxist, or how it may be explained in different ways by different people at different times, they will have missed the point that there is a difference between theories as ideologies versus theories as analytical tools.

So, one may see the huge concentrations of wealth and economic power in the hands of MegaCorps, understand that this is politically enabled by powerful states whose governments practice CorpoCapitalism, and conclude that a Marxist analysis seems to "fit" the reality rather well. And so it does, but does that make you a Marxist? Not necessarily, because *both* Adam Smith and Karl Marx focused on the emancipation of populations from those who controlled the means of production in their time: the monarchical state for Smith and the capitalist class for Marx. Today, neither would have been comfortable with the power enjoyed by MegaCorps through CorpoCapitalism. Marx would have wanted a revolution to overthrow the transnational capitalist class that uses MegaCorps as the organizational form for oppressing and exploiting the masses. Smith would have preferred their replacement by a multitude of competitive entrepreneurial businesses, guided by the "invisible hand" of competitive markets in which individuals are empowered to make choices.

In other words, if they were alive today, they would agree on the problems while disagreeing on what to do about them, because their values differed. As we possess liberal values, we want capitalism to realize its liberal promise, but how do we get out of the current vicious circle in which states use their power to support MegaCorps rather than their citizens directly, and MegaCorps in turn prop up governments? This is our focus in this chapter. We first reprise the political implications of the reality of controlled markets, but not powerless governments, in rich countries. Then, we consider the liberal values necessary to put us on the road to Liberal Capitalism in theory, as well as some examples of what this means in practice, rather than the current reality of CorpoCapitalism. This leads to our conclusion that governments are central to institutionally building better states to underpin, rather than undermine, Liberal Capitalism.

Controlled Markets, but Not Powerless Governments

As explained in chapter 4, almost every industry is controlled by a handful of powerful MegaCorps. Control rather than competition is the norm. *The free market is dead.* The public benefits that theory proclaims to be derived from the free market are confronted by the reality that only what benefits MegaCorps matters. For example, in its special report on the world's most powerful companies, *The Economist* speaks of a "tech aristocracy" comprised of Alphabet, Amazon, Microsoft, Apple, and Facebook at whose pleasure smaller firms are permitted to do business. This corporate royalty now outsources its risk and R&D either to government or to entrepreneurial start-ups expecting to own the results produced, much as states hired mercenaries in the past to fight their wars. It is so powerful that it can readily absorb even large, mature enterprises like Instagram and WhatsApp, which were acquired by Facebook for US$1 billion and nearly US$22 billion, respectively, in 2012 and 2014. Or LinkedIn bought by Microsoft in 2018 for US$26.2 billion.[1]

The patterns of corporate control in the high value-added, technologically advanced industries are spreading to other parts of the economy. Small retailers have always been challenged by bigger chains. Bookstores have found it hard to compete against the likes of Waterstones and Barnes & Noble. General retailers like Macys now face annihilation by Amazon's and other online retail platforms. The bigger chains like Walmart are in turn forced to enter Amazon's cyberspace in their attempts to compete on its terms. Those offering services like hotels have always had to dramatically differentiate themselves or compete on price against the likes of the Hilton and Sheraton chains. Now such firms risk being rendered obsolete by Airbnb,[2] just as taxi and car hire firms are by Uber. Like their larger competitors, they must join rather than compete with these platforms to survive. The result for workers, as discussed in chapter 5, is a "hellscape" on the factory floor, or precarious employment as temporary contractors to the new market "disruptors."

The current arrangements are neither natural nor inevitable, but they will be hard to change because they have been politically enabled. MegaCorps arose from, but did not cause, CorpoCapitalism. The governments of rich countries did, through the rules they made, and the international agreements they negotiated. Supposedly liberal states have in reality had governments practicing CorpoCapitalism, which in so doing have attacked rather than underpinned the liberal values on which their countries were founded and are supposed to function. The result is that while politics should be about democratic processes and elected representatives, too often it is about corporate interests and corporate control.

It could be argued that the political traffic is not all one way, and in fact that the MegaCorp–government relationship is symbiotic.

As Joshua Barkan notes in *Corporate Sovereignty: Law and Government under Capitalism*:

> Corporations and states *model* each other's defining features. Likewise, modern corporate power *emerges from* and *mobilizes* apparatuses of sovereignty, discipline, and government. In this manner, corporate power and state sovereignty depend on one another, each establishing the other's condition of possibility.[3]

But even if it is true that corporations and states model each other's defining features, it is MegaCorps and their shareholders that benefit from the status quo. Liberal values are antithetical to serving their interests, and therefore it is the governments of states that must drive the changes necessary.

Liberal Values

Politics, as invented by the Greeks, is a way of getting what you want without killing somebody. It is about winning the argument, rather than possessing the brute force to win the fight. And it is about establishing the basis on which the arguments are held before they are held. So, politics is all about values. These come before power, satisfying interests, and having control over outcomes. They come before institutions. Politics is a contest of ideas aimed at changing outcomes and challenging (or supporting) the existing order. So, there is always an opportunity to change the basis of political arguments by supporting certain values applicable to all everywhere. In the process, the interests of the main protagonists, or those whom they serve, are often promoted. Sometimes, undermining existing values is a project embarked on in order to ensure others' interests are served. For example, the rise of populism in democratic, rich states is driven by their citizens' growing appetite for change and for their interests to be served rather than those of "elites."

The values behind this appetite are the problem. Too often populism is devoid of values but suffused with personal interests, perhaps to grab power for the aggrandizement of the populist by forcefully rejecting the status quo. For example, in the 2020 US election Donald Trump never offered a set of positive values to pursue or a policy platform to achieve them. He merely trashed the Democrats and claimed he would be a great president, effectively demanding a personal vote. We might agree with some of Trump's supporters on some of the structural changes that are necessary, but because we hold liberal values we hope that political leaders—including populist ones—deliver us from CorpoCapitalism to Liberal Capitalism rather than the extreme nationalist, potentially even fascist, alternatives that sometimes seem more likely (see chapter 8).

What are the characteristics of a beneficial populist, that Pied Piper who rids the town of rats and not children, and might lead the people to their liberal wellbeing? Max Weber defined that person as a politician who balances two ethics, one of ideals (or "values") and one of responsibility:

> It is immensely moving when a *mature* man—no matter whether old or young in years—is aware of a responsibility for the consequences of his conduct and really feels such responsibility with heart and soul. He then acts by following an ethic of responsibility and somewhere he reaches the point where he says: "Here I stand; I can do no other." . . . an ethic of ultimate ends and an ethic of responsibility are not absolute contrasts but rather supplements, which only in unison constitute a genuine man—a man who can have the "calling for politics."[4]

To put it another way, this truly beneficial populist accepts responsibility for how he or she follows the path to the ultimate end of the peoples' autonomous pursuit of their individual wellbeing, and recognizes that absolutes may be a guide but not a goal in a democracy.

Today's populists fail the responsibility test, pursuing their absolutist ends by any means possible whomever they injure. Populists are often strong leaders, with a fervent desire to wield their power. As they are drawn to rule with the stroke of a pen or a sword, rather than through liberal institutions such as parliaments and parliamentary processes, they are a threat to liberal freedoms and thence wellbeing. In addition to observing that "power tends to corrupt, and absolute power corrupts absolutely" Lord Acton declared that "great men are almost always bad men."[5] But beneficial populists are not just strong leaders. They are those who promote clear values and aspire to be *great*. And if they are great, then they are not just great on their own account. They act through the legitimate power of government for all the people, not because they know what is good for them, but because they give their citizens the freedom to choose what is good for themselves. They know what institutions to construct and reinforce (rather than just those to tear down or ignore) to ensure this.

That all sounds very utopian, but not if we accept that it is an ultimate end toward which we all may strive. A bit like justice or righteousness are elusive yet worthy goals, surely something approximating Weber's ideal politician is needed in many countries, now even more than ever. We observe that Liberal Capitalism has a track record of producing jobs, economic growth, opportunities for progress, and a whole host of other positive results in addition to the negative ones. Others with different values will disagree and may say that, based on their ideologies arising from these values, alternative institutional arrangements produce "better" results. Setting aside the obscured value debate in any such proclamation, we reject institutional change that is so revolutionary it takes us into uncharted, and no doubt shark-infested, postcapitalist waters. Regimes that have previously attempted to steer their ships of state into them are not countries where we would choose to live. So, then the question is: how do we bring about these changes without a revolution or dystopian upheaval, whether environmental or sociopolitical?

As a starting point, there is always the need for a balance between "private opulence and public squalor" as John Kenneth Galbraith put it in his 1958 classic *The Affluent Society*.[6] He declared that believing public squalor—whether caused from environmental degradation, or extreme inequality of wealth and income, and especially from inequality of opportunity—is untenable in the midst of plenty "suggests no revolutionary dalliance with socialism."[7] Nor any other more radical alternatives. What it does suggest is that Liberal Capitalism needs institutional underpinnings that work on the basis of liberal values, and governments that act to regulate based on these liberal institutions, as opposed to permitting a slide toward authoritarianism or anarchy.

This slide is in progress. The pathologies of CorpoCapitalism are not just untenable; they are unsustainable—economically, socially, and ecologically. They run the risk of bringing about the end of capitalism, which is what the Marxists also desire albeit not in the same way as the populists would wish to deliver its demise, and along with this end any hope of Liberal Capitalism. So, the role of government must be to create a virtuous circle in which the state supports people who support corporations, rather than supporting corporations in the belief that as they become MegaCorps they will support the people.

Liberal Values in Practice

It is hard to generalize on what this means in practice, because the political institutions necessary are not some global institutional blueprint to be applied to all states, societies, and governments. Such a prescription, in fact the very nature of it as a *prescription*, would hardly be liberal! What we can say, as a start, is that from a liberal perspective, the institutional arrangements necessary are those that stimulate the people to demand their birthright: freedom. In the beginning this must be through values that happen to be common to both rich and poor, and therefore potentially receive broad support. But in the end, this must translate into prevention of concentrated and uncompetitive markets, promotion of competition, and prevention of monopolies. At all times, or at least as much as possible, government should be at arm's length from business to allow markets to coordinate economic activity unless intervention is required to protect people from harm.

But there is a fundamental problem in saying this. If the free market has been killed by MegaCorps with the support of CorpoCapitalist governments, then the reality is that governments are not at arm's length. The intimate relationship between MegaCorps and governments must be acknowledged, yet it must somehow be transformed as the basis for regulation of the former by the latter in the interests of individuals and the societies in which they live. This is a fairly standard conclusion in mainstream liberal economics. It is what public authorities are meant to do when prices are set on the basis of market power not market forces, where production happens not on the basis of efficiency but dominance, and where investment levels can be low in the absence of competitive pressures to innovate. In other words, all the pathologies of CorpoCapitalism we have demonstrated.

Can governments effectively regulate MegaCorps despite being so close to them? In other words, to regulate them *as if* being at arm's length was the rule rather than the exception. Unfortunately, we do not think this very likely as the horse has long bolted on Milton Friedman's ideal of business doing business and government doing government, with a big gulf separating the two.[8] Or to use another metaphor, you cannot unscramble an omelet to extract an egg.

Yet, it may be possible for the omelet to be scrambled differently. As we noted in chapter 5, John Braithwaite's arguments around regulatory capitalism are the hopeful flipside to those about powerless states.[9] We have our doubts if this is on the basis of MegaCorps' CSR, but one of his main points not discussed in that chapter was that markets that are characterized by a handful of big operators are easier to control, and tax, than those comprised of an enormous number of small firms. So, MegaCorps are *potentially* more regulable at both the national and global levels as they can be more easily "seen."[10] This is especially the case if we stop talking in obtuse terms about the evils of neoliberalism, the power of capital, of the marketization of daily life, and instead focus on the employment practices of Amazon, the control of social relations by Facebook, and the attempted domination of environmental and social policymaking by ExxonMobil.[11]

What is needed is for rich countries' governments to be pressured to regulate MegaCorps in the interests of the citizens they represent by populists espousing liberal capitalist values. This pressure at the national level will have to be matched at the global level. Only then may we hope that in the process they will address challenges such as climate change, fixing their broken welfare states, and take back responsibility for enabling individuals in their societies, including in respect of technological innovation.

Climate Change

Before governments do more, they must first do less. As pointed out in chapter 4, the subsidies and protections for fossil fuel industries amount to trillions of dollars each year. Before any other measures are taken, these must be wound back. This is the point made by Arnold Schwarzenegger, movie star and former governor of the State of California turned YouTube vlogger. In his clip of 28 June 2018, he says that as renewable energy sources are to coal, so are streaming services like Netflix to the video rental stores of the 1990s, like Blockbuster. Only by the government protecting, subsidizing, or forcing people to drive to video stores to rent DVDs could Blockbuster survive today, just as it is only economic for electricity utilities to use coal if government mandates they do so.[12] There is a wealth of data to back his argument, like that which shows that renewable energy generation is already cheaper than fossil fuel generated energy.[13] If the environmental costs are factored in as well, then there is literally no comparison. Also, renewable energy employs more workers. For example, it is estimated that there are now 855,000 workers employed in renewable energy industries in the US, by comparison to around 50,000 in mining coal.[14]

Renewable energy is cheaper, employs more workers, is better for the environment, and if the market was allowed to work, and was competitive, there would be greater access to it. Then, because it is socially as well as environmentally desirable, governments could take the trillions of dollars no longer spent on propping up and protecting uncompetitive fossil fuel industries and spend it on socially and environmentally desirable outcomes instead. That is what liberal governments are meant to do: govern to enhance the welfare of their citizens, not the aristocracy, not cronies with the right connections from the right families, and not MegaCorps. As a first step governments should remove subsidies for inefficient polluting industries and channel the funds elsewhere to address, rather than ensure, the threat of climate change.

The Welfare State

In fact, governments should spend public funds differently in all sorts of ways. The current welfare arrangements can neither equalize incomes and wealth, nor provide opportunities for individuals to look after themselves. This is because providing a basic social safety welfare net while allowing markets to work is no longer sufficient, when the legacy of CorpoCapitalism is that competitive markets for goods or labor have been destroyed by MegaCorps. Therefore, a new approach to welfare is required. UBI, as mentioned in chapter 10, is one component of such an approach. It empowers workers to speak up and negotiate their conditions from a position of greater financial security. It empowers them to make choices, such as through having the ability to walk away from forced labor. It empowers them to take risks, such as on new entrepreneurial ventures, rather than forcing them into the arms of MegaCorps that hire contract staff for other MegaCorps. Or to start up small businesses, perhaps to challenge and compete with MegaCorps rather than hoping that they will be bought by them. Or to do something else entirely that better fits their personal wellbeing.

It is not up to us to say what individuals should or shouldn't do with their freedom, but we can say that rather than serving MegaCorps backed by governments practicing CorpoCapitalism, individuals backed by governments with welfare arrangements that enable them to look after their own wellbeing should be at the center of Liberal Capitalism. This, to our mind, is more desirable than governments that make collective decisions for them. In line with the liberal guiding ideas of conflict and power prevention, liberal governments should instead support the open negotiation between management and workers that was lost when labor unions were crushed. This does not mean that they should bring back what was lost. But they do need to bring back the potential for negotiation and contestation.

Chapter 8 concluded that governments are not responsible for our wellbeing, but they are responsible for so arranging the contexts within which we live so that each of us may better discover what our wellbeing entails. For example, as we noted in chapter 6, social democracies to a large extent take over functions that we believe should be left to individuals and families. But that does not mean that the role of government is to punish those who are unable to look after themselves. The function of welfare in rich countries should not be so punitive that it actually *prevents* individuals from getting back on their own two feet and serving their own interests. Therefore, public investment in education should be greatly increased, because of its links to social mobility. Like UBI, education enables individuals to make choices and enhances the potential for them to serve their own interests, rather than those of MegaCorps. It also again means that they can better bargain with those MegaCorps from a position of strength, rather than accepting what they are offered while relying on government welfare subsidies, such as tax credits for the working poor as we pointed out in chapter 7.

These examples are by no means exhaustive, but they serve to illustrate the point that not only have governments handed MegaCorps the right to control their markets, not to compete in them, if they do not reform their welfares states to empower individual workers they risk also handing MegaCorps the role of governing over society.

Social Responsibility

It is time for governments to not simply attack MegaCorps but to change the way MegaCorps themselves are governed. They are, after all, the legal constructions of states as opposed to leading an autonomous existence separate from them. It could of course be contended that MegaCorps can govern others as well as themselves, because they now espouse CSR. It also may seem nice that their CEOs now promise to take responsibility for addressing the major challenges faced by society, as noted in chapter 5. However, these extremely well-remunerated managers of shareholders' interests are not the representatives of citizens. Their claims to act on behalf of society are not democratically legitimate. It therefore falls to governments to legally require MegaCorps to address social issues arising from their operations, and not to just leave it up to their boards and senior managers to decide what these are and how to "fix" them. If the business of business is now to be socially responsible, and business is increasingly monopolistic, then it surely follows that the role of government in representing society is to legally stipulate the parameters by which business fulfills a public or social role.

We need to change the way we think about business in the process. Not as serving private interests but as performing a public service. For example, it may not be too far-fetched to regard some MegaCorps like Facebook and Amazon as akin to public utilities. The former provides communications and media platforms and services akin to the telecommunications, mail, and public broadcasting of years gone by. The latter is like an augmented, virtual main street, where all manner of retail products and services are browsed and purchased. They are nothing less than the economic infrastructure of the twenty-first century. They need to be legally regarded as such, with corporate governance obligations that flow from the role they play in reality as opposed to the mythology of them existing as private competitive entities in markets.

Technological Innovation

Apart from such obvious measures as banning the manipulation of the share price by using their revenues and reserves to buy and sell their own shares, what kinds of legal obligations should governments impose on MegaCorps? Mariana Mazzucato's research, discussed in chapter 9, gives an indication of what might be a good starting point for considering them. She challenges the conventional wisdom that the private sector is dynamic and innovative, whereas the state is slow and bureaucratic. By presenting a range of pertinent examples, she shows that it is the government that does basic research and development, and that drives economic and social change. For example, she points out that 67 percent of the pharmaceutical industry's research is directed to variations of existing drugs, or what she calls "me too drugs," on which its MegaCorps hold patents. The reality is that 75 percent of radically new drugs are produced in government funded and/or run laboratories. This permits

"CEOs to spend most of their time focusing on how to boost their stock prices (e.g., through stock repurchase programmes)."[15]

It is not just the pharmaceutical industry that gets to have its research done for it, make money from the results, and is given monopoly price-setting power through intellectual property protection to do so. There are other examples, like Apple, which became a trillion-dollar company largely because of its iPod, iPad, and iPhones. It did so with enormous government support, though not in direct subsidies as the pharmaceutical industry enjoys, but in the sense that almost everything from the touchscreen, to the Internet, to the GPS and storage systems that drive its products were initially researched and developed by the government.[16] The results produced are not all "bad." Society gets delightful electronic devices, the sick get healed, and there is the possibility of that great liberal goal of *progress*. Yet, this is often achieved in a funding merry-go-round on which public funds go to MegaCorps to produce products that the public pays for. These products masquerade as the result of private innovation, when they are really the result of publicly backed, and often publicly conducted, research.

The role of government in addressing the challenges we face must be in stepping back and allowing that which is truly private and competitive to be so and allowing the private sector to fund all the technological innovation from which it profits. Then, in addition to legally codifying the social obligations of MegaCorps in recognition that they are now public as well as private entities, with public as well as private functions and responsibilities, governments should fund only the technological innovation necessary to meet social ends, as we proposed in chapter 9.

Building Better States

The purpose of politics under Liberal Capitalism is not to define what is good for people, what they deserve, and what they should desire. Politics is about values that create institutions, and if free enterprise and competitive markets are valued, as are individual freedoms, then the current institutional arrangements undermine these. The populists are right: we need to be on another political path. Yet, the current right-wing populists offer the wrong path because it is likely to take us toward autocracy, a path too many countries have traveled before, and which they should never travel again.

The alternative to CorpoCapitalism does not have to be nationalism, fascism, or even communism for that matter. It can instead be Liberal Capitalism, because if politics is about values then it is also about choices. In fact, it is values that allow choices to be made by each of us, not for us, by MegaCorps or governments. CorpoCapitalism is not some institutional prison that states and their governments are locked in. Nor do they need to break out. The reality is that governments built the walls. They always do. The MegaCorps they serve like the walls that have been built to "house" them because they helped to design them. But it is the citizens of their countries that are locked in, and who are increasingly restive when told they must work harder for lower real wages to satisfy the interests of MegaCorps whose managers and shareholders enjoy freedoms their workers cannot imagine.

Instead, governments need to construct a house where their citizens want to *live* rather than escape from. They could choose to do nothing. They could allow the walls to come crashing down from a climate crisis or a populist revolution borne of dissatisfaction with the status quo, but to us that seems like a bad choice. Ironically, the role of government is one of the central planks for both ensuring the economy is more liberal and that its liberal promise is realized, as well as ensuring that now it is not. But so is the role of individuals empowered to make choices and shape their own destinies. In the next and penultimate chapter, we explore another important role of government: building resilience throughout society and economy in the face of unknown challenges. While the role played by the government in underpinning the institutions of the state is crucial, it does not follow that all changes to make capitalism more liberal can only be made by states. Indeed, from a liberal perspective, as far as possible the changes should be made by, as well as for, every individual in their societies.

Chapter 12

The Resilience of Liberal Capitalism

It is well accepted that markets cannot produce public goods. That is the responsibility of states and their governments. Like national security, mitigating climate change so that the world enjoys a stable and equable climate is a public good. So, mitigation is something that states and their governments should be doing, and they should be doing it before, and in addition to, global efforts.[1] They must be ready to address in advance, as well as react to, this and other threats to their citizens, even if some of these threats are hard to predict or quantify in advance. They need to ensure that Liberal Capitalism is resilient to, rather than undermined by, present and future threats. Even when they are "unknown."

In chapter 3, we introduced several unknowns, notably climate change, but also AI and automation. Both are, or rather were, *known unknowns*, in the sense that we knew they would probably occur but did not know exactly when or how, or what impacts they would have. We have a better idea of this now. Since drafting that chapter, the world has been hit by the COVID-19 pandemic. To prevent the spread of this highly contagious and deadly virus most states curtailed economic activity, closed their borders, and encouraged or required all but essential workers to remain at home for weeks. A few short months ago the pathogen was unknown. It was an *unknown unknown*: we neither knew it would happen nor what effects it would have. Now it is the cause of a massive increase in unemployment and government debt, a decline in the economies of every rich country, and a rise in inequality in most.

Pandemics have infrequently decimated populations. The Black Death of the fourteenth century killed up to 40 percent of the population in many countries; and in some European cities over half the population died. But even today, with all our science, we can be blindsided by new pathogens. Surely, if states mean anything, they should prepare for the unexpected in ways that each of us cannot do alone. That preparedness for the unknown, that resilience building, is a public good of the first order. It is part of national security, and together with economic security protects the potential wellbeing of everyone.

It is inefficient to build resilience, but resilience is necessary to *be* efficient. To build resilience draws economic, political, and social resources out of the present to manage a possible future challenge. Because we know that pandemics happen, states have public health systems stocked with laboratories, equipment, and personnel whose job it is to identify and respond to a pandemic as soon as possible. Unknowns are also why we build fire stations and employ specially trained firefighters. So, it is inefficient today. But when a future crisis hits, resilience may prevent the ultimate inefficiency: death and destruction. The primary difference between a pandemic and climate change—as with automation—is that we know what these challenges are but do not know exactly what the nature and magnitude of their impacts will be. In other words, we can anticipate in general terms what the effects will be without having to know how quickly environmental and social impacts will manifest and exactly how large they will be. So, building resilience for such known unknowns is easier and cheaper than for unknown unknowns. In the case of the former we know about where and when the battle will be fought; in the case of the latter both are guesswork.

Resilience for climate change differs from resilience for AI and automation. But for either, rational decision-making is radically challenged. Designing institutions and retaining resources "just in case" opposes everything that markets teach. Generally, centralized political decision-making is only useful for setting aside the resources resilience demands. How and when to use those resources must be determined locally, in proportion to where impacts are suffered and expected to be suffered. Not coincidentally, as we will show in this chapter, Liberal Capitalism is the best political-economic system for building resilience throughout society. We do so by first exploring in more detail the nature of resilience, and then showing why CorpoCapitalism is, despite what many may think, so fragile by comparison.

About Resilience

In 2013, on its fortieth anniversary, *Time* magazine declared resilience the buzzword of the year.[2] But resilience emerged earlier as a way to describe the life cycle of ecosystems. Forests, for example, enjoy an adaptive cycle of growth, collapse, regeneration, and new growth.[3] Even without changes in their external conditions they are constantly changing, with few periods of stability, yet they endure. They also have the ability to do so when their external conditions change, as in 1988 when Yellowstone National Park caught fire. After many years of fire suppression, the fuel load from dead trees and bushes was high but that year the park administrators let the fires burn and only fought to protect structures. The following year some areas that had been forested were instead grassland with brilliant flowers. Herds of deer, elk, and smaller critters moved in and fattened on the lush grasslands.[4] The number of birds, wolves, and foxes grew in response. Eventually, new trees grew where the old ones had died, including some new species previously choked out by old-growth Lodgepole Pine. Fires have always happened in the forests in the American Mountain West—they are part of their ecosystems' life cycle, and so they are known unknowns. The forests normally adapt to them and recover. Without the distortions introduced by humans, including fire suppression and climate change, they are resilient and endure.

The Yellowstone fires illustrate the enduring resilience of natural systems, yet this is not the popular image of resilience. In common usage in the social sciences, resilience is a profoundly conservative idea. It is popularly thought to be a measure of how well a social system can "bounce back," implying a return to a prior normal scenario after some external disturbance. Yet, this is too limiting a conception for social systems as they are constantly evolving toward an ill-defined and hoped for future. Recent debates specifically reflecting the concern that social systems are likely to soon face large and novel challenges have substantially enlarged the idea. Resilience thinking is now "about how periods of gradual changes interact with abrupt changes, and the capacity of people, communities, societies, cultures to adapt or *even transform into new development pathways* in the face of dynamic change."[5] Healthy social systems at any scale are not static and resilience cannot only mean a return to a prior state, but the opening of opportunities to change the trajectory of society, for either better or worse. Unlike forests and other ecosystems, social systems can choose their development pathway, which as we showed in chapter 11, is a primary purpose of politics. From a liberal perspective, it should be for the better because, as explained in chapter 3, for liberals the future should involve *progress* rather than stasis or regression. As David Chandler writes, society "survives *and thrives* on the basis of its ability to adapt or dynamically relate to its socio-ecological environment."[6] Societies travel along a "development pathway" that may be transformed in productive ways by interaction with external events and even crises. So, rather than returning to the prior state or even a prior pathway, challenging external events may stimulate internal changes by which the social system transitions to a more beneficial pathway. Hopefully, this takes them away from CorpoCapitalism.

The Fragility of CorpoCapitalism

CorpoCapitalism looks, on the surface, to be resilient. A system based on big government, looking after big business, to suppress competition and individual freedoms seems unassailable. There is so much concentrated power exercised in supporting it, and preventing it from changing, that it seems it should more easily endure than a system that is less centrally controlled and supported, with power more diffuse in the hands of individuals. But the exact opposite is the case. Research into natural ecosystems illustrates why, because it makes abundantly clear that systems with many diverse parts are much more resilient than simpler systems in which many of the parts are alike.

There are many examples to support this observation. The agricultural monocultures of the American Midwest are efficient but critically fragile. They use the same soil to grow the same few crops every year, and the result is fields of corn, or other single crops, as far as the eye can see. The bounty of what is produced is clearly evident, yet the mass production of what is produced, and the lack of diversity in it year after year, leads to increased risks of pathogens and diseases. The result is that Midwest agriculture works against nature rather than with it.[7] Likewise, overfishing of a single species can collapse whole aquatic systems, and plantation forests comprised of a single species can be devastated by an invasion of insects that attacks every single tree. Such systems are sometimes therefore described as *robust-yet-fragile*. They are productive and robust within a narrow range of external conditions but readily fail when changes in external conditions are more dramatic. And they tend to need propping up with extensive chemical—for example, pesticides and herbicides for agriculture—or regulatory interventions and controls for overexploitation of a single resource.

Natural systems are more resilient when they are composed of diverse interacting species. Ecologists have found that "variability in responses of species within functional groups to environmental change is critical to ecosystem resilience."[8] Each species of plant, insect, or animal adjusts its behavior—for example, to wetter or dryer summers or colder winters—and from these individual behavioral changes emerges the ability of the ecosystem to adapt to changing conditions. The same goes for the economy. There is no clearer illustration of this than the way a lack of diversity among financial firms almost brought down the global financial system during the Great Recession. As noted in chapter 4, the financial system had become extraordinarily dependent on a few large banks. It has become more so since, but just before the crisis hit, it was already known that "large banks were disproportionately connected to small banks, and vice versa" such that "75% of the payment flows involve fewer than 0.1% of the nodes."[9] This meant that there was a risk to the system from "contagion dynamics" due to the mutual financial obligations and exposures that linked all the banks to a handful of enormous banks. In other words, to MegaCorps. Thus, a later analysis of what actually happened concluded that in addition to being too *big* to fail, these banks were also too *central* to fail—a handful of them were at the center of the entire financial system.[10]

To explain, in the US, where it all started, essentially the problem was that all the major banks calculated their risk profiles in a similar fashion without consideration of systemic risk from the cross-collateralization among them.[11] This means that they used the collateral from one loan against other loans, in essence allowing multiple loans to be secured against the same asset. But then they went further and used collateralized debt obligations (CDOs), bundles of residential mortgages often issued by other major banks, to cross-collateralize among themselves. And then they went further still to "insure" against the risk of defaults in their CDOs with credit default swaps (CDSs), again among each other. That all sounds rather complex, but in fact it is quite simple. Too simple, because what it means is that a handful of enormous banks were sharing the same assets against their loans, then taking out insurance with each other for losses from debtors defaulting on these loans. A bit like the soil becoming degraded because of the agricultural monocultures of the American Midwest, eventually many of their high-risk mortgages collapsed, and all the banks that were too big and too central to fail nearly did fail, as they each claimed on the CDSs with each other. Then, to make matters worse, because the CDSs had been freely traded, nobody really knew who owed what to whom. So, the banks then tried to unload their CDOs to generate cash to anyone who would buy them just as their value was sinking fast. The system was ultimately bailed out by the government.

This is yet another tale of MegaCorps supported by CorpoCapitalism, as ultimately the financial crisis that started the Great Recession was caused by a small number of systemically important banks all following the same investment strategies, all doing it together, all at the same time, then all failing at once from the same cause. So, prior to 2009 the US financial system was "robust-yet-fragile." It was well designed to handle the normal variations in context and was highly efficient, delivering an ever-greater proportion of the nation's income to a few massive banks and their traders. And it was supported in so doing by a government that allowed these MegaCorps to do whatever they liked with minimal regulation. Yet, it was fragile to the unanticipated risk of a decline in house prices that the banks had themselves created.

The fragility of international finance has also been recognized in other ways. In January 2020 the Bank for International Settlements published a lengthy report called *The Green Swan: Central Banking and Financial Stability in the Age of Climate Change*.[12] It analyzed the potential for climate change to completely unravel the global financial system. The concern was that a changing climate could cause a collapse in asset values in many places—imagine the impacts of extensive floods, hurricane destruction, persistent droughts, and so on. In addition, where, when, and how these changes might occur is characterized by deep uncertainty, as well as unpredictability. The report concludes that, because climate change encompasses "physical and transition risks that interact with complex, far-reaching, nonlinear, chain reaction effects," predicting the social and economic impacts is extremely difficult if not impossible as "exceeding climate tipping points could lead to catastrophic and irreversible impacts that would make quantifying financial damages impossible."[13] In other words, expected unpredictable and catastrophic changes that the financial system is not designed to handle. Central banks cannot foresee when and where challenges to the financial system will emerge and even if they could their ability to repair the damage as it occurs is problematic. So, central banks should engage in ambitious actions to increase the resilience of the financial system and treat climate stability as a global public good. They should also coordinate their actions to equitably distribute the costs of mitigation, adaptation, and harms. In other words, the report recommended building resilience into the global financial system in anticipation of a catastrophic change in the climate.

It might be argued that our recent experience of the COVID-19 pandemic shows that CorpoCapitalism can have a stabilizing influence. Because the virus is highly contagious and deadly to many people, governments reacted by shutting down much economic activity and preventing social gatherings from in-house restaurant dining to large sports events and political rallies. At the same time states have lavished economic support on corporations either to pay their furloughed workers or to purchase their debt and prevent bankruptcies. Even though in many countries fiscal policies were aimed at small to medium-sized businesses, nevertheless they have found it hardest to bear the economic pain, while monetary policies principally supported larger corporations and their debts. After an early hiccup in response to uncertainty, once states stepped in stock markets around the world soared, principally benefiting the rich. This tale might be told in support of MegaCorps in the sense that during a crisis they can more easily survive where smaller enterprises are more easily crushed. But that is not the whole story. Because they tend to persist where their less well-funded, smaller competitors fail or are purchased by them, this only serves to embed MegaCorps deeper in the economy and society. As every crisis is also an opportunity, they therefore potentially also more deeply institutionally embed CorpoCapitalism. This takes us further down the path of big government in support of big business. It will not make our economies more resilient to the long-term effects of climate change. Liberal Capitalism will.

The Resilience of Liberal Capitalism

As noted earlier, thinking about resilience began in the natural sciences, and especially in biology, but soon gained a foothold in the social sciences. As a result, social sciences research has begun to move from a classical physics model of society as a complicated machine with clear causes and effects to a model of biological complexity that sketches human systems as constantly varying, never in equilibrium, and unpredictable.[14]

Understood from this perspective human systems are, like natural systems, more resilient when they are more diverse. But actually, this is not so far from the model of the economy originally proposed by Adam Smith.

As he intuited, the economy is not the work of any one of the agents involved but of them all, each choosing for themselves. In so doing, "every individual . . . neither intends to promote the public interest, nor knows how much he is promoting it . . . he intends only his own security . . . he intends only his own gain, and he is in this, as in many other cases, led by an invisible hand to promote an end which was no part of his intention."[15] Adam Smith's classic insight tells us that a great diversity of economic agents makes free markets more resilient than the concentrated markets that are dominated by MegaCorps with the backing of CorpoCapitalist governments. The whole CorpoCapitalist economic system is robust-yet-fragile, as the aforementioned financial example demonstrates. It may be efficient for its owners and executives during the good times, but lacks the diversity needed for resilience. When times are good, they are very good, but if conditions change substantially the whole society it supports might collapse. This has happened to many civilizations in the past, and the fragility of our current prosperity, underlined by gross inequality, could add another to the list of sorry tales from history.[16] Climate change or AI or a pandemic might be enough to tip the economic system and the society it supports into complete disarray and collapse.

With freedom of thought and speech, democratic systems also ought to be resilient. In a free and democratic society, the nation and its interests emerge from the choices of the people, what they think and believe, how they vote, and how they interact among themselves. States, cities, towns, and even the global political-economy—indeed, almost any social group—emerge from the interactions of "agents." These may be people or organizations who act for themselves but in so doing create the system that in turn influences their choices through formal and informal institutions. These institutions were formed by history and the natural and human context of the state. At any point in time, changes in international relations, or the basis for trade, or unanticipated economic booms and busts, new techno-economic paradigms, political ideologies, and the natural environment may affect the trajectory of a society and the institutions that guide how it functions. But, as discussed in the previous chapter, it is the *political* institutions that determine which values are most desired in any society. The institutions of CorpoCapitalism value economic growth and economic dominance most highly, but Liberal Capitalism is more desirable because it prioritizes opportunities for individual wellbeing, and in supporting individuals to make choices it encourages diversity and complexity, and thereby resilience.

Another example demonstrates the point. When the price of oil rocketed to over US$150 a barrel in May 2008 and stayed over US$100 per barrel for most of the next six years, US consumers switched from buying light trucks and SUVs to small cars. Because American auto manufacturers were more adept at making and selling SUVs (which also were more profitable) than cars, they lost market share. Meanwhile, the market shrank as total US car sales fell by nearly 50 percent between 2006 and 2009 and only slowly recovered thereafter. The upshot of these changes was an increase in the fuel efficiency of the fleet of private vehicles, driven by the sale of vehicles by non-US auto manufacturers. It also caused the bankruptcy of General Motors and Chrysler in 2008 and necessitated government bailouts with the resultant loss of thousands of well-paid manufacturing jobs, and reduced benefits to the remaining employees. These were all the unintended consequences of the decisions by millions of consumers intending their "own gain" in a highly concentrated market dominated by a handful of MegaCorps. Voters like to think that the government they choose will regulate the economy to produce the outcomes they desire, whether is it more jobs or less work, lower prices, or economic growth. Yet, if the auto market had been more competitive—indeed, more liberal—then the industry and those depending on it may have been more resilient and adaptive in the face of an external shock to the system. It also illustrates how the economic impact of the unintentional emergent aspects of socioeconomic systems often overrule governmental intentions—the US government was forced to provide over US$80 billion in a bailout package. That is why asking the government to fix things after the fact is remarkably inefficient. Instead, what is required is governance for resilience.

Governance for Resilience

Challenges like climate change and automation are "wicked" problems. They are wicked because they occur where the data are incomplete, contradictory, or constantly changing such that there is no single or simple solution. They are also wicked because they are multidimensional and therefore too complex to be viewed or solved in one way or in a single dimension. For pandemics, climate change, and automation, rationally designing the formal institutions and policies needed to "solve" them, or to mitigate or adapt to their consequences as if they are stand-alone problems, is impossible. Actually, to see and respond to them as such is ridiculous. For example, automation is tied up with inequality, globalization, and technological development. One country directly preventing the development of true AI only opens it up to another country outcompeting it in the innovation race. Also, AI offers more uses than automation of manufacturing, it is expected to have other spin-offs in medical diagnosis and treatment, pharmaceuticals, material science, and alternative energy. In addition, of course, military matters. As AI essentially increases the leverage of capital at a cost to labor, policy on AI must integrate with national security and income distribution issues, which in turn affect tax policy, foreign relations, and incentives for innovation.

To take another example, mitigating climate change requires modifying most production and distribution systems, and many personal behaviors. It potentially demands the redesign of energy and transportation systems, cities, housing, workplaces, and much more. In the rich countries, even adapting to rapid climate change might demand moving large populations away from surging seas, protecting millions from new diseases, and redesigning agriculture. As we showed in chapter 9, relying on technology alone to reduce GHG emissions will not save societies from wrenching change, including that from novel technologies designed for mitigation or adaptation. As it is not possible to forecast when and where the effects of climate change will occur, adaptation to a hotter reality will be less planned and no easier than mitigation, and more ad hoc.

Yet again, income and wealth inequality are difficult problems, as are the related ones of declining happiness and political extremism, but the potential impacts of a rapidly changing climate on human health, food sufficiency, or even the existence of coastal cities housing half the world's population can only be guessed at. Global circulation models differ on where and how the climate is likely to change and social scientists (as usual) disagree on how those impacts might affect social systems.

Furthermore, it is unclear how society will respond to each of the scenarios proffered by forecasters. The potential disruption of these changes is enormous, and we are as reliant on scientists' guesses as medieval kings on the local soothsayer. Under such conditions, normal rational cost-benefit decision-making will not suffice. Policymakers commonly look for levers to pull to make specific changes to achieve promised social goals and seek an optimal balance between the costs and benefits of any action. But policymaking today on wicked problems is an art dressed up as a science. And not just today. In 1959, Charles Lindblom showed that rational policymaking for complex problems is largely impossible.[17] It would require knowing all possible values—such as economic growth, social capital, environmental conservation, inequality, wealth, and so on—and the ability to comprehensively and accurately assess their relative importance. It also would require using all available knowledge and theories to evaluate all possible responses to the problem, and the ability to determine how they would maximize as many of those values as possible. In place of attempts at fully rational policymaking Lindblom recommends a system of what he calls "Successive Limited Comparisons," a limited and cautious stepwise approach to policymaking to help protect from large, unanticipated consequences in which each policy is a cautious experiment that tests the effectiveness of a policy, and its acceptance by the broader community.

In short, policymakers should have more limited ambitions (and voters more limited expectations of their representatives). J. Brian Arthur goes further. Not only can government not be rational in its decision-making, but the whole process must change:

> You want to keep as many options open as possible. You go for viability, something that's workable, rather than what's "optimal." . . . because optimization isn't well defined anymore. What you're trying to do is maximize robustness, or survivability, in the face of an ill-defined future. And that, in turn, puts a premium on becoming aware of nonlinear relationships and causal pathways as best we can. You observe the world very, very carefully, and you don't expect circumstances to last.[18]

In other words, "good" governance is not about optimizing efficiency (and profits) of a handful of MegaCorps, the economy as a whole, or of the decision process. Instead, it must be consistently aimed at maintaining and improving the social system in the face of many known, unknown, and ill-defined challenges. In other words, the goal must be resilience. A resilient society will maintain and improve itself despite and as a result of critical external stresses whether known or unknown.

Resilience through Liberal Capitalism

To be fair, many governments and levels of governance have already begun to adopt resilience thinking to drive decisions.[19] However, the most CorpoCapitalist countries have eschewed such thinking at the national level, with expected dire consequences for all but the MegaCorps, their executives and investors, and their rich advisers. And maybe even them too. Climate change probably most clearly illustrates the point. The Earth has never had a climate changing as rapidly as is now expected. It will likely adapt and recover, and life will continue. What we do not know is what that life then will be (the biodiversity problem) and whether it will include human populations as large as today's and how they will be organized (social impacts).[20] Yet, if countries are to continue to develop and improve the lives of their citizens, they must begin to plan for uncertain changes in conditions and unpredictable social impacts. In short, governments must begin to consider resilience of what and for whom to continue to develop society and improve the lives of their people. Liberal Capitalism is the way to do that.

The problem is that social scientists are not as social as they profess. They hive off into competing tribes or "disciplines." However, in reality economic, political, and social activities interact both within the state, in communities and cities, and across borders. And they all interact with and depend on complex ecosystems, including the global climate. For a state to be resilient it must be resilient throughout, through sub-state governance all the way down to its communities and individuals.

Community resilience to climate change has been defined as: "the ability of communities to reduce exposure to, prepare for, cope with, recover better from, adapt and transform as needed to, the direct and indirect effects of climate change, where these effects can be both shocks and stresses."[21] Shocks are the acute impacts such as flash floods, or heat waves; stresses are the chronic impacts, including those on the housing market of insurance costs. However, community resilience should not be solely about climate change; it must include resilience against unknown unknowns (like pandemics) as well as known unknowns. An essential component of community resilience is its ability to identify the community's collective values, develop its skills and abilities (in for instance food production), build its social capital through existing organizations and new volunteer associations, and organize and mobilize its collective resources. Resilient communities encourage a degree of buy-in by the people that nationally mandated policies can never achieve. Given their liberal freedom to choose, and with support to do so by their governments, communities can even participate in mitigation of GHG emissions. And then at the smallest scale, the individual, Liberal Capitalism with its more equal distribution of resources, opportunity, and luck builds more resilient people who would be well willing and able to participate in community resilience.

Divisive politics and populist right-wing negation of proactive resilience-building could fatally weaken even the wealthiest countries. Big government supporting big business, in other words CorpoCapitalism for MegaCorps, is no better. Resilience-building is a community and collective endeavor, and Liberal Capitalism is the best way to organize it.

Chapter 13

Progressing to Liberal Capitalism

It is popular to complain that capitalism has lost its way. The common diagnosis is that ungoverned markets have caused the social strife and natural destruction we see around us. We see the effect but disagree with the cause. As we have shown, for us the cause is not that markets are ungoverned but that they are governed in the wrong way through states practicing not Liberal Capitalism, but CorpoCapitalism. We agree that states have drawn back, but the result is not neoliberal free markets running wild. Nor is it that they are governed in the interests of "capital," or more colloquially "business" to the detriment of society. No, markets are governed by giant corporations, which we call MegaCorps. They dominate countries' economies, and because they are multinational, they also dominate the global economy. Like giant squids whose supply chains are the tentacles that encircle the globe, they work in multiple countries where they are instrumental in regulating production.

This is not how it was meant to be. In the imagination of the great liberal philosophers like Adam Smith, capitalism would serve the needs of the many not solely those of the few. He argued that liberating the masses from serfdom to a hereditary aristocracy and autocratic monarch would be not only morally good for society but economically beneficial for states. He did not imagine an absence of government but a government that turned its attention from control of the people, and the employment of them in service of the national interest, to a government that ensured individuals could pursue their enlightened self-interest to the unwitting advancement of the common good. As Smith admitted, this would be an ideal outcome that the weaknesses of human nature—such as ego, greed, and avarice—would destroy unless controlled by a powerful yet benign government. Unfortunately, the withdrawal of government in recent decades has permitted these darker angels of human nature to stifle the desire of most of the people to live full lives of their own choosing. In a Sophoclean tragedy the child born of liberal capitalism unintentionally but naturally murders its parent.

As capitalism has matured it has forgotten the liberal lessons to value the individual. It has grown big and bloated to become CorpoCapitalism that applauds the concentration of economic power so that MegaCorps may usurp the power of government, perpetuate their profits for the benefit of the wealthy few, and employ them to master the masses. Governments, conveniently believing that the economic growth CorpoCapitalism promises will cure all social ills, have withdrawn from their liberal democratic role of governing for their people. Meanwhile, capitalism is undermining the ability of most people to sustain themselves through meaningful work that automation will further erode while ignoring existential threats like climate change.

So, unhappiness grows, and divisions are easily stoked by populists expressing nostalgia for a fake history of national greatness along with hatred of the outsider and of difference. This social fracturing serves no beneficial purpose, but only reduces resilience and wellbeing while grand challenges like a changing climate, and unexpected events like the COVID-19 global pandemic, further threaten prosperity and social cohesion.

This process has progressed differently in every country. Geography, culture, and history have channeled these changes to local interpretations of capitalism. We have held up the US as the most extreme example of CorpoCapitalism and have done so as a warning to other countries that have gone some way down its path or have so far successfully resisted doing so. Indeed, the US is the exemplar of where other countries should fear to tread. European countries have stronger welfare states that cushion the calamities that capitalism too often imposes on their citizens. But as every country has bent toward the CorpoCapitalist extreme, like wheat stalks in an ideological wind, their states are under internal threat from across the political spectrum. A threat they themselves cultivated by accepting greater insecurity and inequality for most of their people as the cost of an assumed higher rate of economic growth. The US appears more innovative than most countries, its economy grows faster than many, and its military is mighty. But need most Americans sacrifice their health, happiness, and wellbeing for these goods? As each of us has but one life to live, we think that is a poor bargain.

If governments do not work for the people, how can they be persuaded to change? The prevailing ideology of CorpoCapitalism proclaims free markets as always efficient. Leaving aside for the moment the fact that markets are actually dominated by MegaCorps—indeed, they are the destroyers of the free market—and therefore not necessarily efficient because they are not competitive, the more pertinent question is whether efficiency is the appropriate goal of markets and economic activity. Under CorpoCapitalism efficiency serves the goal of increasing GDP without regard to the environmental or social consequences. By contrast the purpose of the economy, what it is for, under Liberal Capitalism is to provide the resources and opportunities by which every individual may seek his or her wellbeing in his or her own way. We have offered several suggestions about how to achieve this, and thereby to promote the guiding ideas of liberalism that we introduced in chapter 2: *conflict mitigation, power prevention, personal and collective progress*, and *respect*. Efficiency then becomes the means by which these goals are achieved, rather than the sole purpose of the economy. And to ensure this is the case, there must be a continual shift in the purpose of politics and the institutions it creates, but not once and for all. Dynamism must be the aim, otherwise the ever-present danger is a slide back into the cozy arrangements between MegaCorps and governments that produces CorpoCapitalism, or something worse than the current populist backlash. Therefore, the relationship between dynamism and institutions is our starting point.

Dynamism and Institutions

Life, as a scientist once said, exists on the knife-edge between chaos and order. The late eighteenth and early nineteenth-century poet, novelist, playwright, and biologist Johann von Goethe explained it more lyrically:

> The Divinity works in the living, not in the dead; in the *becoming and changing*, not in the become and the fixed. Therefore Reason, with its tendency toward the divine, has only to do with the becoming, the living; but Understanding with the become, the already fixed, that it may make use of it.[1]

Simply put, the essence of life is change. The essence of a healthy and resilient society is dynamism, constant evolution, and development toward a more human life for all. In other words, the liberal idea of *progress*. This dynamic social process has rules, for if it did not it would be governed by randomness. It would be chaotic. But too many rules, too much order, is like death, when nothing can change, and everything is fixed.

As we have shown, CorpoCapitalism is governance of, by, and for MegaCorps. Even without governments making regulations this is too orderly to support a healthy society, one that is able to adapt to the impacts of AI and climate change, and can continue to flourish. Governments have forgotten that their primary responsibility is to the people, not to MegaCorps; to individuals, not national statistics; and to growing opportunities for wellbeing, not to private fortunes built on inadequate wages. In contrast, the purpose of Liberal Capitalism is to enable progress toward a more *human*—indeed, humane—future for everyone. One which each person chooses to define for themselves, rather than having defined for them, or demanded of them, by their overlords. Through progress and respect for individual life choices, Liberal Capitalism prevents excessive conflict, yet it proscribes the excessive use of power. Its institutions frame the "rules of the game" for both economy and society, the limits beyond which personal choices harm others directly or indirectly. In short, the objective of the institutions that underpin Liberal Capitalism is to encourage life, change, and innovation, without permitting chaos.

We cannot offer a playbook to transition to Liberal Capitalism, because countries differ in their culture and institutional history. However, from the concepts of freedom and the guiding ideas (or "principles") of liberalism we can frame ways that states can dismantle CorpoCapitalism and begin to govern for the people.

Personal and Collective Progress

Everybody wants progress, but what is it? At present, many states understand it only as economic growth. Yet, economic growth comes from both construction and destruction: war creates growth because it does both so well. Environmental destruction and GHG emissions increase GDP but cycling to work and wearing warm clothes in the home do not. So, there are always conundrums to be considered, but by pursuing economic growth at all costs, and supporting MegaCorps as the primary agents to deliver it, clearly denies too much to too many.

Liberal Capitalism measures progress in the opportunities it creates for everyone to live an enjoyable life according to their personal beliefs and desires. This means enabling wellbeing with life chances and providing the resources for individuals to seize opportunities as they arise. For most of us this means having the skills to take a job with decent pay and benefits, sufficient for a commonly accepted quality of life, one that does not "denote a disgraceful degree of poverty."[2] In the rich countries this is more than the basic physical needs of food and shelter. It may include a telephone, television, and an adequate means of transportation. If states cannot provide the *opportunity* for work that at a minimum sustains life and provides such basic resources, they should otherwise provide the necessary *means*. Modern liberal welfare states are failing to do either. They require massive bureaucracies to set multiple trip wires to receiving the means when individuals are lacking the opportunity. A UBI could remedy the current failures and reduce the bureaucratic costs of governance. It would rebalance power relations between MegaCorp employers and their workers. It would be part of the twenty-first-century institutional architecture of the liberal welfare state.

Such a fundamental change in thinking is also necessary for climate change. Climate deniers reject the possibility of progress. They look at the world as it is now and cite the cost of mitigation for why they oppose taking action. Yet, like all innovation, a search for technologies that mitigate or adapt to a changing climate would likely increase economic growth and job opportunities in new industries. Automation and AI are part of the story as they can help drive a "green" TEP, and the opportunities this will create may offset the jobs lost in old industries that were once the source of well-paid jobs for the less skilled. For example, in many countries, clean energy provides more well-paid jobs than coal-fired energy production and a transition to clean transportation would radically change production techniques and raw material demand. And while AI could reduce employment in vehicle assembly, the transition may generate more jobs elsewhere in the economy. But fundamentally, whether moving to a green TEP produces progress, or merely provides another opportunity for the incumbent wealthy and powerful elites that benefit from the status quo, is down to the institutions that channel the life of society and economy. For example, a liberal state would recognize and mitigate the social costs of these industrial transitions and a UBI would help individuals make necessary changes. Likewise, encouraging a green TEP and mitigating its social impacts requires a change in thinking, and an institutional shift from the CorpoCapitalist orthodoxy.

Conflict Mitigation

Dictators restrict ideas and monopolists oppose new entrants. But people intrinsically have different ideas, religions, and beliefs. It has been well established that difference breeds resilience from debate, if it does not devolve into chaos.[3] What is true in general is also true specifically for capitalism. The greater the range of ideas about future challenges, and the greater the expression of them in markets—such as in the latter stages of technological innovation where competition is most effective—the more likely states will be prepared to maintain progress as conditions change.[4] The more companies compete in markets, as well as people being able to choose in them, the faster the evolution of products and services, the higher the efficiency of production, and the lower the prices. If more researchers work on climate innovation, then it is more likely that effective technologies will be discovered. In every case larger numbers and greater diversity are good.

Ultimately, it is not the amount of conflict that is important but how it is expressed. Boundaries placed around conflict processes prevent a devolution into the chaos of all-against-all. Freedom of speech and freedom of the press are essential but any form of violence, threat of violence, or incitement to violence, or the use of power to control speech are beyond the pale. Unfortunately, business is currently permitted a massive megaphone that can drown out opposition or control the direction of debate. Through control of newspapers, media outlets, and websites, and (in some countries) through unlimited political donations, those controlling MegaCorps can use their economic power for political ends. They can use it as an effective bulwark protecting CorpoCapitalism.

Liberal Capitalism demands more conflict in markets (that is, competition) than CorpoCapitalism permits. It would liberate markets that are now increasingly ordered (and, therefore, lack resilience) by the interests of MegaCorps that dominate whole industries. Free markets do not reject governments as surplus to economic requirements but leave to government the responsibility to navigate the state through the construction of appropriate institutions in the direction of its national interests and the betterment of its citizens' lives and to prepare for grand future challenges, both known and unknown. Government has a legitimate role preventing excess order or ungoverned chaos, and to encourage dynamic competition while enhancing resilience in the face of grand challenges. Only government can build the guardrails that prevent markets damaging social or ecological systems.

This is especially true for inequality. It is "human" to measure oneself against others. In grossly unequal societies, in addition to the reality of diminished economic and social status the *recognition* of them breeds resentment and even anger. Therefore, not only is it economically important to provide the opportunities to reduce inequality, it also is morally appropriate to do so. This is especially the case when wealth is unearned, but simply from a pragmatic viewpoint it is important that the potential for unnecessary social conflict is diminished. States, therefore, use various tools—including progressive taxation, minimum wages, corporate governance regulations, and labor unions—to reduce inequality, though the evidence (as we have shown) suggests it has so far been without great success. With Liberal Capitalism these efforts would have to increase by taxing wealth and inheritances directly and forcefully, raising minimum wages, in addition to providing a UBI to increase worker bargaining power.

Yet, the primary way to reduce inequality is to bolster social mobility. The tools for this are readily at hand: expansive public education from an early age through academic or vocational college to ready students for work and an autonomous life that they can enjoy. Not only does democracy demand educated citizens, but those citizens are good for society too. They can better seek their wellbeing both at work and in society and more quickly acquire new skills as the market demands. As in liberalism more generally, though it may not be their intention, individuals freely acting in their personal interests nevertheless build national resilience and grow the economy.

Respect

States that respect their citizens are concerned about their wellbeing. Wellbeing as we have defined it would construct the institutions of Liberal Capitalism in two distinct ways. First, their wellbeing must be wholly personal. It is a set of activities, a way of life, that each of us chooses so as to fulfill our potential *in our own way*. Negative rights that keep government out of personal lives are necessary but insufficient. Government has further duties. For example, it must provide security and protection against all enemies foreign and domestic, social or economic, human or natural. It also should increase trust, with robust institutions for minimizing corruption, as this is the grease between the gears of commerce that also is essential to building social capital and resilience. Rich countries' governments have the means to remove evident obstacles to wellbeing such as poverty, hunger, and violence. All they need is a cohesive moral and practical plan that Liberal Capitalism supplies.

Second, liberal institutions must challenge the raw capitalism of overweening self-interested profiteering. Because wellbeing is not merely pleasure, capitalism on its own cannot improve it. Capitalism efficiently produces material goods and personal services to alleviate pain or increase pleasure, and to meet the basic conditions of life such as food, shelter, clothing, and social relations, if one can afford them. But it contributes little or nothing to the less tangible (more internal and personal) aspects of wellbeing. The current fads of yoga, meditation (repackaged as mindfulness), and other New Age simplifications of oriental religious practices provide only small assistance in this intensely personal and effortful lifestyle choice. Social media is likewise a poor substitute for real social connectedness.[5] Rampant materialism encouraged by corporations and governments to drive economic growth distracts from wellbeing and condemns life for many to trudging on an unsatisfying hedonic treadmill. Liberal Capitalism directs governments back to their essential purpose: *creating the context in which people may increase their wellbeing.* From personal and economic security to education and free time, this implies a reorientation of social, economic, and political institutions. New Zealand and Iceland have moved cautiously in that direction, but most governments remain fixated on growth at all costs.

UBI is, again, a step further in that direction. It accords to everyone a *personhood* aside from roles as worker or consumer and allows them freedom to develop themselves as best they can. Public education that increases social mobility is an accepted idea nearly everywhere and provides the skills to obtain work to sustain life; UBI provides the means to make that life valuable and enjoyable. UBI is no panacea but it would release many from being supplicants for work to stay alive. Can Liberal Capitalism in rich countries sustain a basic income out of the national income from accumulated wealth? We think it can if wealth not employed in productive enterprise pays the bill.

Power Prevention

Liberal Capitalism does not control, command, or instruct. It guides, promotes, regulates, and allows.[6] It is not about having or not having taxes, so much as what these taxes are for and who pays them. It is not pro– or anti–private enterprise, so much as it is about the institutional environment in which private enterprise is pursued and personal lives lived. It is about making the rules so that they ensure the growth of undemocratic power centers—like MegaCorps—outside of democratically elected government are neither promoted nor served at the expense of individuals' freedoms.

We have outlined some ways to correct the central failings of modern CorpoCapitalism, particularly high and growing inequality. But that is not the whole story. Because, as we have shown, wellbeing is more than material consumption, income, and wealth; governments at all scales can do more to open opportunities for everyone to grow their wellbeing by reducing economic and climate insecurity; rebalancing power relations between employer and employee and enforcing fair labor practices (ever more necessary as unions decline); reducing corruption to increase trust in government and business; and supporting social spaces to bring communities together. Some of these actions are the responsibility of national governments but others would fall to provincial, city, or municipal governments. For example, voluntary collective responses to local challenges are valuable aids to governance throughout society. Because volunteering increases wellbeing, government power can initiate a virtuous circle that would bolster community and social resilience.

So, it is not a matter of governments having or not having a role to play. It is about the role government must play in Liberal Capitalism. It is governing for the people not MegaCorps and not by forcing individuals into becoming passive servants of the economy. Instead, Liberal Capitalism ensures that they have a stake and benefit from being active participants in society and economy.

Releasing the Death Grip

CorpoCapitalism's ideological stranglehold is killing capitalism. Yet how can liberalism be restored in this world in which the mere name is reviled in leading countries? By what means would it be possible to loosen the death grip of MegaCorps on governments and the social effects they permit? We have laid out the need for, and the pattern of, a liberal version of capitalism that places the personal projects of people ahead of collective and corporate goals.

Given today's crippling CorpoCapitalism—together with its toxic politics by-product—the vision of Liberal Capitalism as we have described it appears utopian, and unlikely to be realized. Our vision of personal liberty—sailing free toward self-actualization on an ocean of economy—is threatened by the jagged MegaCorp rocks of political reality. Quite simply, what would require the rich and powerful to deny themselves the satisfaction (and profit) of control? What are commonly called "vested interests" are actually attempts by the few to expropriate excess value from the many. In a free (that is, liberal) society they are symbols of power to be challenged not coddled, to be fought not favored. But who can challenge and fight them? Who has the power to persuade them to release their grip on, and guidance of, society and the people's lives? It cannot come from the governments that have been captured and tamed by the ideology of CorpoCapitalism. It cannot come from the international organizations that are bequeathed their small power by those same governments. Nor do we anticipate the voluntary withdrawal of MegaCorps and their wealthy investors from the policy forum, whatever pablum they publish about stakeholders' rights. The only power to return capitalism to its liberal roots for the good of the people is the people themselves. They have to want the promise of liberalism and to create a capitalism for all, one that will not emerge from the current politics of populist fearmongering.

Representative democracy is not an unalloyed good. It makes government of the people more practical by leaving the decisions of state in the hands of seasoned practitioners who have long studied the problems in their portfolio. Still, by removing the people from matters of state it makes many of them ignorant and incurious about the complexities of policy and more inclined to hire on their behalf politicians who seek office through platitudes. With the rise of fake news—intentional factually erroneous statements, written or spoken, that appear to be news or statements of fact—electorates are confused and uncertain and, therefore, more likely to become emotionally attached to certain candidates. A broad education that includes learning critical thinking reduces this effect and creates the "developed person."[7]

Yet, populism need not be as dangerous as the current versions are. An ideal populist would represent the needs of all the people by combining an ethic of ultimate ends (for example, the wellbeing of the people) and an ethic of responsibility (for example, planning to mitigate and adapt to climate change). While waiting for this ideal populist to appear, people still have some ability to reduce the influence of MegaCorps and improve their conditions, particularly through engagement in local politics. At the same time, a small movement in the direction of improving wellbeing for the masses might snowball into national resilience from the bottom up. The possibility of local success building to something bigger is buttressed by international comparisons in which smaller countries like Finland, Norway, or the Netherlands have lower levels of inequality, stronger welfare systems, and much higher levels of happiness. While these benefits may be the result of culture, history, or homogeneity, they also may have emerged from closer physical and political engagement of people with elites.

Rejecting revolution, we propose an evolution to a fairer, more sustainable world. We oppose the tearing down of institutions that have demonstrated their value and support the construction of new ones that guide capitalism toward liberalism. Through the power of the people governments may begin to change and to claw back freedom from the stranglehold of CorpoCapitalism. If a journey of a thousand miles begins with one step, that first step might be to stop paying fossil fuel MegaCorps to generate GHG emissions. Next it could redirect government support for innovation to climate innovation as we suggested in chapter 9. The next step would be to tinker with corporate governance to prevent executives managing their rewards, with that followed by denial of mergers and acquisitions that do not increase wellbeing for all. And so it goes, a death of CorpoCapitalism by a thousand cuts, each one directed by the overall goal of making capitalism liberal once again. We hope, with Martin Luther King, that "the arc of the moral universe is long, but it bends toward justice," the justice of equal freedom to choose one's life. And, therefore, toward Liberal Capitalism.

Notes

Chapter 1. The Fading Promise of Capitalism

1. Throughout the book we refer to "rich nations" or "rich countries," by which we mean the thirty-seven members of the Organisation for Economic Co-operation and Development (OECD).

2. Throughout the book, we refer to "countries" (sometimes "nations"), "governments," and "states." A country is a geographical area. The term is synonymous with, and a more casual form of, the term "nation," which refers to the population occupying the land within a certain area and "sharing a common culture, language, and ethnicity with strong historical continuity" (Ian McLean and Alistair McMillan, *Oxford Concise Dictionary of Politics*, 2nd ed. [Oxford: Oxford University Press, 2003], 364). The government is the group of people, or entities, with the authority to govern a country. The state is "the set of political institutions whose specific concern is with the organization of domination, in the name of the common interest, within a delimited territory" (512). It encompasses the government of a country and also all its institutions—both formal and informal—of how the social and economic affairs of a country are run and regulated, including the cultural rules and beliefs that are the basis on which it is ordered. Therefore, we are talking about ideas and ideologies, the mutual understandings, the "rules of the game," and "standard operating procedures," including beliefs about the role of government. So, a liberal state should have a liberal government, but as we will show this is not necessarily the case.

3. Giorgos Kallis, *Degrowth* (Newcastle upon Tyne: Agenda, 2018); Giacomo D'Alisa, Federico Demaria, and Giorgos Kallis, *Degrowth: A Vocabulary for a New Era* (Abingdon: Routledge, 2014).

4. Colin Crouch, "Neoliberalism, Nationalism and the Decline of Political Traditions," *Political Quarterly* 88, no. 2 (2017): 221–229, https://doi.org/10.1111/1467-923X.12321.

5. Noam Chomsky and Robert W. McChesney, *Profit over People: Neoliberalism and the Global Order* (New York: Seven Stories Press, 1998), 8.

6. Quinn Slobodian, *Globalists: The End of Empire and the Birth of Neoliberalism* (Cambridge, MA: Harvard University Press, 2018).

7. Chomsky and McChesney, *Profit over People*, 8.

8. Slobodian, *Globalists*, 6.

9. Robert Powell, "Anarchy in International Relations Theory: The Neorealist-Neoliberal Debate," *International Organization* 48, no. 2 (Spring 1994): 313–344; Robert O. Keohane and Joseph S. Nye, *Power and Interdependence: World Politics in Transition* (Boston: Little, Brown, 1977).

10. John Mikler, *The Political Power of Global Corporations* (Cambridge: Polity Press, 2018).

11. James H. Stock and Mark W. Watson, "Has the Business Cycle Changed and Why?," *NBER Macroeconomics Annual* 17 (2002): 159–218.

12. Lawrence H. Summers, "Low Equilibrium Real Rates, Financial Crisis, and Secular Stagnation," in *Across the Great Divide: New Perspectives on the Financial Crisis*, ed. Martin Neil Baily and John B. Taylor (Stanford, CA: Hoover Institution Press, 2014), 37–50.

13. Mark Blyth and Matthias Matthijs, "Black Swans, Lame Ducks, and the Mystery of IPE's Missing Macroeconomy," *Review of International Political Economy* 24, no. 2 (2017), https://doi.org/10.1080/09692290.2017.1308417.

14. Robert J. Gordon, *The Rise and Fall of American Growth: The US Standard of Living since the Civil War* (Princeton, NJ: Princeton University Press, 2017).

15. Donella H. Meadows, *Thinking in Systems: A Primer*, ed. Diana Wright Sustainability Institute (White River Junction, VT: Chelsea Green, 2008).

16. Anne Case and Angus Deaton, *Deaths of Despair and the Future of Capitalism* (Princeton, NJ: Princeton University Press, 2020).

17. Margaret Thatcher, interview with *Woman's Own*, Downing Street, 23 September 1987, https://www.margaretthatcher.org/document/106689.

18. Helena Rosenblatt, *The Lost History of Liberalism: From Ancient Rome to the Twenty-First Century* (Princeton, NJ: Princeton University Press, 2020).

19. The five-year-old grandson of one of the authors wants nearly every toy he sees, especially if it is some sort of model motor vehicle. Retailers recognize this and make the supermarket check-out a harrowing experience with knickknacks, geegaws, and candy arrayed all around for the unsuspecting impulse shopper. And small children are the most impulsive.

20. Will Steffen et al., "Trajectories of the Earth System in the Anthropocene," *Proceedings of the National Academy of Sciences* 115, no. 33 (2018): 8252–8259, http://www.pnas.org/content/pnas/115/33/8252.full.pdf.

Chapter 2. What's Been Lost: The Dream of Liberalism

1. Adam Smith, *An Inquiry into the Nature and Causes of the Wealth of Nations*, ed. R. H. Campbell and A. S. Skinner, 2 vols., vol. 1, Glasgow Edition

of the Works and Correspondence of Adam Smith (Indianapolis: Liberty Classics, 1976). His primary work in liberal philosophy, which he continued to revise until shortly before his death, is Adam Smith, *The Theory of Moral Sentiments*, ed. D. D. Raphael and A. L. Macfie (Indianapolis: Liberty Classics, 1984).

2. In this chapter we do not attempt a historical review of the development of liberalism as a political philosophy. That has been done by others; in particular, see Edmund Fawcett, *Liberalism: The Life of an Idea* (Princeton, NJ: Princeton University Press, 2018).

3. Thomas E. Ricks, *Churchill and Orwell: The Fight for Freedom* (New York: Penguin Books, 2018).

4. Quoted, Ricks, *Churchill and Orwell*, 222.

5. World Commission on Environment and Development, *Our Common Future* (Oxford: Oxford University Press, 1987), 43. Note that the present does not have to allow for the wants of the future. However, the wants of some may be the needs of others.

6. These rules were first described in John Rawls, *A Theory of Justice* (Cambridge, MA: The Belknap Press of Harvard University Press, 1971), but expressed in this fashion in a later article: John Rawls, "Justice as Fairness: Political Not Metaphysical," *Philosophy and Public Affairs* 14, no. 3 (1985): 227.

7. Simone de Beauvoir, *Must We Burn de Sade?* (London: Peter Nevill, 1953).

8. Smith, *Theory of Moral Sentiments*, IV.i.2.8.

9. Edward Luce, *The Retreat of Western Liberalism* (Toronto: CNIB, 2017), 13.

10. Luce, *Retreat of Western Liberalism*, 191.

11. Gøsta Esping-Andersen, *The Three Worlds of Welfare Capitalism* (Cambridge: Polity Press, 1990).

12. Patrick J. Deneen, *Why Liberalism Failed* (New Haven, CT: Yale University Press, 2018), 179.

13. Deneen, *Why Liberalism Failed*, 5.

14. Definition from *Oxford English Dictionary* online, https://en.oxforddictionaries.com/definition/ideology.

15. Fawcett, *Liberalism*, 13.

16. Ralf Dahrendorf, *Life Chances: Approaches to Social and Political Theory* (Chicago: University of Chicago Press, 1979).

17. Rawls, "Justice as Fairness," 225.

18. Fawcett, *Liberalism*, 2.

19. Fawcett, *Liberalism*, 7.

20. Fawcett, *Liberalism*, 8.

21. Smith, *Theory of Moral Sentiments*, II.ii.3.4.

22. Smith, *Wealth of Nations*, V.i.b.2; 709–710.

23. Smith, *Theory of Moral Sentiments*, III.2.6.

24. Edmund Burke, "Letter to a Member of the National Assembly in Answer to Some Objections on His Book on French Affairs (1791)," http://www.ourcivilisation.com/smartboard/shop/burkee/tonatass/.

25. Comment by Grover Norquist in an interview on NPR's *Morning Edition* on 25 May 2001, http://www.npr.org/templates/story/story.php?storyId=1123439.

26. Letter from John Dahlberg-Acton to Mandell Creighton on 5 April 1887, https://en.wikiquote.org/wiki/ John_Dalberg-Acton,_1st_Baron_Acton.

27. Fawcett, *Liberalism*, 9.

28. Fawcett, *Liberalism*, 9.

29. Fawcett, *Liberalism*, 10.

30. Denis Goulet, *The Cruel Choice: A New Concept in the Theory of Development* (New York: Atheneum, 1977), x.

31. Fawcett, *Liberalism*, 10–11.

32. Fawcett, Liberalism, 11.

33. Dissent in *Citizens United, Appellant v. Federal Election Commission*, https://www.law.cornell.edu/supct/ html/08-205.ZX.html.

34. Charles Dickens, *Oliver Twist* (London: Tom Doherty Associates, 1998), 451.

35. Smith, *Theory of Moral Sentiments*, I.iii.2.1.

Chapter 3. The Present and Future Challenges of Liberalism

1. Wilhelm von Humboldt, *The Sphere and Duties of Government*, trans. Junior Joseph Coulthard (London: John Chapman, 1854), 2.

2. William Beveridge, *Social Insurance and Allied Services* (London: His Majesty's Stationery Office, 1942), 6–7.

3. Abraham H. Maslow, *The Farther Reaches of Human Nature* (New York: Viking Press, 1971).

4. Jeffrey D. Sachs, "America's Health Crisis and the Easterlin Paradox," in *World Happiness Report 2018*, ed. John Helliwell, Richard Layard, and Jeffrey Sachs (New York: Sustainable Development Solutions Network, 2018), 149–159.

5. Richard A. Easterlin, "Does Economic Growth Improve the Human Lot?," in *Nations and Households in Economic Growth: Essays in Honor of Moses Abramovitz*, ed. Paul A. David and Melvin W. Reder (New York: Academic Press, 1974), 89–125.

6. Quoted from Easterlin, "Does Economic Growth Improve the Human Lot?," 92. For the technical reader, Easterlin, like many after him, used "Gallup-poll-type" surveys that asked a direct question and a more sophisticated procedure, a "self-Anchoring Striving Scale" that seeks to include the "spectrum of values a person is preoccupied or concerned with and by means of which he evaluates

his own life." In other words, it includes people's hopes and fears for the future as it may directly affect them. This method was pioneered by Hadley Cantril, *Pattern of Human Concerns* (New Brunswick, NJ: Rutgers University Press, 1965).

7. Daniel Kahneman and Angus Deaton, "High Income Improves Evaluation of Life but Not Emotional Well-Being," *Proceedings of the National Academy of Sciences* 107, no. 38 (2010): 16489–16493, https://doi.org/10.1073/pnas.1011492107.

8. Arthur Cecil Pigou, *The Economics of Welfare*, 4th ed. (London: Macmillan, 1932), I.I.6.

9. Philip Brickman, Dan Coates, and Ronnie Janoff-Bulman, "Lottery Winners and Accident Victims: Is Happiness Relative?," *Journal of Personality and Social Psychology* 36, no. 8 (1978): 917–927; P. Brickman and D. T. Campbell, "Hedonic Relativism and Planning the Good Society," in *Adaptation Level Theory: A Symposium*, ed. M. H. Appley (New York: Academic Press, 1971), 287–302.

10. Ed Diener, Richard E. Lucas, and Christie Napa Scollon, "Beyond the Hedonic Treadmill: Revising the Adaptation Theory of Well-Being," *American Psychologist* 61, no. 4 (2006): 305–314.

11. Leaf Van Boven, "Experientialism, Materialism, and the Pursuit of Happiness," *Review of General Psychology* 9, no. 2 (2005): 132–142; Emily G. Solberg, Edward Diener, and Michael D. Robinson, "Why Are Materialists Less Satisfied?," in *Psychology and Consumer Culture: The Struggle for a Good Life in a Materialistic World*, ed. T. Kasser and A. D. Kanner (Washington, DC: American Psychological Association, 2004); Tim Kasser, *The High Price of Materialism* (Cambridge, MA: MIT Press, 2002).

12. John Helliwell, Richard Layard, and Jeffrey Sachs, eds., *World Happiness Report 2017* (New York: Sustainable Development Solutions Network, 2017), 3. The seventh category is a catch-all for poll responses that do not fall within the other categories. It is an error or unknown factor. For poorer countries, this category may hold a quarter or more of the responses but for rich countries it is a much smaller proportion of responses.

13. Andrew T. Jebb et al., "Happiness, Income Satiation and Turning Points around the World," *Nature Human Behaviour* 2, no. 1 (2018): 33–38, https://doi.org/10.1038/s41562-017-0277-0.

14. Alan S. Waterman, "On the Importance of Distinguishing Hedonia and Eudaimonia When Contemplating the Hedonic Treadmill," *American Psychologist* 62, no. 6 (September 2007): 612–613, https://doi.org/10.1037/0003-066X62.6.612.

15. Aristotle, *Nicomachean Ethics* (Oxford: Oxford University Press, 2009).

16. Abraham Maslow, *The Farther Reaches of Human Nature* (New York: Viking Press, 1971); Edward L. Deci and Richard M. Ryan, "Hedonia, Eudaimonia, and Well-Being: An Introduction," *Journal of Happiness Studies* 9, no. 1 (2008): 1–11.

17. Dan Buettner, *The Blue Zones of Happiness: Lessons from the World's Happiest People* (Washington, DC: National Geographic Partners, 2019).

18. David Wallace-Wells, *The Uninhabitable Earth* (New York: Tim Duggan Books, 2019).

19. Transcript of US Department of Defense news briefing (12 February 2002), accessed at https://archive.defense.gov/Transcripts/Transcript.aspx?TranscriptID=2636.

20. David Wallace-Wells, "The Uninhabitable Earth," *New York Magazine*, 10 July 2017; Wallace-Wells, *Uninhabitable Earth*, https://nymag.com/intelligencer/2017/07/climate-change-earth-too-hot-for-humans.html.

21. IPCC, *Climate Change 2014: Synthesis Report*, Contribution of Working Groups I, II, and III to the Fifth Assessment Report of the Intergovernmental Panel on Climate Change, Core Writing Team R. K. Pachauri and L. A. Meyer, eds. (Geneva: IPCC, 2015).

22. IPCC, *Climate Change 2014*, 64–74.

23. This is set as the "Objective" of the United Nations Framework Convention on Climate Change signed in 1992, https://unfccc.int/resource/docs/convkp/conveng.pdf.

24. The Copenhagen Accord (United Nations Decision-/CP.15), https://unfccc.int/files/ meetings/cop_15/application/pdf/cop15_cph_auv.pdf.

25. United Nations "Paris Agreement," https://unfccc.int/sites/default/files/english_paris_agreement.pdf.

26. V. Masson-Delmotte et al., eds., *Global Warming of 1.5°C. An IPCC Special Report on the Impacts of Global Warming of 1.5°C above Pre-Industrial Levels and Related Global Greenhouse Gas Emission Pathways, in the Context of Strengthening the Global Response to the Threat of Climate Change, Sustainable Development, and Efforts to Eradicate Poverty* (Geneva: World Meteorological Organization, 2018).

27. Joeri Rogelj et al., "Probabilistic Cost Estimates for Climate Change Mitigation," *Nature* 493, no. 7430 (2013): 79–83.

28. Nicholas Stern, *Stern Review Report on the Economics of Climate Change* (London: H.M. Treasury, 2006).

29. William D. Nordhaus, "A Review of the Stern Review on the Economics of Climate Change," *Journal of Economic Literature* 45 (September 2007): 687–702; William Nordhaus, "Projections and Uncertainties about Climate Change in an Era of Minimal Climate Policies," *American Economic Journal: Economic Policy* 10, no. 3 (2018): 333–360.

30. Nordhaus, "Projections and Uncertainties."

31. IPCC, *Climate Change 2014*, v.

32. US White House, "Remarks by President Trump Before Marine One Departure," 26 November 2018, https://www.whitehouse.gov/briefings-statements/remarks-president-trump-marine-one-departure-26/.

33. Japan Ministry of Internal Affairs and Communications, Statistics Bureau, *Statistical Handbook of Japan* (Tokyo: Japan Ministry of Internal Affairs and Communications, 2017).

34. Daron Acemoglu and Pascual Restrepo, "Robots and Jobs: Evidence from US Labor Markets," NBER Working Paper no. 23285, March 2017, https://ssrn.com/abstract=2941263.

35. Illah Reza Nourbakhsh, "The Coming Robot Dystopia," *Foreign Affairs* 94, no. 4 (2015): 23–28, https://www.foreignaffairs.com/articles/2015-06-16/coming-robot-dystopia.

36. Erik Brynjolfsson and Andrew McAfee, *Race against the Machine: How the Digital Revolution Is Accelerating Innovation, Driving Productivity, and Irreversibly Transforming Employment and the Economy* (Tokyo: Digital Frontier Press, 2012).

37. James Manyika et al., *An Economy That Works: Job Creation and America's Future*, McKinsey Global Institute (Washington, DC: McKinsey, 2011).

38. Kerwin Kofi Charles, Erik Hurst, and Matthew Notowidigdo, "Manufacturing Decline, Housing Booms, and Non-Employment," NBER Working Paper no. 18949, 2013, 13–57.

39. Frank Levy and Richard J. Murnane, *The New Division of Labor: How Computers Are Creating the Next Job Market* (Princeton, NJ: Princeton University Press, 2005).

40. John Krafcik [CEO of Waymo, part of Alphabet], *Status*, 20 July 2018, https://twitter.com/johnkrafcik/status/1020343952266973186?lang=en.

41. Carl Benedikt Frey and Michael A Osborne, "The Future of Employment: How Susceptible Are Jobs to Computerisation?," *Technological Forecasting and Social Change* 114 (2017): 254–280.

42. Nedelkoskam Ljubica and Glenda Quintini, *Automation, Skills Use and Training*, Labour and Social Affairs Directorate for Employment, OECD, 14 March (Paris: OECD, 2018), https://www.oecd-ilibrary.org/employment/automation-skills-use-and-training_2e2f4eea-en.

43. Jacques Bughin et al., *Skill Shift: Automation and the Future of the Workforce*, McKinsey Global Institute (Washington, DC: McKinsey, 2018).

44. Bughin et al., *Skill Shift*, 7.

45. Eduardo Porter, "Don't Fight the Robots, Tax Them," *New York Times*, 23 February 2019, https://www.nytimes.com/2019/02/23/sunday-review/tax-artificial-intelligence.html.

46. Bertrand Russell, *The Conquest of Happiness* (New York: Horace Liveright, 1930); John Maynard Keynes, "Economic Possibilities for Our Grandchildren (1930)," in *Essays in Persuasion* (New York: Springer, 2010), 321–332.

47. Quoted in Paul Krugman, *The Conscience of a Liberal* (New York: W. W. Norton, 2009).

Chapter 4. MegaCorps: Malefactors of Great Wealth

1. Susan Strange, "The Future of Global Capitalism; or Will Divergence Persist Forever?," in *Political Economy of Modern Capitalism: Mapping Convergence and Diversity*, ed. Colin Crouch and Wolfgang Streeck (London: Sage, 1997), 4.

2. Strange, "Global Capitalism," 6.

3. Strange, "Global Capitalism," 6.

4. Strange, "Global Capitalism," 14.

5. Jagdish Bhagwati, *In Defense of Globalization* (New York: Oxford University Press, 2004); David Harvey, *A Brief History of Neoliberalism* (Oxford: Oxford University Press, 2005).

6. Thomas Friedman, *The Lexus and the Olive Tree* (London: Harper-Collins, 2000).

7. Peter Nolan, Dylan Sutherland, and Jin Zhang, "The Challenge of the Global Business Revolution," *Contributions to Political Economy* 21, no. 1 (2002): 91–110.

8. Jonathan Tepper and Denise Hearn, *The Myth of Capitalism: Monopolies and the Death of Competition* (Hoboken: John Wiley and Sons, 2019).

9. "Fortune Global 500," *Fortune*, 2015, http://fortune.com/global500/.

10. World Bank, *Gross Domestic Product 2015*, World Development Indicator Database, 11 October 2016, http://databank.worldbank.org/data/download/GDP.pdf.

11. Genevieve LeBaron, "Subcontracting Is Not Illegal, but Is It Unethical? Business Ethics, Forced Labour, and Economic Success," *Brown Journal of World Affairs* 20, no. 2 (2014): 237–249; Walmart, *Walmart 2103 Annual Report*, 2013, http://c46b2bcc0db5865f5a76–91c2ff8eba65983a1c33d367b8503d02.r78.cf2.rackcdn.com/88/2d/4fdf67184a359fdef07b1c3f4732/2013-annual-report-for-walmart-storesinc_130221024708579502.pdf; Walmart, *Apply to Be a Supplier*, 2017, http://corporate.walmart.com/suppliers/apply-to-be-a-supplier.

12. Richard Dobbs et al., *Playing to Win: The New Global Competition for Corporate Profits*, McKinsey Global Institute, September 2015, http://www.mckinseycom/business-functions/strategy-and-corporate-finance/our-insights/thenew-global-competition-for-corporate-profits.

13. His famous nineteenth-century illustration was that Britain was better at producing cloth, while Portugal was better at producing wine. Being endowed with these abilities, it followed that it would be best if each country specialized in what its industry could most efficiently produce, and that free trade between them was permitted for mutual gains.

14. Adam Smith, *The Wealth of Nations* (New York: Bantam Classic, 2003), xvii.

15. For example, John Braithwaite, *Regulatory Capitalism: How It Works, Ideas for Making It Work Better* (Cheltenham: Edward Elgar, 2008).

16. For example, John Micklethwait and Adrian Wooldridge, *The Company: A Short History of a Revolutionary Idea* (London: Phoenix, 2003).

17. Strange, "Global Capitalism," 184.

18. Alan Rugman and Alain Verbeke, "Location, Competitiveness, and the Multinational Enterprise," in *The Oxford Handbook of International Business*, 2nd ed., ed. Alan Rugman (Oxford: Oxford University Press, 2009), 146–181.

19. Clifford L. Staples, "Board Globalisation in the World's Largest TNCs 1993–2005," *Corporate Governance* 15, no. 2 (2017): 311–321.

20. Kees van Veen and Ilse Marsman, "How International Are Executive Boards of European MNCs? National Diversity in 15 European Countries," *European Management Journal* 26 (2008): 188–198.

21. Ha-Joon Chang, *Bad Samaritans: The Myth of Free Trade and the Secret History of Capitalism* (New York: Bloomsbury Press, 2008), 32.

22. Alan Rugman, *The End of Globalization* (London: Random House Business Books, 2000); Raymond L. Bryant and Sinéad Bailey, *Third World Political Ecology* (London: Routledge, 1997).

23. Annebritt Dullforce, "FT Global 500 2015," *Financial Times* (International Edition), 20 June 2015, www.ft.com/ft500.

24. Jeffrey Harrod, "The Century of the Corporation," in *Global Corporate Power*, ed. Christopher May (Boulder, CO: Lynne Rienner, 2006), 27–28.

25. IMF, *World Economic Outlook Database: April 2015 Edition*, 2015, http://www.imf.org/external/pubs/ft/weo/2015/01/weodata/index.aspx.

26. Kun-Chin Lin, "Protecting the Petroleum Industry: Renewed Government Aid to Fossil Fuel Producers," *Business and Politics* 16, no. 4 (2014): 549–578.

27. These data are presented in Nathan Jensen and Edmund Malesky, *Incentives to Pander: How Politicians Use Corporate Welfare for Political Gain* (Cambridge: Cambridge University Press, 2018). One example they give is the US$8.5 billion paid to Amazon for it to establish a headquarters in Maryland, along with a promise to pay back 5.75 percent of every worker's salary. This is equal to Maryland's minimum state income tax rate. In other words, Amazon paid its taxes like a good corporate citizen, and these were then paid back to Amazon.

28. Fabio Panetta et al., "An Assessment of Financial Sector Rescue Programmes," Bank for International Settlement, BIS Papers no. 48, Basel, Switzerland, 2009, http://www.bis.org/publ/bppdf/bispap48.pdf, 1.

29. Australia, Canada, France, Germany, Italy, Japan, the Netherlands, Spain, Switzerland, the UK, and the US.

30. "Prospering in the Pandemic: the Top 100 Companies," *Financial Times*, 18 June 2020, https://www.ft.com/content/844ed28c-8074-4856-bde0-20f3bf4cd8f0.

31. Panetta et al., "Assessment of Financial Sector Rescue Programmes."

32. OECD, *Concentration of the Banking Sector: Assets of Three Largest Banks as a Share of Assets of All Commercial Banks, Percent, 2011*, OECD Economic Surveys, Netherlands, April 2014, http://10.1787/eco_surveys-nld-2014-graph31-en; Thorsten Beck, Asli Demirguc-Kunt, and Ross Levine, "Bank Concentration and Fragility: Impact and Mechanics," NBER Working Paper no. 11500, 2005, http://www.nber.org/papers/w11500; OECD, *Bank Competition and Financial Stability*, 2011, http://www.oecd.org/finance/financial-markets/48501035.pdf.

33. IMF, *Global Financial Stability Report: Restoring Confidence and Progressing Reforms* (Washington, DC: IMF, 2012), http://www.imf.org/external/pubs/ft/gfsr/2012/02/pdf/text.pdf.

34. Banks around the World, *Top 100 Banks in the World*, 2015, http://www.relbanks.com/worlds-top-banks/assets.

35. World Bank, *Gross Domestic Product 2015*, World Development Indicator Database, 11 October 2016, http://databank.worldbank.org/data/download/.GDP.pdf.

Chapter 5. CorpoCapitalism and the Misery of Work

1. David Korten, *When Corporations Rule the World*, 3rd ed. (Oakland: Berrett-Koehler, 2015).

2. Genevieve LeBaron and Nicola Phillips, "States and the Political Economy of Unfree Labour," *New Political Economy* 24, no. 1 (2019): 1–21. They point out that it is not just a matter of deregulation but also a failure to enforce labor standards that still exist. For example, in the US there was one inspector per 11,000 workers in 1941, while by 2008 there was one per 141,000 workers. There is not enough being done not just because there is a lack of regulations, but because the agencies enforcing them have been attacked by the government.

3. For example, Michael Horn, "Uber, Disruptive Innovation and Regulated Markets," *Forbes*, 20 June 2016, https://www.forbes.com/sites/michaelhorn/2016/06/20/uber-disruptive-innovation-and-regulated-markets/#6de654d237fb; Clayton M. Christensen et al., "What Is Disruptive Innovation?," *Harvard Business Review*, December 2015, https://hbr.org/2015/12/what-is-disruptive-innovation.

4. Sui-Lee Wee and Paul Mozur, "Amazon Wants to Disrupt Health Care in America. In China, Tech Giants Already Have," *New York Times*, 31 January 2018, https://www.nytimes.com/2018/01/31/technology/amazon-china-health-care-ai.html.

5. Patrick Hatch, "In Amazon's 'Hellscape,' Workers Face Insecurity and Crushing Targets," *Sydney Morning Herald*, 7 September 2018, https://www.smh.com.au/business/workplace/in-amazon-s-hellscape-workers-face-insecurity-and-crushing-targets-20180907-p502ao.html.

6. Genevieve LeBaron, "Subcontracting Is Not Illegal, but Is It Unethical? Business Ethics, Forced Labour, and Economic Success," *Brown Journal of World Affairs* 20, no. 2 (2014): 237–249.

7. Martin Wolf, *Why Globalization Works* (New Haven, CT: Yale University Press, 2004); Robert Wade, "Is the Globalization Consensus Dead?," *Antipode* 41, no. S1 (2010): 141–165; Ha-Joon Chang, *Bad Samaritans: The Myth of Free Trade and the Secret History of Capitalism* (New York: Bloomsbury Press, 2008).

8. "The Purse of the One Percent," *The Economist*, 14 October 2014, https://www.economist.com/node/21625355/. In this article it is noted that

"wealth is so unevenly distributed, that you need just $3,650 (net of debts) to count yourself among the richest half of the world's population."

9. Anthony Shorrocks, James Davies, and Rodrigo Lluberas, *Global Wealth Report* (Zurich: Credit Suisse Research Institute, 2019), https://www.credit-suisse.com/about-us/en/reports-research/global-wealth-report.html.

10. Tansy Hopkins, "Reliving the Rana Plaza Factory Collapse: A History of Cities in 50 Buildings, day 22," *The Guardian*, 23 April 2015, https://www.theguardian.com/cities/2015/apr/23/rana-plaza-factory-collapse-history-cities-50-buildings; Julhas Alam and Farid Hossain, "Bangladesh Collapse Search Over; Death Toll 1,127," Yahoo News, 14 May 2013, https://news.yahoo.com/bangladesh-collapse-search-over-death-toll-1-127-122554495.html.

11. John Braithwaite, *Regulatory Capitalism: How It Works, Ideas for Making It Work Better* (Cheltenham: Edward Elgar, 2008).

12. Eric Posner, "Milton Friedman Was Wrong," *Atlantic*, 22 August 2019, https://www.theatlantic.com/ideas/archive/2019/08/milton-friedman-shareholder-wrong/596545/; Milton Friedman, "The Social Responsibility of Business Is to Increase Its Profits," *New York Times Magazine*, 13 September 1970, 32–33 and 122–126.

13. Fortune, *World's Most Admired Companies 2015*, 2015, http://fortune.com/worlds-most-admired-companies/2015/; Fortune, *World's Most Admired Companies Ranked by Key Attributes*, 2015, http://fortune.com/2015/02/19/wmac-ranked-by-key-attribute/; Fortune, *How to Become the World's Most Admired Company*, 2015, http://fortune.com/video/2015/02/19/how-to-become-the-worlds-most-admiredcompany/.

14. David Vogel, "Taming Globalization? Civil Regulation and Corporate Capitalism," in *The Oxford Handbook of Business and Government*, ed. David Coen, Win Grant, and Graham Wilson (Oxford: Oxford University Press, 2010), 478.

15. Angela K. Davis, David A. Guenther, and Linda K. Krull, "Do Socially Responsible Firms Pay More Taxes?," *Accounting Review* 91, no. 1 (2016): 65.

16. Fiona G. Tam, "Foxconn Factories Are Labor Camps: Report," *South China Morning Post*, 11 October 2010, https://www.scmp.com/article/727143/foxconn-factories-are-labour-camps-report; Susan Adams, "Apple's New Foxconn Embarrassment," *Forbes*, 12 September 2012, http://www.forbes.com/sites/susanadams/2012/09/12/apples-new-foxconn-embarrassment/#103b24a28ae6.

17. Connor Myers, "Corporate Social Responsibility in the Consumer Electronics Industry: A Case Study of Apple Inc.," Georgetown University Edmund A. Walsh School of Foreign Service, 2013, 11, http://lwp.georgetown.edu/wp-content/uploads/Connor-Myers.pdf.

18. René Schmidpeter and Christopher Stehr, "A History of Research on CSR in China: The Obstacles for the Implementation of CSR in Emerging Markets," in *Sustainable Development and CSR in China: A Multi-Perspective*

Approach, ed. René Schmidpeter, Hualiang Lu, Christopher Stehr, and Haifeng Huang (New York: Springer International, 2015), 1–12.

19. Adams, "Foxconn Embarrassment."

20. Myers, "Corporate Social Responsibility," 3.

21. Doris Fuchs, *Business Power in Global Governance* (Boulder, CO: Lynne Rienner, 2007).

22. Apple, *Apple Supplier Responsibility 2019 Progress Report*, https://www.apple.com/au/supplier-responsibility/pdf/Apple_SR_2019_Progress_Report.pdf.

23. Mario Christodoulou, "UK Auditors Criticized on Bank Crisis," *Wall Street Journal*, 30 March 2011, https://www.wsj.com/articles/SB10001424052748703806304576232231353594682; PwC, *PwC's Global Annual Review 2018*, https://www.pwc.com/gx/en/about/global-annual-review-2018/clients.html.

24. LeBaron, "Subcontracting Is Not Illegal," 245.

25. Adam Smith, *The Wealth of Nations* (New York: Bantam Classics, 2003), 621.

26. This is a central point of Colin Crouch, *The Strange Non-Death of Neoliberalism* (Cambridge: Polity Press, 2011).

27. Jan de Loecker and Jan Eeckhout, "The Rise of Market Power and the Macroeconomic Implications," NBER Working Paper no. 23687, August 2017, http://www.nber.org/papers/w23687. For examples of the price increases in particular industries, see also Jonathan Tepper and Denise Hearn, *The Myth of Capitalism: Monopolies and the Death of Competition* (Hoboken, NJ: John Wiley and Sons, 2019), 43. Also see Thomas Philippon, *The Great Reversal: How America Gave Up on Free Markets* (Cambridge, MA: The Belknap Press of Harvard University Press, 2019).

28. Milton Friedman, "The Social Responsibility of Business Is to Increase Profits," *New York Times Magazine*, 13 September 1970.

Chapter 6. Providing for Individual Wellbeing

1. Peter Hall and David Soskice, "An Introduction to Varieties of Capitalism," in *Varieties of Capitalism: The Institutional Foundations of Comparative Advantage*, ed. Peter Hall and David Soskice (Oxford: Oxford University Press, 2001), 9.

2. Justin R. Pierce and Peter K. Schott, "The Surprisingly Swift Decline of US Manufacturing Employment," *American Economic Review* 106, no. 7 (2016): 1632–1662; David H. Autor, David Dorn, and Gordon H. Hanson, "The China Syndrome: Local Labor Market Effects of Import Competition in the United States," *American Economic Review* 103, no. 6 (2013): 2121–2168.

3. Both figures are produced from data on the World Inequality Database (WID) accessed at https://wid.world on 1 July 2019. The figures should only

be considered generally indicative as we do not present here all the possible permutations of income and wealth by source, age, or other grouping available on the WID.

4. Melike Wulfgramm, Tonia Bieber, and Stephan Leibfried, eds., *Welfare State Transformations and Inequality in OECD Countries* (London: Palgrave Macmillan, 2016), 6–7.

5. OECD, "Real Minimum Wages" Dataset on OECD.Stat, https://stats.oecd.org/.

6. Richard G. Wilkinson and Kate E. Pickett, "Income Inequality and Social Dysfunction," *Annual Review of Sociology* 35 (2009): 493–511.

7. Robert Putnam, *Bowling Alone: The Collapse and Revival of American Community* (New York: Simon and Schuster, 2000); see also Robert Putnam, *Making Democracy Work: Civic Traditions in Modern Italy* (Princeton, NJ: Princeton University Press, 1993).

8. Gøsta Esping-Andersen, *The Three Worlds of Welfare Capitalism* (Cambridge: Polity Press, 1990), 18–19. See also Robert E. Goodin, Bruce Headey, Ruud Muffels, and Henk-Jan Dirven, *The Real Worlds of Welfare Capitalism* (Cambridge: Cambridge University Press, 1999).

9. John Rawls, *A Theory of Justice* (Cambridge, MA: The Belknap Press of Harvard University Press, 1971), 14–15.

10. Rawls, *A Theory of Justice*, 73 and 83–90.

11. Matthew Watson, "Ricardian Political Economy and the 'Varieties of Capitalism' Approach: Specialization, Trade and Comparative Institutional Advantage," *Comparative European Politics* 1, no. 2 (2003): 227.

12. John Braithwaite, *Regulatory Capitalism: How It Works, Ideas for Making It Work Better* (Cheltenham: Edward Elgar, 2008); Stephen Wilks, *The Political Power of the Business Corporation* (Cheltenham: Edward Elgar, 2013).

13. For example, Kathleen Thelen, "Varieties of Labour Politics in the Developed Democracies," in *Varieties of Capitalism: The Institutional Foundations of Comparative Advantage*, ed. Peter Hall and David Soskice (Oxford: Oxford University Press, 2001), 71–103; Torben Iversen and Jonas Pontusson, "Comparative Political Economy: A Northern European Perspective," in *Unions, Employers and Central Banks: Macroeconomic Coordination and Institutional Change in Social Market Economies*, ed. Torben Iversen, Jonas Pontusson, and David Soskice (New York: Cambridge University Press, 2000), 1–37; Peter Hall and David Soskice, "Varieties of Capitalism and Institutional Change: A Response to Three Critics," *Comparative European Politics* 1, no. 2 (2003): 241–250; Peter Hall, "The Evolution of Varieties of Capitalism in Europe," in *Beyond Varieties of Capitalism: Contradictions, Complementarities and Change*, ed. Bob Hancke, Martin Rhodes, and Mark Thatcher (Oxford: Oxford University Press, 2007), 39–88; Peter Hall and Daniel Gingerich, "Varieties of Capitalism and Institutional Complementarities in the Political Economy," *British Journal of Political Science* 39, no. 3 (2009):

449–482; Peter Hall and Kathleen Thelen, "Institutional Change in Varieties of Capitalism," *Socio-Economic Review* 7 (2009): 7–34.

14. David Harvey, *A Brief History of Neoliberalism* (Oxford: Oxford University Press 2005), 11.

15. Wolfgang Streek, "The Return of the Repressed," *New Left Review* 104 (March/April 2017): 14.

Chapter 7. Taxation and Representation

1. For example: "The Nine Most Terrifying Words in the English Language Are: I'm From the Government, and I'm Here to Help," News Conference, 12 August 1986, https://www.reaganfoundation.org/ronald-reagan/reagan-quotes-speeches/news-conference-1/.

2. Milton Friedman, "The Social Responsibility of Business Is to Increase Profits," *New York Times Magazine*, 13 September 1970, 32.

3. William Lazonick, "Profits without Prosperity," *Harvard Business Review* (September 2014): 46–55.

4. Lazonick, "Profits without Prosperity," 50.

5. Share buybacks avoid the double taxation of profits through dividends as they are deemed a distribution of capital.

6. Ronald Dore, "Will Global Capitalism Be Anglo-Saxon Capitalism?," *New Left Review* 6 (2000): 103.

7. Kim Doyle, "Facebook, WhatsApp and the Commodification of Affective Labour," *Communication, Politics and Culture* 48, no. 1 (2015): 51–65.

8. Smith, *Wealth of Nations*, IV.1.3, quoted in Stephen Wilks, *The Political Power of the Business Corporation* (Cheltenham: Edward Elgar, 2013), 10.

9. Lazonick, "Profits without Prosperity," 52.

10. IMF, "World Economic Outlook Database," April 2015, http://www.imf.org/external/pubs/ft/weo/2015/01/weodata/index.aspx.

11. Elke Asen, "Corporate Tax Rates around the World 2019," *The Tax Foundation*, Fiscal Fact #679, 10 December 2019, accessed at https://taxfoundation.org/corporate-tax-rates-around-the-world-2019/ on 28 April 2020.

12. OECD, "Tax Revenue," 2018, https://data.oecd.org/tax/tax-revenue.htm. Social security contributions are broadly what are termed "employment" or "payroll" taxes in the US.

13. Philip Cerny, "Political Globalization and the Competition State," in *Political Economy and the Changing Global Order*, ed. Richard Stubbs and Geoffrey Underhill (Oxford: Oxford University Press, 2000), 302. See also Philip Cerny, "The Competition State Today: From Raison d'État to Raison du Monde," *Policy Studies* 31, no. 1 (2010): 5–21.

14. Ernesto Crivelli et al., "Base Erosion, Profit Shifting and Developing Countries," *FinanzArchiv: Public Finance Analysis* 72, no. 3 (2016): 268–301; Jane

Gravelle, *Tax Havens: International Tax Avoidance and Evasion* (Washington, DC: Congressional Research Services, 2015); OECD, *OECD Secretary-General Report to G20 Finance Ministers and Central Bank Governors* (Paris: OECD, 2019), http://www.oecd.org/tax/oecd-secretary-general-tax-report-g20-finance-ministers-june-2019.pdf.

15. For example, see Richard Eccleston, "BEPS and the New Politics of Corporate Tax Justice," in *Business, Civil Society and the 'New' Politics of Corporate Tax Justice*, ed. Richard Eccleston and Ainsley Elbra (Cheltenham: Edward Elgar, 2018), 40–67.

16. Australian Senate, *Australian Senate Economic References Committee Hearing into Corporate Tax Avoidance*, 9 April 2015, https://parlinfo.aph.gov.au/parlInfo/search/display/display.w3p;query=Id:"committees/commsen/aa68d895-38dc-4165-bce7-2082c796519b/0000". Also, see the analysis in John Mikler, Ainsley Elbra, and Hannah Murphy-Gregory, "Defending Harmful Tax Practices: Mining Companies' Responses to the Australian Senate Inquiry into Tax Avoidance," *Australian Journal of Political Science* 54, no. 2 (2019): 238–254; John Mikler and Ainsley Elbra, "Paying a Fair Share: Multinational Corporations' Perspectives on Taxation," *Global Policy* 8, no. 2: 181–190.

17. Ronen Palan, Richard Murphy, and Christian Chavagneux, *Tax Havens: How Globalization Really Works* (Ithaca: Cornell University Press, 2013), 217; see also Jason Sharman, *Havens in a Storm: The Struggle for Global Tax Regulation* (Ithaca: Cornell University Press, 2006).

18. US Department of the Treasury, "Treasury Secretary O'Neill Statement on OECD Tax Havens," News Release no. PO-366, 5 October 2001, http://www.treasury.gov/press-center/press-releases/Pages/po366.aspx.

19. "The Global 500, the World's Largest Public Companies," 2 July 2002, https://www.forbes.com/global/2002/0722/global.html#71aac2ad47f6.

20. For example, see Leonard Seabrooke and Duncan Wigan, *Emergent Entrepreneurs in Transnational Advocacy Networks: Professional Mobilization in the Fight for Global Tax Justice* (Warwick: Centre for the Study of Globalisation and Regionalisation, 2013); Palan, Murphy, and Chavagneux, *Tax Havens*.

21. Laura Stampler, "Amazon Will Pay a Whopping $0 in Federal Taxes on $11.2 Billion Profits," *Fortune*, 14 February 2019, https://fortune.com/2019/02/14/amazon-doesnt-pay-federal-taxes-2019/.

22. Megan Cerullo, "60 of America's Biggest Companies Paid No Federal Income Tax in 2018," CBS News, 12 April 2019, https://www.cbsnews.com/news/2018-taxes-some-of-americas-biggest-companies-paid-little-to-no-federal-income-tax-last-year/.

23. Owen Jones, *The Establishment and How They Get Away with It* (London: Allen Lane, 2014), 178.

24. John Schwartz, "We Went to the Moon. Why Can't We Solve Climate Change?," *New York Times*, 19 July 2019, https://www.nytimes.com/2019/07/19/climate/moon-shot-climate-change.html.

Chapter 8. Capitalism and Its Discontents

1. Thomas Piketty, *Capital in the Twenty-First Century*, trans. Arthur Goldhammer (Cambridge, MA: The Belknap Press of Harvard University Press, 2014).

2. Credit Suisse Research Institute, *Global Wealth Databook 2018*, Credit Suisse Research Institute, 2019, https://www.credit-suisse.com/about-us/en/reports-research/global-wealth-report.html.

3. Joseph Stiglitz, *People, Power, and Profits: Progressive Capitalism for an Age of Discontent* (New York: W. W. Norton, 2019), 35.

4. Michael Kumhof, Romain Rancière, and Pablo Winant, "Inequality, Leverage, and Crises," *American Economic Review* 105, no. 3 (March 2015): 1217–1245.

5. White House Council of Economic Advisers, "Labor Market Monopsony: Trends, Consequences, and Policy Responses," October 2016, 20161025_monopsony_labor_mrkt_cea.pdf (archives.gov).

6. OECD, *Tax Reforms Accelerating with Push to Lower Corporate Tax Rates*, 5 September (Paris: OECD Centre for Tax Policy and Administration, 2018). Because MegaCorps can potentially move operations, competition between countries has precipitated this decline.

7. Calculated as a simple average of statutory personal income tax rates and top rate income thresholds from date at https://stats.oecd.org/.

8. Anna Stansbury and Lawrence Summers, "Declining Worker Power and American Economic Performance," Brookings Papers on Economic Activity, BPEA Conference Drafts, 19 March 2020; Lawrence H. Summers, "Low Equilibrium Real Rates, Financial Crisis, and Secular Stagnation," in *Across the Great Divide: New Perspectives on the Financial Crisis*, ed. Martin Neil Baily and John B. Taylor (Stanford, CA: Hoover Institution Press, 2014), 37–50.

9. Joseph E. Stiglitz, "Inequality and Economic Growth," in *Rethinking Capitalism: Economics and Policy for Sustainable and Inclusive Growth*, ed. Michael Jacobs and Mariana Mazzucato (Chichester, UK: John Wiley and Sons, 2016), 134–155; Joseph E. Stiglitz, "Monetary Policy in a Multi-Polar World," in *Taming Capital Flows: Capital Account Management in an Era of Globalization*, ed. J. E. Stiglitz and R. S. Gürkaynak, International Economic Association Series (London: Palgrave Macmillan, 2015), 124–170.

10. Richard G. Wilkinson and Kate E. Pickett, "Income Inequality and Social Dysfunction," *Annual Review of Sociology* 35 (2009): 493–511.

11. Cameron Anderson, John Angus D. Hildreth, and Laura Howland, "Is the Desire for Status a Fundamental Human Motive? A Review of the Empirical Literature," *Psychological Bulletin* 141, no. 3 (2015): 574–601, DOI:10.1037/a0038781; Joey T. Cheng, Jessica L. Tracy, and Joseph Henrich, "Pride, Personality, and the Evolutionary Foundations of Human Social Status," *Evolution and Human Behavior* 31, no. 5 (2010): 334–347.

12. Keith Payne, *The Broken Ladder: How Inequality Affects the Way We Think, Live, and Die* (New York: Penguin Books, 2018).

13. Payne, *Broken Ladder*, 4.

14. Payne, *Broken Ladder*, 29.

15. Adam Smith, *An Inquiry into the Nature and Causes of the Wealth of Nations*, ed. R. H. Campbell and A. S. Skinner, 2 vols., vol. 1, Glasgow Edition of the Works and Correspondence of Adam Smith (Indianapolis: Liberty Classics, 1976), V.ii.k, 870.

16. Payne, *Broken Ladder*, 200.

17. Sarah McCue Horwitz et al., "Language Delay in a Community Cohort of Young Children," *Journal of the American Academy of Child and Adolescent Psychiatry* 42, no. 8 (2003): 932–940.

18. Christian H. Cooper, "Why Poverty Is Like a Disease," *Nautilus*, 20 April 2017, http://nautil.us/issue/47/consciousness/why-poverty-is-like-a-disease.

19. Quote from Cooper, "Why Poverty Is Like a Disease," based on Kimberly G. Noble, M. Frank Norman, and Martha J. Farah, "Neurocognitive Correlates of Socioeconomic Status in Kindergarten Children," *Developmental Science* 8, no. 1 (2005): 74–87; Jens Ludwig et al., "Neighborhoods, Obesity, and Diabetes—a Randomized Social Experiment," *New England Journal of Medicine* 365, no. 16 (2011): 1509–1519.

20. OECD StatLink, http://dx.doi.org/10.1787/784787325068, and "Opportunity Insights," 2019, https://opportunityinsights.org/.

21. Sam Harris, *Free Will* (New York: Free Press, 2014).

22. John Rawls, *A Theory of Justice* (Cambridge, MA: The Belknap Press of Harvard University Press, 1971).

23. Robert H. Frank and Philip J. Cook, *The Winner-Take-All Society: Why the Few at the Top Get So Much More than the Rest of US* (New York: Penguin, 1996).

24. OECD, *GDP per Hour Worked* (Paris: OECD, 2018), https://data.oecd.org/lprdty/gdp-per-hour-worked.htm.

25. Thijs Bol, "Has Education Become More Positional? Educational Expansion and Labour Market Outcomes, 1985–2007," *Acta Sociologica* 58, no. 2 (2015): 105–120, https://doi.org/10.1177%2F0001699315570918.

26. Fred Hirsch, *Social Limits to Growth* (Cambridge, MA: Harvard University Press, 1976).

27. Robert D. Putnam, *Our Kids: The American Dream in Crisis* (New York: Simon and Schuster, 2016), 229.

28. Alberto Alesina, Stefanie Stantcheva, and Edoardo Teso, "Intergenerational Mobility and Preferences for Redistribution," *American Economic Review* 108, no. 2 (2018): 521–554.

29. Cas Mudde, "Populist Radical Right Parties in Europe Today," in *Transformations of Populism in Europe and the Americas: History and Recent Trends*,

ed. John Abromeit, York Norman, Gary Marotta, and Bridget Maria Chesterton (London: Bloomsbury, 2015), 295–307.

30. Jochen I. Menges et al., "The Awestruck Effect: Followers Suppress Emotion Expression in Response to Charismatic but Not Individually Considerate Leadership," *Leadership Quarterly* 26, no. 4 (2015): 626–640.

31. Ronald F. Inglehart and Pippa Norris, "Trump, Brexit, and the Rise of Populism: Economic Have-Nots and Cultural Backlash," HKS Working Paper no. RWP16-026, 2016, SSRN: https://ssrn.com/abstract=2818659 or http://dx.doi.org/10.2139/ssrn.2818659.

32. Noam Gidron and Peter A. Hall, "The Politics of Social Status: Economic and Cultural Roots of the Populist Right," *British Journal of Sociology* 68, no. S1 (2017): S57–S84. The notable exception to all these trends has been Hungary.

33. John Sides, Michael Tesler, and Lynn Vavreck, *Identity Crisis: The 2016 Presidential Campaign and the Battle for the Meaning of America* (Princeton, NJ: Princeton University Press, 2019).

34. Colin Crouch, *The Strange Non-Death of Neoliberalism* (Cambridge: Polity Press, 2011).

35. David F. Larcker and Brian Taya, CEO *Compensation—Data Spotlight*, Corporate Governance Research Initiative, Corporate Governance Research Initiative, Stanford Graduate School of Business, 2018, https://www.gsb.stanford.edu/sites/gsb/files/publication-pdf/cgri-quick-guide-17-ceo-compensation-data.pdf.

36. Matthew Weinzierl, "Popular Acceptance of Inequality Due to Innate Brute Luck and Support for Classical Benefit-Based Taxation," *Journal of Public Economics* 155 (2017): 54–63.

37. Evelyne Huber, Jingjing Huo, and John D. Stephens, "Power, Markets, and Top Income Shares," Kellogg Institute for International Studies Working Paper 404, April 2015.

38. Lydia Dishman, "How U.S. Employee Benefits Compare to Europe's," *Fast Company*, 17 February 2016, https://www.fastcompany.com/3056830/how-the-us-employee-benefits-compare-to-europe.

39. Smith, *Wealth of Nations*, V.i.b.2; 709–710.

40. Putnam, *Our Kids*, 234.

41. Anthony B. Atkinson, *Inequality* (Cambridge, MA: Harvard University Press, 2015).

42. Atkinson, *Inequality*, 62–64.

Chapter 9. Technological Innovation for the People

1. IPCC, *Climate Change 2014: Synthesis Report. Contribution of Working Groups I, II and III to the Fifth Assessment Report of the Intergovernmental Panel*

on Climate Change, Core Writing Team R. K. Pachauri and L. A. Meyer, eds. (Geneva: IPCC, 2015), v.

2. Neil E. Harrison and John Mikler, eds., *Climate Innovation: Liberal Capitalism and Climate Change* (London: Palgrave Macmillan, 2014).

3. Harrison and Mikler, *Climate Innovation*, 5.

4. Harrison and Mikler, *Climate Innovation*.

5. Nokia Bell Labs, "Our History," https://www.bell-labs.com/about/history-bell-labs/.

6. William Lazonick, "Profits without Prosperity," *Harvard Business Review* 92, no. 9 (2014): 46–55; William Lazonick and Mariana Mazzucato, "The Risk-Reward Nexus in the Innovation-Inequality Relationship: Who Takes the Risks? Who Gets the Rewards?," *Industrial and Corporate Change* 22, no. 4 (2013): 1093–1128.

7. Mariana Mazzucato and Gregor Semieniuk, "Public Financing of Innovation: New Questions," *Oxford Review of Economic Policy* 33, no. 1 (2017): 24–48; Andrew G. Haldane, "The Costs of Short-Termism," *Political Quarterly* 86, no. 1 (2015): 66–76.

8. R. J. Gilson, "Controlling Shareholders and Corporate Governance: Complicating the Comparative Taxonomy," Review, *Harvard Law Review* 119, no. 6 (April 2006): 1641–1679.

9. Mariana Mazzucato, "Mission-Oriented Innovation Policies: Challenges and Opportunities," *Industrial and Corporate Change* 27, no. 5 (2018): 803.

10. Mariana Mazzucato and Caetano Penna, *The Brazilian Innovation System: A Mission-Oriented Policy Proposal* (Brazilia: Centro de Gestão e Estudos Estratégico, 2016), 6.

11. Mariana Mazzucato, "From Market Fixing to Market-Creating: A New Framework for Innovation Policy," *Industry and Innovation* 23, no. 2 (2016): 2.

12. Mazzucato, "Mission-Oriented Innovation Policies," 804.

13. Defense Advanced Research Projects Agency, "A Selected History of DARPA Innovation," https://www.darpa.mil/Timeline/index.html.

14. Erica R. H. Fuchs, "Rethinking the Role of the State in Technology Development: DARPA and the Case for Embedded Network Governance," *Research Policy* 39, no. 9 (2010): 1117.

15. ARPA-E, "About," https://arpa-e.energy.gov/?q=arpa-e-site-page/about.

16. Jeffrey Mervis, "Department of Energy Broke Law in Blocking Research Funds, Report Says," *Science*, 13 December 2017, http://www.sciencemag.org/news/2017/12/department-energy-broke-law-blocking-research-funds-report-says.

17. Mariana Mazzucato and Gregor Semieniuk, "Financing Renewable Energy: Who Is Financing What and Why It Matters," *Technological Forecasting and Social Change* 127 (2018): 8–22.

18. William D. Nordhaus, "To Tax or Not to Tax: Alternative Approaches to Slowing Global Warming," *Review of Environmental Economics and Policy* 1, no. 1 (2007): 2.

19. Shelagh Whitley and Laurie Van Der Burg, *Fossil Fuel Subsidy Reform: From Rhetoric to Reality* (London: World Resources Institute, 2015), http://newclimateeconomy.report/misc/working-papers, 3; Laura Merrill et al., *Tackling Fossil Fuel Subsidies and Climate Change: Levelling the Energy Playing Field* (Copenhagen: Nordic Council of Ministers, 2015).

20. Merritt Roe Smith and Leo Marx, *Does Technology Drive History? The Dilemma of Technological Determinism* (Boston: MIT Press, 1994).

21. Ronald R. Kline, "Technological Determinism," in *International Encyclopedia of the Social and Behavioral Sciences (Second Edition)*, ed. James D. Wright, 109–112 (Oxford: Elsevier, 2015); Langdon Winner, *Autonomous Technology: Technics-Out-of-Control as a Theme in Political Thought* (Boston: MIT Press, 1978).

22. Lewis Mumford, *Technics and Civilization* (New York: Harcourt, Brace, 1934).

23. Jack Kerouac, *On the Road* (New York: New American Library, 1958).

24. Donald MacKenzie and Judy Wajcman, *The Social Shaping of Technology* (London: Open University Press, 1999); Trevor J. Pinch and Wiebe E. Bijker, "The Social Construction of Facts and Artefacts: Or How the Sociology of Science and the Sociology of Technology Might Benefit Each Other," *Social Studies of Science* 14, no. 3 (1984): 399–441.

25. Carlota Perez, "Technological Revolutions and Techno-Economic Paradigms," *Cambridge Journal of Economics* 34, no. 1 (2010): 9.

26. Ha-Joon Chang, *23 Things They Don't Tell You about Capitalism* (New York: Bloomsbury Press, 2011), 34–37.

Chapter 10. The Purpose of the Economy

1. Thomas Piketty, *Capital in the Twenty-First Century*, trans. Arthur Goldhammer (Cambridge, MA: The Belknap Press of Harvard University Press, 2014).

2. Sam Wren-Lewis, "Well-Being as a Primary Good: Towards Legitimate Well-Being Policy," *Philosophy and Public Policy Quarterly* 31, no. 2 (2013): 7.

3. Business Roundtable, "Our Commitment," https://opportunity.businessroundtable.org/ourcommitment/.

4. Joseph Stiglitz, *People, Power, and Profits: Progressive Capitalism for an Age of Discontent* (New York: W. W. Norton, 2019).

5. Arthur M. Okun, *Equality and Efficiency: The Big Tradeoff* (Washington, DC: Brookings Institution, 1975), 13, emphasis added.

6. Okun, *Equality and Efficiency*, 119.

7. Milton Friedman, "The Social Responsibility of Business Is to Increase Profits," *New York Times Magazine*, 13 September 1970, Section SM, 17.

8. Robert Nozick, *Anarchy, State, and Utopia* (New York: Basic Books, 1974).

9. Marshall David Sahlins, *Stone Age Economics* (Chicago: Aldine-Atherton, 1972).

10. Kristin L. Leimgruber, Alexandra G. Rosati, and Laurie R. Santos, "Capuchin Monkeys Punish Those Who Have More," *Evolution and Human Behavior* 37, no. 3 (2016): 236–244.

11. Adam Smith, *An Inquiry into the Nature and Causes of the Wealth of Nations*, ed. R. H. Campbell and A. S. Skinner, 2 vols., vol. 1, Glasgow Edition of the Works and Correspondence of Adam Smith (Indianapolis: Liberty Classics, 1976), I.ii.1, 25.

12. Yanis Varoufakis and Jacob Moe, *Talking to My Daughter about the Economy, or, How Capitalism Works—And How It Fails* (New York: Farrar, Straus and Giroux, 2018), 178.

13. Jeffrey D. Sachs, "The 2019 Hubert Curien Memorial Lecture," https://www.youtube.com/watch?v=NIWJg5ZmeN8.

14. Daron Acemoglu and James Robinson, *Why Nations Fail: The Origins of Power, Prosperity, and Poverty* (New York: Crown Business, 2012).

15. Richard Abrams, letter to the editor, *The Economist*, 21 September 2019.

16. William J. Baumol, "Entrepreneurship: Productive, Unproductive, and Destructive," *Journal of Business Venturing* 11, no. 1 (1996): 3–22.

17. Thomas Piketty, Emmanuel Saez, and Gabriel Zucman, "Rethinking Capital and Wealth Taxation," 2013, http://piketty. pse. ens. fr/files/PikettySaez2014RKT. pdf.

18. Thomas Piketty, "About Capital in the 21st Century," *American Economic Review* 105, no. 5 (2015): 48–53.

19. Thomas Piketty and Emmanuel Saez, "A Theory of Optimal Inheritance Taxation," *Econometrica* 81, no. 5 (2013): 1851–1886. Yet rates in many countries are significantly less and include substantial exclusions. For example, the US estate tax has an exemption of more than $11 million before a 40 percent rate kicks in, and Japan has a complex *inheritance* tax with a rate of 55 percent after a basic allowance of about $300,000 on the estate plus $60,000 for each heir.

20. The Giving Pledge, "A Commitment to Philanthropy," https://givingpledge.org/About.aspx.

21. Anthony B. Atkinson, *Inequality* (Cambridge, MA: Harvard University Press, 2015).

22. David Neumark and William L. Wascher, "Minimum Wages and Employment," *Foundations and Trends in Microeconomics* 3, no. 1–2 (2007): 1–182.

23. OECD.Stat. Data for real minimum wages expressed in US$ at Purchasing Power Parity, https://stats.oecd.org/Index.aspx?DataSetCode=RMW.

24. Basic Income Earth Network, "History of Basic Income," 2019, https://basicincome.org/basic-income/history/.

25. Don Arthur, "Basic Income, a Radical Idea Enters the Mainstream," *Australian Parliamentary Library Research Paper Series*, 18 November 2016, https://

parlinfo.aph.gov.au/parlInfo/download/library/prspub/4941916/upload_binary/4941916.pdf.

26. Citizen's Basic Income Trust, *What Is It?*, 2019, https://citizensincome.org/citizens-income/what-is-it/.

27. Dina Bowman, Shelley Mallett, and Diarmuid Cooney-O'Donoghue, *Basic Income: Trade-Offs and Bottom Lines* (Fitzroy, Australia: Research & Policy Center, Brotherhood of St Laurence, 2017), http://library.bsl.org.au/jspui/bitstream/1/10141/2/Bowman_etal_Basic_income_2017.pdf.

28. Damon Jones and Ioana Marinescu, "The Labor Market Impacts of Universal and Permanent Cash Transfers: Evidence from the Alaska Permanent Fund," NBER Working Paper no. 24312, February 2018.

29. Anthony Painter and Chris Thoung, *Creative Citizen, Creative State: The Principled and Pragmatic Case for a Universal Basic Income* (London: RSA, 2015). 4.

30. Kati Pohjanpalo, "Finland's Landmark Trial Finds Basic Income Brings Happiness but Not Jobs," Bloomberg, https://www.bloomberg.com/news/articles/2020-05-06/milestone-free-money-study-shows-happiness-grows-but-jobs-don-t?sref=LspfQlRv.

31. Joseph Zeballos-Roig, "Spain Is Moving to Establish Permanent Basic Income in the Wake of the Coronavirus Pandemic," https://www.businessinsider.com/spain-universal-basic-income-coronavirus-yang-ubi-permanent-first-europe-2020-4.

32. Anon., "Spain's Embattled Government Proposes a New Anti-Poverty Scheme," *The Economist*, 4 June 2020, https://www.economist.com/europe/2020/06/04/spains-embattled-government-proposes-a-new-anti-poverty-scheme.

33. Theodore Roosevelt, "Citizenship in a Republic," speech delivered at the Sorbonne in Paris, France, 23 April 1910, http://www.theodore-roosevelt.com/trsorbonnespeech.html.

34. Theodore Roosevelt, *The Key to Success in Life*, Theodore Roosevelt Digital Library, Dickinson State University, https://www.theororerooseveltcenter.org/Research/Digital-Library/Record?libID-o283099.

Chapter 11. The Purpose of the Politics

1. Anon., "Special Report: The Dark Arts," *The Economist*, 15 September 2016. https://www.economist.com/special-report/2016/09/15/the-rise-of-the-superstars.

2. Presuming it survives the bust in travel due to COVID-19 at the time of writing.

3. Joshua Barkan, *Corporate Sovereignty: Law and Government under Capitalism* (Minneapolis: University of Minnesota Press, 2013), 6.

4. H. H. Gerth and C. Wright Mills, eds., *Max Weber: Essays in Sociology* (Abingdon: Routledge, 1948), 127.

5. From a letter to Bishop Mandell Creighton on 5 April 1887. The transcript is published in John Neville Figgis and Reginald Vere Laurence, eds., *Historical Essays and Studies* (London: Macmillan, 1907).

6. John Kenneth Galbraith, *The Affluent Society* (London: Hamish Hamilton, 1958), 200.

7. Galbraith, *Affluent Society*, 196.

8. Milton Friedman, "The Social Responsibility of Business Is to Increase Its Profits," *New York Times Magazine*, 13 September 1970, 32–33 and 122–126.

9. John Braithwaite, *Regulatory Capitalism: How It Works, Ideas for Making It Work Better* (Cheltenham: Edward Elgar, 2008).

10. He does not call them this, but he does speak of "mega-corporate capitalism."

11. For example, Steve Coll, "Gusher: The Power of ExxonMobil," *New Yorker*, 9 April 2012, https://www.newyorker.com/magazine/2012/04/09/gusher. He points out that the company "functions as a corporate state within the American state—constructing its own foreign, economic, and human rights policies—and its executives are self-conscious about their sovereignty." It does not just accept enormous subsidies from the US government but in turn overwhelmingly funds the Republican Party and, partially as a result of so doing, manages to have officials in the White House that carry out its policies. In fact, it has a "Political Action Committee" that aims to "control what's going on in the House."

12. Arnold Schwarzenegger, "Arnold Schwarzenegger Has a New Blunt Message for Donald J. Trump," YouTube, 28 June, 2018, https://www.youtube.com/watch?v=_Ise8Mvzub4.

13. Giles Parkinson, "The Stunning Wind, Solar and Battery Costs the Coalition Refuses to Accept," *Renew Economy*, 23 November, 2018, https://reneweconomy.com.au/the-stunning-wind-solar-and-battery-costs-the-coalition-refuses-to-accept-31985/; Ken Baldwin, "FactCheck Q&A: Is Coal Still Cheaper than Renewables as an Energy Source?," *The Conversation*, 14 August, 2018, http://theconversation.com/factcheck-qanda-is-coal-still-cheaper-than-renewables-as-an-energy-source-81263; International Energy Agency, *World Energy Outlook 2019*, https://www.iea.org/reports/world-energy-outlook-2019/renewables#abstract.

14. Niall McCarthy, "The State of Global Renewable Energy Employment," *Forbes*, 23 July 2019, https://www.forbes.com/sites/niallmccarthy/2019/07/23/the-state-of-global-renewable-energy-employment-infographic/#10980100e63f; Bureau of Labor Statistics, "Occupational Employment Statistics: May 2017 National Industry-Specific Occupational Employment and Wage Estimates, NAICS 212100—Coal Mining," *Occupational Employment Statistics*, 2019, https://www.bls.gov/oes/2017/may/naics4_212100.htm.

15. Mariana Mazzucato, *The Entrepreneurial State: Debunking Public vs. Private Sector Myths* (New York: Public Affairs, 2015), 72–73.

16. Mazzucato, *Entrepreneurial State*, chapter 5.

Chapter 12. The Resilience of Liberal Capitalism

1. They should also be planning for adaptation should their mitigation efforts fall short. However, adaptation is not inherently a public good; it can be (and often is) provided privately.

2. Katrina Brown, "Global Environmental Change I: A Social Turn for Resilience?," *Progress in Human Geography* 38, no. 1 (2014): 107–117.

3. C. S. Holling, "Resilience and Stability in Ecological Systems," *Annual Review of Ecology and Systematics* 4 (1973): 1–24.

4. Monica G. Turner, William H. Romme, and Daniel B. Tinker, "Surprises and Lessons from the 1988 Yellowstone Fires," *Frontiers in Ecology and the Environment* 1, no. 7 (2003): 351–358.

5. Carl Folke, "Resilience (Republished)," *Ecology and Society* 21, no. 4 (2016): 44, emphasis added, https://doi.org/10.5751/ES-09088-210444, http://www.ecologyandsociety.org/vol21/iss4/art44/.

6. David Chandler, *Resilience: The Governance of Complexity* (New York: Routledge, 2014), 7, emphasis added.

7. Karen Perry Sillerman, "The Midwest's Food System Is Failing. Here's Why," *Blog: Union of Concerned Scientists*, 17 July 2018, https://blog.ucsusa.org/karen-perry-stillerman/the-midwests-food-system-is-failing-heres-why.

8. Thomas Elmqvist et al., "Response Diversity, Ecosystem Change, and Resilience," *Frontiers in Ecology and the Environment* 1, no. 9 (2003): 488.

9. Robert M. May, Simon A. Levin, and George Sugihara, "Ecology for Bankers," *Nature* 451, no. 7181 (2008): 894.

10. Stefano Battiston et al., "Complexity Theory and Financial Regulation," *Science* 351, no. 6275 (2016).

11. Andrew Zolli and Ann Marie Healy, *Resilience: Why Things Bounce Back* (New York: Simon and Schuster, 2014).

12. Patrick Bolton et al., *The Green Swan: Central Banking and Fnancial Stability in the Age of Climate Change* (Basel: Bank for International Settlements, 2020), https://www.bis.org/publ/othp31.pdf.

13. Bolton et al., *Green Swan*,1.

14. For example, Murray Gell-Mann, *The Quark and the Jaguar: Adventures in the Simple and the Complex* (New York: W. H. Freeman, 1994); Ilya Prigogine, *The End of Certainty: Time, Chaos, and the New Laws of Nature* (New York: The Free Press, 1997); Philip W. Anderson, Kenneth J. Arrow, and David Pines, *The Economy as an Evolving Complex System*, Santa Fe Institute Studies in the Sciences of Complexity (Redwood City, CA: Addison-Wesley, 1988); Niklas Luhmann, *Social Systems*, trans. John Bednarz Jr., with Dirk Baecker (Stanford, CA: Stanford University Press, 1995); Didier Sornette, *Why Stock Markets Crash: Critical Events in Complex Financial Systems* (Princeton, NJ: Princeton University Press, 2002); M. Mitchell Waldrop, *Complexity: The Emerging Science at the Edge of Order and Chaos* (New York: Simon and Schuster, 1992).

15. Adam Smith, *An Inquiry into the Nature and Causes of the Wealth of Nations*, ed. R. H. Campbell and A. S. Skinner, 2 vols., vol. 1, Glasgow Edition of the Works and Correspondence of Adam Smith (Indianapolis: Liberty Classics, 1976), IV.ii.9; 456.

16. Joseph A. Tainter, *The Collapse of Complex Societies* (Cambridge: Cambridge University Press, 1988).

17. Charles E. Lindblom, "The Science of Muddling Through," *Public Administration Review* 14 (Spring 1959): 79–88.

18. Quoted in Waldrop, *Complexity*, 331–334.

19. Chandler, *Resilience*.

20. James E. Lovelock, *Gaia: A New Look at Life on Earth* (Oxford: Oxford University Press, 1979).

21. Clare Twigger-Ross et al., *Community Resilience to Climate Change: An Evidence Review* (York: Joseph Roundtree Foundation, 2015), 1, http://sro.sussex.ac.uk/id/eprint/69092/1/resilience-to-climate-change-full.pdf.

Chapter 13. Progressing to Liberal Capitalism

1. Johann Wolfgang von Goethe, Johann Peter Eckermann, and J. K. Moorhead, *Conversations of Goethe*, 1st ed. (Cambridge, MA: Da Capo Press, 1998), 294, emphasis added.

2. Adam Smith, *An Inquiry into the Nature and Causes of the Wealth of Nations*, ed. R. H. Campbell and A. S. Skinner, 2 vols., vol. 1, Glasgow Edition of the Works and Correspondence of Adam Smith (Indianapolis: Liberty Classics, 1976),V.ii.k.3; 870.

3. James Surowiecki, *The Wisdom of Crowds* (New York: Anchor Books, 2005).

4. Paul J. H. Schoemaker and Philip E. Tetlock, "Superforecasting: How to Upgrade Your Company's Judgment," *Harvard Business Review* 94 (2016): 72–78; Lyle Ungar et al., *The Good Judgment Project: A Large Scale Test*, AAAI Technical Report (Philadelphia, PA: University of Philadelphia, 2012).

5. Research suggests that lonely people use Facebook rather than that Facebook makes people lonely. Yet, Facebook cannot cure the current "epidemic of loneliness." Only high-quality social relations can do that. See Hayeon Song et al., "Does Facebook Make You Lonely? A Meta Analysis," *Computers in Human Behavior* 36 (July 2014): 446–452.

6. By "regulation" we do not mean control with authority as one regulates a machine. Rather it is the setting of boundaries to prevent chaos or harm to essential social or environmental functions.

7. Stephen D. Brookfield, *Developing Critical Thinkers: Challenging Adults to Explore Alternative Ways of Thinking and Acting* (San Francisco: Jossey-Bass, 1987).

Bibliography

Abrams, Richard. Letter to the editor. *The Economist*, 21 September 2019.

Acemoglu, Daron, and Pascual Restrepo. "Robots and Jobs: Evidence from US Labor Markets." NBER Working Paper no. 23285, National Bureau of Economic Research, March 2017. https://ssrn.com/abstract=2941263.

Acemoglu, Daron, and James Robinson. *Why Nations Fail: The Origins of Power, Prosperity, and Poverty*. New York: Crown Business, 2012.

Adams, Susan. "Apple's New Foxconn Embarrassment." *Forbes*, 12 September 2012. http://www.forbes.com/sites/susanadams/2012/09/12/apples-new-foxconn-embarrassment/#103b24a28ae6.

Alam, Julhas, and Farid Hossain. "Bangladesh Collapse Search Over; Death Toll 1,127." Yahoo News, 14 May 2013. https://news.yahoo.com/bangladesh-collapse-search-over-death-toll-1-127-122554495.html.

Alesina, Alberto, Stefanie Stantcheva, and Edoardo Teso. "Intergenerational Mobility and Preferences for Redistribution." *American Economic Review* 108, no. 2 (2018): 521–554.

Anderson, Cameron, John Angus D. Hildreth, and Laura Howland. "Is the Desire for Status a Fundamental Human Motive? A Review of the Empirical Literature." *Psychological Bulletin* 141, no. 3 (2015): 574–601. DOI:10.1037/a0038781.

Anderson, Philip W., Kenneth J. Arrow, and David Pines. *The Economy as an Evolving Complex System*. Santa Fe Institute Studies in the Sciences of Complexity. Redwood City, CA: Addison-Wesley, 1988.

Anon. "Spain's Embattled Government Proposes a New Anti-Poverty Scheme." *The Economist*, 4 June 2020. https://www.economist.com/europe/2020/06/04/spains-embattled-government-proposes-a-new-anti-poverty-scheme.

Anon. "Special Report: The Dark Arts." *The Economist*, 15 September 2016. https://www.economist.com/special-report/2016/09/15/the-rise-of-the-superstars, accessed 5 November 2019.

Apple. *Apple Supplier Responsibility 2019 Progress Report*. https://www.apple.com/au/ supplier-responsibility/pdf/Apple_SR_2019_Progress_Report.pdf.

Aristotle. *Nicomachean Ethics*. Oxford: Oxford University Press, 2009.

ARPA-E. "About." https://arpa-e.energy.gov/?q=arpa-e-site-page/about.

Arthur, Don. "Basic Income, a Radical Idea Enters the Mainstream." *Australian Parliamentary Library Research Paper Series*. 18 November 2016. https://parlinfo.aph.gov.au/parlInfo/download/library/prspub/4941916/upload_binary/4941916.pdf.

Asen, Elke. "Corporate Tax Rates around the World 2019." The Tax Foundation, Fiscal Fact #679, 10 December 2019. https://taxfoundation.org/corporate-tax-rates-around-the-world-2019/.

Atkinson, Anthony B. *Inequality*. Cambridge, MA: Harvard University Press, 2015.

Australian Senate. *Australian Senate Economic References Committee Hearing into Corporate Tax Avoidance*. 9 April 2015. https://parlinfo.aph.gov.au/parlInfo/search/display/display.w3p;query=Id:"committees/commsen/aa68d895-38dc-4165-bce7-2082c796519b/0000".

Autor, David H., David Dorn, and Gordon H. Hanson. "The China Syndrome: Local Labor Market Effects of Import Competition in the United States." *American Economic Review* 103, no. 6 (2013): 2121–2168.

Baldwin, Ken. "FactCheck Q&A: Is Coal Still Cheaper than Renewables as an Energy Source?" *The Conversation*, 14 August 2018, http://theconversation.com/factcheck-qanda-is-coal-still-cheaper-than-renewables-as-an-energy-source-81263.

Banks around the World. *Top 100 Banks in the World*. 2015. http://www.relbanks.com/worlds-top-banks/assets.

Barkan, Joshua. *Corporate Sovereignty: Law and Government Under Capitalism*. Minneapolis: University of Minnesota Press, 2013.

Basic Income Earth Network. "History of Basic Income." 2019. https://basicincome.org/basic-income/history/.

Battiston, Stefano, J. Doyne Farmer, Andreas Flache, Diego Garlaschelli, Andrew G. Haldane, Hans Heesterbeek, Cars Hommes, et al. "Complexity Theory and Financial Regulation." *Science* 351, no. 6275 (2016): 818–819.

Baumol, William J. "Entrepreneurship: Productive, Unproductive, and Destructive." *Journal of Business Venturing* 11, no. 1 (1996): 3–22.

Beck, Thorsten, Asli Demirguc-Kunt, and Ross Levine. "Bank Concentration and Fragility: Impact and Mechanics." NBER Working Paper no. 11500, National Bureau of Economic Research, 2005. http://www.nber.org/papers/w11500.

Beveridge, William. *Social Insurance and Allied Services*. London: His Majesty's Stationery Office, 1942.

Bhagwati, Jagdish. *In Defense of Globalization*. New York: Oxford University Press, 2004.

Blyth, Mark, and Matthias Matthijs. "Black Swans, Lame Ducks, and the Mystery of IPE's Missing Macroeconomy." *Review of International Political Economy* 24, no. 2 (2017): 203–231. https://doi.org/10.1080/09692290.2017.1308417.

Bol, Thijs. "Has Education Become More Positional? Educational Expansion and Labour Market Outcomes, 1985–2007." *Acta Sociologica* 58, no. 2 (2015): 105–120. https://doi.org/10.1177%2F0001699315570918.

Bolton, Patrick, Morgan Despres, Pereira Da Silve, Luiz Awazu, Frédéric Samama, and Romain Svartman. *The Green Swan: Central Banking and Financial Stability in the Age of Climate Change*. Basel: Bank for International Settlements, 2020. https://www.bis.org/publ/othp31.pdf.

Bowman, Dina, Shelley Mallett, and Diarmuid Cooney-O'Donoghue. *Basic Income: Trade-Offs and Bottom Lines*. Fitzroy: Research & Policy Centre, Brotherhood of St Laurence, 2017. http://library.bsl.org.au/jspui/bitstream/1/10141/2/Bowman_etal_Basic_income_2017.pdf.

Braithwaite, John. *Regulatory Capitalism: How It Works, Ideas for Making It Work Better*. Cheltenham: Edward Elgar, 2008.

Brickman, P., and D. T. Campbell. "Hedonic Relativism and Planning the Good Society." In *Adaptation Level Theory: A Symposium*, edited by M. H. Appley, 287–302. New York: Academic Press, 1971.

Brickman, Philip, Dan Coates, and Ronnie Janoff-Bulman. "Lottery Winners and Accident Victims: Is Happiness Relative?" *Journal of Personality and Social Psychology* 36, no. 8 (1978): 917–927.

Brookfield, Stephen D. *Developing Critical Thinkers: Challenging Adults to Explore Alternative Ways of Thinking and Acting*. San Francisco: Jossey-Bass, 1987.

Brown, Katrina. "Global Environmental Change I: A Social Turn for Resilience?" *Progress in Human Geography* 38, no. 1 (2014): 107–117.

Bryant, Raymond L., and Sinéad Bailey. *Third World Political Ecology*. London: Routledge, 1997.

Brynjolfsson, Erik, and Andrew McAfee. *Race against the Machine: How the Digital Revolution Is Accelerating Innovation, Driving Productivity, and Irreversibly Transforming Employment and the Economy*. Tokyo: Digital Frontier Press, 2012.

Buettner, Dan. *The Blue Zones of Happiness: Lessons from the World's Happiest People*. Washington, DC: National Geographic Partners, 2019.

Bughin, Jacques, Eric Hazan, Susan Lund, Peter Dahlström, Anna Wiesinger, and Amresh Subramaniam. *Skill Shift: Automation and the Future of the Workforce*. McKinsey Global Institute. Washington, DC: McKinsey, 2018.

Bureau of Labor Statistics. "May 2017 National Industry-Specific Occupational Employment and Wage Estimates, NAICS 212100—Coal Mining." *Occupational Employment and Wage Statistics* (2019). https://www.bls.gov/oes/2017/may/naics4_212100.htm.

Burke, Edmund, "Letter to a Member of the National Assembly in Answer to Some Objections on His Book on French Affairs (1791)." http://www.ourcivilisation.com/smartboard/shop/burkee/tonatass/.

Business Roundtable. "Our Commitment." https://opportunity.businessroundtable.org /ourcommitment/.

Cantril, Hadley. *Pattern of Human Concerns*. New Brunswick, NJ: Rutgers University Press, 1965.

Case, Anne, and Angus Deaton. *Deaths of Despair and the Future of Capitalism*. Princeton, NJ: Princeton University Press, 2020.

Cerny, Philip. "The Competition State Today: From Raison d'État to Raison du Monde." *Policy Studies* 31, no. 1 (2010): 5–21.

Cerny, Philip. "Political Globalization and the Competition State." In *Political Economy and the Changing Global Order*, edited by Richard Stubbs and Geoffrey Underhill, 300–309. Oxford: Oxford University Press, 2000.

Cerullo, Megan. "60 of America's Biggest Companies Paid No Federal Income Tax in 2018." CBS News, 12 April 2019. https://www.cbsnews.com/news/2018-taxes-some-of-americas-biggest-companies-paid-little-to-no-federal-income-tax-last-year/.

Chandler, David. *Resilience: The Governance of Complexity*. New York: Routledge, 2014.

Chang, Ha-Joon. *23 Things They Don't Tell You about Capitalism*. New York: Bloomsbury Press, 2011.

Chang, Ha-Joon. *Bad Samaritans: The Myth of Free Trade and the Secret History of Capitalism*. New York: Bloomsbury Press, 2008.

Charles, Kerwin Kofi, Erik Hurst, and Matthew Notowidigdo. "Manufacturing Decline, Housing Booms, and Non-Employment." NBER Working Paper no. 18949, National Bureau of Economic Research, 2013, 13–57.

Cheng, Joey T., Jessica L. Tracy, and Joseph Henrich. "Pride, Personality, and the Evolutionary Foundations of Human Social Status." *Evolution and Human Behavior* 31, no. 5 (2010): 334–347.

Chomsky, Noam, and Robert W. McChesney. *Profit over People: Neoliberalism and the Global Order*. New York: Seven Stories Press, 1999.

Christensen, Clayton M., Michael E. Raynor, and Rory McDonald. "What Is Disruptive Innovation?" *Harvard Business Review*, December 2015. https://hbr.org/2015/12/what-is-disruptive-innovation.

Christodoulou, Mario. "UK Auditors Criticized on Bank Crisis." *Wall Street Journal*, 30 March 2011. https://www.wsj.com/articles/SB10001424052748703806304576232231353594682.

Citizen's Basic Income Trust. *What Is It?* 2019. https://citizensincome.org/citizens-income/what-is-it/.

Coll, Steve. "Gusher: The Power of ExxonMobil." *New Yorker*, 9 April 2012. https://www.newyorker.com/magazine/2012/04/09/gusher, accessed 20 June 2018.

Cooper, Christian H. "Why Poverty Is Like a Disease." *Nautilus*, 20 April 2017. http://nautil.us/issue/47/consciousness/why-poverty-is-like-a-disease.

Corak, Miles. "Income Inequality, Equality of Opportunity, and Intergenerational Mobility." *Journal of Economic Perspectives* 27, no. 3 (2013): 79–102.

Credit Suisse Research Institute. *Global Wealth Databook 2018*. Credit Suisse Research Institute, 2019. https://www.credit-suisse.com/about-us/en/reports-research/global-wealth-report.html.

Crivelli, Ernesto, Ruud De Mooij, and Michael Keen. "Base Erosion, Profit Shifting and Developing Countries." *FinanzArchiv: Public Finance Analysis* 72, no. 3 (2016): 268–301.

Crouch, Colin. "Neoliberalism, Nationalism and the Decline of Political Traditions." *Political Quarterly* 88, no. 2 (2017): 221–229.

Crouch, Colin. *The Strange Non-Death of Neoliberalism*. Cambridge: Polity Press, 2011.

Dabla-Norris, Era, Kalpana Kochhar, Nujin Suphaphiphat, Frantisek Ricka, and Evridiki Tsounta. *Causes and Consequences of Income Inequality: A Global Perspective*. Paris: International Monetary Fund, 2015.

Dahrendorf, Ralf. *Life Chances: Approaches to Social and Political Theory*. Chicago: University of Chicago Press, 1979.

D'Alisa, Giacomo, Federico Demaria, and Giorgos Kallis. *Degrowth: A Vocabulary for a New Era*. Abingdon: Routledge, 2014.

Davis, Angela K., David A. Guenther, Linda K. Krull, and Brian M. Williams. "Do Socially Responsible Firms Pay More Taxes?" *Accounting Review* 91, no. 1 (2016): 47–68.

de Beauvoir, Simone. *Must We Burn de Sade?* London: Nevill, 1953.

Deci, Edward L., and Richard M. Ryan. "Hedonia, Eudaimonia, and Well-Being: An Introduction." *Journal of Happiness Studies* 9, no. 1 (2008): 1–11.

Defense Advanced Research Projects Agency. "A Selected History of DARPA Innovation." https://www.darpa.mil/Timeline/index.html.

Deneen, Patrick J. *Why Liberalism Failed*. New Haven, CT: Yale University Press, 2018.

de Loecker, Jan, and Jan Eeckhout. "The Rise of Market Power and the Macroeconomic Implications." NBER Working Paper no. 23687, National Bureau of Economic Research, August 2017. http://www.nber.org/papers/w23687.

Dickens, Charles. *Oliver Twist*. London: Tom Doherty Associates, 1998.

Diener, Ed, Richard E. Lucas, and Christie Napa Scollon. "Beyond the Hedonic Treadmill: Revising the Adaptation Theory of Well-Being." *American Psychologist* 61, no. 4 (2006): 305–314.

Dishman, Lydia. "How U.S. Employee Benefits Compare to Europe's." *Fast Company*, 17 February 2016. https://www.fastcompany.com/3056830/how-the-us-employee-benefits-compare-to-europe.

Dobbs, Richard, Tim Koller, Sree Ramaswamy, Jonathan Woetzel, James Manyika, Rohit Krishnan, and Nicoló Andreula. *Playing to Win: The New Global Competition for Corporate Profits*. McKinsey Global Institute. New York: McKinsey, 2015. http://www.mckinseycom/business-functions/strategy-and-corporate-finance/our-insights/thenew-global-competition-for-corporate-profits.

Dore, Ronald. "Will Global Capitalism be Anglo-Saxon Capitalism?" *New Left Review* 6 (2000): 101–119.

Doyle, Kim. "Facebook, Whatsapp and the Commodification of Affective Labour." *Communication, Politics and Culture* 48, no. 1 (2015): 51–65.

Dullforce, Annebritt. "FT Global 500 2015." *Financial Times* (International Edition), 20 June 2015. www.ft.com/ft500.

Easterlin, Richard A. "Does Economic Growth Improve the Human Lot?" In *Nations and Households in Economic Growth: Essays in Honor of Moses Abramovitz*, edited by Paul A. David and Melvin W. Reder, 89–125. New York: Academic Press, 1974.

Eccleston, Richard. "BEPS and the New Politics of Corporate Tax Justice." In *Business, Civil Society and the 'New' Politics of Corporate Tax Justice*, edited by Richard Eccleston and Ainsley Elbra, 40–67. Cheltenham: Edward Elgar, 2018.

Elmqvist, Thomas, Carl Folke, Magnus Nyström, Garry Peterson, Jan Bengtsson, Brian Walker, and Jon Norberg. "Response Diversity, Ecosystem Change, and Resilience." *Frontiers in Ecology and the Environment* 1, no. 9 (2003): 488–494.

Esping-Andersen, Gøsta. *The Three Worlds of Welfare Capitalism*. Cambridge: Polity Press, 1990.

Fawcett, Edmund. *Liberalism: The Life of an Idea*. Princeton, NJ: Princeton University Press, 2018.

Figgis, John Neville, and Reginald Vere Laurence, eds. *Historical Essays and Studies*. London: Macmillan, 1907.

Folke, Carl. "Resilience (Republished)." *Ecology and Society* 21, no. 4 (2016): 44. http://www.ecologyandsociety.org/vol21/iss4/art44/.

"Fortune Global 500." *Fortune*, 2015. http://fortune.com/global500/.

Fortune. *How to Become the World's Most Admired Company*. 2015. http://fortune.com/video/2015/02/19/how-to-become-the-worlds-most-admiredcompany/.

Fortune. *World's Most Admired Companies 2015*. 2015. http://fortune.com/worlds-most-admired-companies/2015/.

Fortune. *World's Most Admired Companies Ranked by Key Attributes*, 2015. http://fortune.com/2015/02/19/wmac-ranked-by-key-attribute/

Frank, Robert H., and Philip J. Cook. *The Winner-Take-All Society: Why the Few at the Top Get So Much More than the Rest of Us*. New York: Penguin, 1996.

Frey, Carl Benedikt, and Michael A. Osborne. "The Future of Employment: How Susceptible Are Jobs to Computerisation?" *Technological Forecasting and Social Change* 114 (2017): 254–280.

Friedman, Milton. "The Social Responsibility of Business Is to Increase Profits." *New York Times Magazine*, 13 September 1970.

Friedman, Thomas. *The Lexus and the Olive Tree*. London: HarperCollins, 2000.

Fuchs, Doris. *Business Power in Global Governance*. Boulder, CO: Lynne Rienner, 2007.

Fuchs, Erica R. H. "Rethinking the Role of the State in Technology Development: DARPA and the Case for Embedded Network Governance." *Research Policy* 39, no. 9 (2010): 1133–1147.

Galbraith, John Kenneth. *The Affluent Society*. London: Hamish Hamilton, 1958.

Gell-Mann, Murray. *The Quark and the Jaguar: Adventures in the Simple and the Complex*. New York: W.H. Freeman, 1994.

Gerth, H. H., and C. Wright Mills, eds. *Max Weber: Essays in Sociology*. Abingdon: Routledge, 1948.

Gidron, Noam, and Peter A. Hall. "The Politics of Social Status: Economic and Cultural Roots of the Populist Right." *British Journal of Sociology* 68, no. S1 (2017): S57–S84.

Gilson, R. J. "Controlling Shareholders and Corporate Governance: Complicating the Comparative Taxonomy." Review. *Harvard Law Review* 119, no. 6 (2006): 1641–1679.

The Giving Pledge. "A Commitment to Philanthropy." https://givingpledge.org/About.aspx.

"The Global 500, the World's Largest Public Companies." *Forbes*, 2 July 2002. https://www.forbes.com/global/2002/0722/global.html#71aac2ad47f6.

Goethe, Johann Wolfgang von, Johann Peter Eckermann, and J. K. Moorhead. *Conversations of Goethe*. 1st ed. Cambridge, MA: Da Capo Press, 1998.

Goodin, Robert E., Bruce Headey, Ruud Muffels, and Henk-Jan Dirven. *The Real Worlds of Welfare Capitalism*. Cambridge: Cambridge University Press, 1999.

Gordon, Robert J. *The Rise and Fall of American Growth: The US Standard of Living since the Civil War*. Princeton, NJ: Princeton University Press, 2017.

Goulet, Denis. *The Cruel Choice: A New Concept in the Theory of Development*. New York: Atheneum, 1977.

Gravelle, Jane. *Tax Havens: International Tax Avoidance and Evasion*. Washington, DC: Congressional Research Services, 2015.

Haldane, Andrew G. "The Costs of Short-Termism." *Political Quarterly* 86, no. 1 (2015): 66–76.

Hall, Peter. "The Evolution of Varieties of Capitalism in Europe." In *Beyond Varieties of Capitalism: Contradictions, Complementarities and Change*, edited by Bob Hancke, Martin Rhodes, and Mark Thatcher, 39–88. Oxford: Oxford University Press, 2007.

Hall, Peter, and Daniel Gingerich. "Varieties of Capitalism and Institutional Complementarities in the Political Economy." *British Journal of Political Science* 39, no. 3 (2009): 449–482.

Hall, Peter, and David Soskice. "Varieties of Capitalism and Institutional Change: A Response to Three Critics." *Comparative European Politics* 1, no. 2 (2003): 241–250.

Hall, Peter, and Kathleen Thelen. "Institutional Change in Varieties of Capitalism." *Socio-Economic Review* 7 (2009): 7–34.

Harris, Sam. *Free Will*. New York: Free Press, 2014.

Harrison, Neil E., and John Mikler, eds. *Climate Innovation: Liberal Capitalism and Climate Change*. London: Palgrave Macmillan, 2014.

Harrod, Jeffrey. "The Century of the Corporation." In *Global Corporate Power*, edited by Christopher May, 23–46. Boulder, CO: Lynne Rienner, 2006.

Harvey, David. *A Brief History of Neoliberalism*. Oxford: Oxford University Press, 2005.

Hatch, Patrick. "In Amazon's 'Hellscape,' Workers Face Insecurity and Crushing Targets." *Sydney Morning Herald*, 7 September 2018. https://www.smh.com.au/business/workplace/in-amazon-s-hellscape-workers-face-insecurity-and-crushing-targets-20180907-p502ao.html.

Helliwell, John, Richard Layard, and Jeffrey Sachs, eds. *World Happiness Report 2017*. New York: Sustainable Development Solutions Network, 2017. http://worldhappiness.report/ed/2017/.

Hirsch, Fred. *Social Limits to Growth*. Cambridge, MA: Harvard University Press, 1976.

Holling, C. S. "Resilience and Stability in Ecological Systems." *Annual Review of Ecology and Systematics* 4 (1973): 1–24.

Hopkins, Tansy. "Reliving the Rana Plaza Factory Collapse: A History of Cities in 50 Buildings, Day 22." *The Guardian*, 23 April 2015. https://www.theguardian.com/cities/2015/apr/23/rana-plaza-factory-collapse-history-cities-50-buildings.

Horn, Michael. "Uber, Disruptive Innovation and Regulated Markets." *Forbes*, 20 June 2016. https://www.forbes.com/sites/michaelhorn/2016/06/20/uber-disruptive-innovation-and-regulated-markets/#6de654d237fb.

Horwitz, Sarah McCue, Julia R. Irwin, Margaret J. Briggs-Gowan, Joan M. Bosson Heenan, Jennifer Mendoza, and Alice S. Carter. "Language Delay in a Community Cohort of Young Children." *Journal of the American Academy of Child and Adolescent Psychiatry* 42, no. 8 (2003): 932–940.

Huber, Evelyne, and John D. Stephens. "Power, Markets, and Top Income Shares." Kellogg Institute for International Studies Working Paper no. 404, April 2015.

IMF. *Global Financial Stability Report: Restoring Confidence and Progressing Reforms*. Washington, DC: IMF, 2012. http://www.imf.org/external/pubs/ft/gfsr/2012/02/pdf/text.pdf.

IMF. *World Economic Outlook Database: April 2015 Edition*. 2015. http://www.imf.org/external/pubs/ft/weo/2015/01/weodata/index.aspx.

Inglehart, Ronald F., and Pippa Norris. "Trump, Brexit, and the Rise of Populism: Economic Have-Nots and Cultural Backlash." HKS Working Paper no. RWP16-026, 2016. SSRN: https://ssrn.com/abstract=2818659 or http://dx.doi.org/10.2139/ssrn.2818659.

International Energy Agency. *World Energy Outlook 2019*. https://www.iea.org/reports/world-energy-outlook-2019/renewables#abstract.

IPCC. *Climate Change 2014: Synthesis Report*. Contribution of Working Groups I, II, and III to the Fifth Assessment Report of the Intergovernmental

Panel on Climate Change. Core Writing Team R. K. Pachauri and L. A. Meyer, eds. Geneva: IPCC, 2015.

Iversen, Torben, and Jonas Pontusson. "Comparative Political Economy: A Northern European Perspective." In *Unions, Employers and Central Banks: Macroeconomic Coordination and Institutional Change in Social Market Economies*, edited by Torben Iversen, Jonas Pontusson, and David Soskice, 1–37. New York: Cambridge University Press, 2000.

Japan Ministry of Internal Affairs and Communications, Statistics Bureau. *Statistical Handbook of Japan*. Tokyo: Japan Ministry of Internal Affairs and Communications, 2017.

Jebb, Andrew T., Louis Tay, Ed Diener, and Shigehiro Oishi. "Happiness, Income Satiation and Turning Points around the World." *Nature Human Behaviour* 2, no. 1 (2018): 33–38.

Jensen, Nathan. "Do Taxpayers Know They Are Handing Out Billions to Corporations?" *New York Times*. 24 April 2018. https://www.nytimes.com/2018/04/24/opinion/amazon-hq2-incentives-taxes.html.

Jensen, Nathan, and Edmund Malesky. *Incentives to Pander: How Politicians Use Corporate Welfare for Political Gain*. Cambridge: Cambridge University Press, 2018.

Jones, Damon, and Ioana Marinescu. "The Labor Market Impacts of Universal and Permanent Cash Transfers: Evidence from the Alaska Permanent Fund." NBER Working Paper no. 24312, National Bureau of Economic Research, February 2018.

Jones, Owen. *The Establishment and How They Get Away with It*. London: Allen Lane, 2014.

Kahneman, Daniel, and Angus Deaton. "High Income Improves Evaluation of Life but Not Emotional Well-Being." *Proceedings of the National Academy of Sciences* 107, no. 38 (2010): 16489–16493. https://doi.org/10.1073/pnas.1011492107.

Kallis, Giorgos. *Degrowth*. Newcastle upon Tyne: Agenda, 2018.

Kambhu, John, Scott Weidman, and Neel Krishnan. "New Directions for Understanding Systemic Risk." *Economic Policy Review* 13, no. 2 (2007): 1–83.

Kasser, Tim. *The High Price of Materialism*. Cambridge, MA: MIT Press, 2002.

Keohane, Robert O., and Joseph S. Nye. *Power and Interdependence: World Politics in Transition*. Boston: Little, Brown, 1977.

Kerouac, Jack. *On the Road*. New York: New American Library, 1958.

Keynes, John Maynard. "Economic Possibilities for Our Grandchildren (1930)." In *Essays in Persuasion*, 321–332. New York: Springer, 2010.

Kline, Ronald R. "Technological Determinism." In *International Encyclopedia of the Social and Behavioral Sciences*, 2nd ed., edited by James D. Wright, 109–112. Oxford: Elsevier, 2015.

Korten, David. *When Corporations Rule the World*, 3rd edition. Oakland: Berrett-Koehler, 2015.

Krafcik, John [CEO of Waymo, part of Alphabet]. *Status*. 20 July 2018, https://twitter.com/johnkrafcik/status/1020343952266973186?lang=en.

Krugman, Paul. *The Conscience of a Liberal*. New York: W. W. Norton, 2009.

Kumhof, Michael, Romain Rancière, and Pablo Winant. "Inequality, Leverage, and Crises." *American Economic Review* 105, no. 3 (March 2015): 1217–1245.

Larcker, David F., and Brian Taya. *CEO Compensation—Data Spotlight*. Corporate Governance Research Initiative, Stanford Graduate School of Business, 2018. https://www.gsb.stanford.edu/sites/gsb/files/publication-pdf/cgri-quick-guide-17-ceo-compensation-data.pdf.

Lazonick, William. "Profits without Prosperity." *Harvard Business Review* 92, no. 9 (2014): 46–55.

Lazonick, William, and Mariana Mazzucato. "The Risk-Reward Nexus in the Innovation-Inequality Relationship: Who Takes the Risks? Who Gets the Rewards?" *Industrial and Corporate Change* 22, no. 4 (2013): 1093–1128.

LeBaron, Genevieve. "Subcontracting Is Not Illegal, but Is It Unethical? Business Ethics, Forced Labour, and Economic Success." *Brown Journal of World Affairs* 20, no. 2 (2014): 237–249.

LeBaron, Genevieve, and Nicola Phillips. "States and the Political Economy of Unfree Labour." *New Political Economy* 24, no. 1 (2019): 1–21.

Leimgruber, Kristin L., Alexandra G. Rosati, and Laurie R. Santos. "Capuchin Monkeys Punish Those Who Have More." *Evolution and Human Behavior* 37, no. 3 (2016): 236–244.

Levy, Frank, and Richard J. Murnane. *The New Division of Labor: How Computers Are Creating the Next Job Market*. Princeton, NJ: Princeton University Press, 2005.

Lin, Kun-Chin. "Protecting the Petroleum Industry: Renewed Government Aid to Fossil Fuel Producers." *Business and Politics* 16, no. 4 (2014): 549–578.

Lindblom, Charles E. "The Science of Muddling Through." *Public Administration Review* 19, no. 2 (1959): 79–88.

Ljubica, Nedelkoskam, and Glenda Quintini. *Automation, Skills Use and Training*. Labour and Social Affairs Directorate for Employment, OECD. Paris: OECD, 2018.

Lovelock, James E. *Gaia: A New Look at Life on Earth*. Oxford: Oxford University Press, 1979.

Luce, Edward. *The Retreat of Western Liberalism*. Toronto: CNIB, 2017.

Ludwig, Jens, Lisa Sanbonmatsu, Lisa Gennetian, Emma Adam, Greg J. Duncan, Lawrence F. Katz, Ronald C. Kessler, et al. "Neighborhoods, Obesity, and Diabetes—a Randomized Social Experiment." *New England Journal of Medicine* 365, no. 16 (2011): 1509–1519.

Luhmann, Niklas. *Social Systems*. Translated by John Bednarz Jr. with Dirk Baecker. Stanford, CA: Stanford University Press, 1995.

MacKenzie, Donald, and Judy Wajcman. *The Social Shaping of Technology*. London: Open University Press, 1999.

Manyika, James, Susan Lund, Byron Auguste, Lenny Mendonca, Tim Welsh, and Sreenivas Ramaswamy. *An Economy That Works: Job Creation and America's Future*. McKinsey Global Institute. Washington, DC: McKinsey, 2011.

Maslow, Abraham H. *The Farther Reaches of Human Nature*. New York: Viking Press, 1971.

Masson-Delmotte, V., P. Zhai, H.-O. Pörtner, D. Roberts, J. Skea, P. R. Shukla, A. Pirani, et al., eds. *Global Warming of 1.5°C. An IPCC Special Report on the Impacts of Global Warming of 1.5°C above Pre-Industrial Levels and Related Global Greenhouse Gas Emission Pathways, in the Context of Strengthening the Global Response to the Threat of Climate Change, Sustainable Development, and Efforts to Eradicate Poverty*. Geneva: World Meteorological Organization, 2018.

May, Robert M., Simon A. Levin, and George Sugihara. "Ecology for Bankers." *Nature* 451, no. 7181 (2008): 893–894.

Mazzucato, Mariana. *The Entrepreneurial State: Debunking Public vs. Private Sector Myths*. New York: Public Affairs, 2015.

Mazzucato, Mariana. "From Market Fixing to Market-Creating: A New Framework for Innovation Policy." *Industry and Innovation* 23, no. 2 (2016): 140–156.

Mazzucato, Mariana. "Mission-Oriented Innovation Policies: Challenges and Opportunities." *Industrial and Corporate Change* 27, no. 5 (2018): 803–815.

Mazzucato, Mariana, and Caetano Penna. *The Brazilian Innovation System: A Mission-Oriented Policy Proposal*. Brazilia: Centro de Gestão e Estudos Estratégico, 2016.

Mazzucato, Mariana, and Gregor Semieniuk. "Financing Renewable Energy: Who Is Financing What and Why It Matters." *Technological Forecasting and Social Change* 127 (2018): 8–22.

Mazzucato, Mariana, and Gregor Semieniuk. "Public Financing of Innovation: New Questions." *Oxford Review of Economic Policy* 33, no. 1 (2017): 24–48.

McCarthy, Niall. "The State of Global Renewable Energy Employment." *Forbes*, 23 July 2019. https://www.forbes.com/sites/niallmccarthy/2019/07/23/the-state-of-global-renewable-energy-employment-infographic/#10980100e63f.

McLean, Ian, and Alistair McMillan. *Oxford Concise Dictionary of Politics*, 2nd ed. Oxford: Oxford University Press, 2003.

Meadows, Donella H. *Thinking in Systems: A Primer*. Edited by Diana Wright Sustainability Institute. White River Junction, VT: Chelsea Green, 2008.

Menges, Jochen I., Martin Kilduff, Sarah Kern, and Heike Bruch. "The Awestruck Effect: Followers Suppress Emotion Expression in Response to Charismatic but Not Individually Considerate Leadership." *Leadership Quarterly* 26, no. 4 (2015): 626–640.

Merrill, Laura, Andrea M. Bassi, Richard Bridle, and Lasse T. Christensen. *Tackling Fossil Fuel Subsidies and Climate Change: Levelling the Energy Playing Field.* Copenhagen: Nordic Council of Ministers, 2015.

Mervis, Jeffrey. "Department of Energy Broke Law in Blocking Research Funds, Report Says." *Science*, 13 December 2017. http://www.sciencemag.org/news/2017/12/department-energy-broke-law-blocking-research-funds-report-says.

Micklethwait, John, and Adrian Wooldridge. *The Company: A Short History of a Revolutionary Idea*. London: Phoenix, 2003.

Mikler, John. *The Political Power of Global Corporations*. Cambridge: Polity Press, 2018.

Mikler, John, and Ainsley Elbra. "Paying a Fair Share: Multinational Corporations' Perspectives on Taxation." *Global Policy* 8, no. 2 (2017): 181–190.

Mikler, John, Ainsley Elbra, and Hannah Murphy-Gregory. "Defending Harmful Tax Practices: Mining Companies' Responses to the Australian Senate Inquiry into Tax Avoidance." *Australian Journal of Political Science* 54, no. 2 (2019): 238–254.

Mudde, Cas. "Populist Radical Right Parties in Europe Today." In *Transformations of Populism in Europe and the Americas: History and Recent Trends*, edited by John Abromeit, York Norman, Gary Marotta, and Bridget Maria Chesterton, 295–307. London: Bloomsbury, 2015.

Mumford, Lewis. *Technics and Civilization*. New York: Harcourt, Brace, 1934.

Myers, Connor. "Corporate Social Responsibility in the Consumer Electronics Industry: A Case Study of Apple Inc." Georgetown University Edmund A. Walsh School of Foreign Service, 2013, 11. http://lwp.georgetown.edu/wp-content/uploads/Connor-Myers.pdf.

Neumark, David, and William L. Wascher. "Minimum Wages and Employment." *Foundations and Trends in Microeconomics* 3, no. 1–2 (2007): 1–182.

Noble, Kimberly G., M. Frank Norman, and Martha J. Farah. "Neurocognitive Correlates of Socioeconomic Status in Kindergarten Children." *Developmental Science* 8, no. 1 (2005): 74–87.

Nokia Bell Labs. "Our History." https://www.bell-labs.com/about/history-bell-labs/.

Nolan, Peter, Dylan Sutherland, and Jin Zhang. "The Challenge of the Global Business Revolution." *Contributions to Political Economy* 21, no. 1 (2002): 91–110.

Nordhaus, William D. "A Review of the Stern Review on the Economics of Climate Change." *Journal of Economic Literature* 45 (September 2007): 686–702.

Nordhaus, William D. "To Tax or Not to Tax: Alternative Approaches to Slowing Global Warming." *Review of Environmental Economics and Policy* 1, no. 1 (2007): 26–44.

Nordhaus, William. "Projections and Uncertainties About Climate Change in an Era of Minimal Climate Policies." *American Economic Journal: Economic Policy* 10, no. 3 (2018): 333–360.

Nourbakhsh, Illah Reza. "The Coming Robot Dystopia." *Foreign Affairs* 94, no. 4 (2015): 23–28. http://0-search.ebscohost.com.catalog.poudrelibraries.org/login.aspx?direct=true&db=aph&AN=103175005&site=ehost-live.

Nozick, Robert. *Anarchy, State, and Utopia*. New York: Basic Books, 1974.

OECD. *Bank Competition and Financial Stability*. 2011. http://www.oecd.org/finance/financial-markets/48501035.pdf.

OECD. *Concentration of the Banking Sector: Assets of Three Largest Banks as a Share of Assets of All Commercial Banks, Percent, 2011*, OECD Economic Surveys: Netherlands, April 2014. http://10.1787/eco_surveys-nld-2014-graph31-en.

OECD. "A Family Affair: Intergenerational Social Mobility across OECD Countries." In *Economic Policy Reforms: Going for Growth*, 183–200. Paris: OECD, 2010.

OECD. *GDP per Hour Worked*. Paris: OECD, 2018. https://data.oecd.org/lprdty/gdp-per-hour-worked.htm.

OECD. *OECD Secretary-General Report to G20 Finance Ministers and Central Bank Governors*. Paris: OECD, 2019. http://www.oecd.org/tax/oecd-secretary-general-tax-report-g20-finance-ministers-june-2019.pdf.

OECD. "Real Minimum Wages" Dataset on OECD.Stat. https://stats.oecd.org/.

OECD. *Tax Reforms Accelerating with Push to Lower Corporate Tax Rates*. 5 September. Paris: OECD Centre for Tax Policy and Administration, 2018.

OECD. "Tax Revenue." 2018. https://data.oecd.org/tax/tax-revenue.htm.

Office of the President. *Economic Report of the President*. Washington, DC: US Government Printing Office, 2012.

Okun, Arthur M. *Equality and Efficiency: The Big Tradeoff*. Washington, DC: Brookings Institution, 1975.

"Opportunity Insights." 2019. https://opportunityinsights.org/.

Painter, Anthony, and Chris Thoung. *Creative Citizen, Creative State: The Principled and Pragmatic Case for a Universal Basic Income*. London: RSA, 2015.

Palan, Ronen, Richard Murphy, and Christian Chavagneux. *Tax Havens: How Globalization Really Works*. New York: Cornell University Press, 2013.

Panetta, Fabio, Thomas Faeh, Giuseppe Grande, Corinne Ho, Michael King, Aviram Levy, Frederico M. Signoretti, Marco Taboga, and Andrea Zaghini. "An Assessment of Financial Sector Rescue Programmes." Bank for International Settlement. BIS Papers no. 48, Basel, Switzerland, 2009. http://www.bis.org/publ/bppdf/bispap48.pdf.

Parkinson, Giles. "The Stunning Wind, Solar and Battery Costs the Coalition Refuses to Accept." *Renew Economy*, 23 November 2018. https://reneweconomy.com.au/the-stunning-wind-solar-and-battery-costs-the-coalition-refuses-to-accept-31985/.

Payne, Keith. *The Broken Ladder: How Inequality Affects the Way We Whink, Live, and Die*. New York: Penguin Books, 2018.

Perez, Carlota. "Technological Revolutions and Techno-Economic Paradigms." *Cambridge Journal of Economics* 34, no. 1 (2010): 185–202.

Philippon, Thomas. *The Great Reversal: How America Gave Up on Free Markets*. Cambridge, MA: The Belknap Press of Harvard University Press, 2019.

Pierce, Justin R., and Peter K. Schott. "The Surprisingly Swift Decline of US Manufacturing Employment." *American Economic Review* 106, no. 7 (2016): 1632–1662.

Pigou, Arthur Cecil. *The Economics of Welfare*, 4th ed. London: Macmillan, 1932.

Piketty, Thomas. "About Capital in the 21st Century." *American Economic Review* 105, no. 5 (2015): 48–53.

Piketty, Thomas. *Capital in the Twenty-First Century*. Translated by Arthur Goldhammer. Cambridge, MA: The Belknap Press of Harvard University Press, 2014.

Piketty, Thomas. "Rethinking Capital and Wealth Taxation." Working Paper, Paris School of Economics, 17 September 2013. http://www.piketty.pse.ens.fr/files/PikettySaez2013RKT.pdf.

Piketty, Thomas, and Emmanuel Saez. "A Theory of Optimal Inheritance Taxation." *Econometrica* 81, no. 5 (2013): 1851–1886.

Piketty, Thomas, Emmanuel Saez, and Gabriel Zucman. "Rethinking Capital and Wealth Taxation." 2013. http://piketty.pse.ens.fr/files/PikettySaez2014RKT.pdf.

Pinch, Trevor J., and Wiebe E. Bijker. "The Social Construction of Facts and Artefacts: Or How the Sociology of Science and the Sociology of Technology Might Benefit Each Other." *Social Studies of Science* 14, no. 3 (1984): 399–441.

Pohjanpalo, Kati. "Finland's Landmark Trial Finds Basic Income Brings Happiness but Not Jobs." Bloomberg. https://www.bloomberg.com/news/articles/2020-05-06/milestone-free-money-study-shows-happiness-grows-but-jobs-don-t?sref=LspfQlRv.

Porter, Eduardo. "Don't Fight the Robots, Tax Them." *New York Times*, 23 February 2019. https://www.nytimes.com/2019/02/23/sunday-review/tax-artificial-intelligence.html.

Posner, Eric. "Milton Friedman Was Wrong." *Atlantic*, 22 August 2019. https://www.theatlantic.com/ideas/archive/2019/08/milton-friedman-shareholder-wrong/596545/.

Powell, Robert. "Anarchy in International Relations Theory: The Neorealist-Neoliberal Debate." *International Organization* 48, no. 2 (Spring 1994): 313–344.

Prigogine, Ilya. *The End of Certainty: Time, Chaos, and the New Laws of Nature*. New York: The Free Press, 1997.

"The Purse of the One Percent." *Economist*, 14 October 2014. https://www.economist.com/node/21625355/.

Putnam, Robert D. *Our Kids: The American Dream in Crisis*. New York: Simon and Schuster, 2016.

Putnam, Robert. *Bowling Alone: The Collapse and Revival of American Community*. New York: Simon and Schuster, 2000.

Putnam, Robert. *Making Democracy Work: Civic Traditions in Modern Italy*. Princeton, NJ: Princeton University Press, 1993.

PwC. *PwC's Global Annual Review 2018*. https://www.pwc.com/gx/en/about/global-annual-review-2018/clients.html.

Rawls, John. "Justice as Fairness: Political Not Metaphysical." *Philosophy and Public Affairs* 14, no. 3 (1985): 223–251.

Rawls, John. *A Theory of Justice*. Cambridge, MA: The Belknap Press of Harvard University Press, 1971.

Ricks, Thomas E. *Churchill and Orwell: The Fight for Freedom*. New York: Penguin Books, 2018.

Rogelj, Joeri, David L. McCollum, Andy Reisinger, Malte Meinshausen, and Keywan Riahi. "Probabilistic Cost Estimates for Climate Change Mitigation." *Nature* 493, no. 7430 (2013): 79–83.

Roosevelt, Theodore. "Citizenship in a Republic." Speech delivered at the Sorbonne in Paris, France, 23 April 1910. http://www.theodore-roosevelt.com/trsorbonnespeech.html.

Roosevelt, Theodore. *The Key to Success in Life*. Theodore Roosevelt Digital Library, Dickinson State University. https://www.theororerooseveltcenter.org/Research/Digital-Library/Record?libID-o283099.

Rosenblatt, Helena. *The Lost History of Liberalism: From Ancient Rome to the Twenty-First Century*: Princeton, NJ: Princeton University Press, 2020.

Rugman, Alan. *The End of Globalization*. London: Random House Business Books, 2000.

Rugman, Alan, and Alain Verbeke. "Location, Competitiveness, and the Multinational Enterprise." In *The Oxford Handbook of International Business*, 2nd ed., edited by Alan Rugman, 150–177. Oxford: Oxford University Press, 2009.

Russell, Bertrand. *The Conquest of Happiness*. New York: Horace Liveright, 1930.

Sachs, Jeffrey D. "The 2019 Hubert Curien Memorial Lecture." https://www.youtube.com/watch?v=NIWJg5ZmeN8.

Sachs, Jeffrey D. "America's Health Crisis and the Easterlin Paradox." In *World Happiness Report 2018*, edited by John F. Helliwell, Richard Layard, Jeffrey D. Sachs, 146–159. New York: Sustainable Development Solutions Network, 2018.

Sahlins, Marshall David. *Stone Age Economics*. Chicago: Aldine-Atherton, 1972.

Schmidpeter, René, and Christopher Stehr. "A History of Research on CSR in China: The Obstacles for the Implementation of CSR in Emerging Markets." In *Sustainable Development and CSR in China: A Multi-Perspective Approach*, edited by René Schmidpeter, Hualiang Lu, Christopher Stehr, and Haifeng Huang, 1–11. New York: Springer International, 2015.

Schoemaker, Paul J. H., and Philip E. Tetlock. "Superforecasting: How to Upgrade Your Company's Judgment." *Harvard Business Review* 94 (2016): 72–78.

Schwartz, John. "We Went to the Moon. Why Can't We Solve Climate Change?" *New York Times*. 19 July 2019. https://www.nytimes.com/2019/07/19/climate/moon-shot-climate-change.html.

Schwarzenegger, Arnold. "Arnold Schwarzenegger Has a New Blunt Message for Donald J. Trump." YouTube, 28 June 2018. https://www.youtube.com/watch?v=_Ise8Mvzub4, accessed 14 January 2019.

Seabrooke, Leonard, and Duncan Wigan. *Emergent Entrepreneurs in Transnational Advocacy Networks: Professional Mobilization in the Fight for Global Tax Justice*. Warwick: Centre for the Study of Globalisation and Regionalisation, 2013.

Sharman, Jason. *Havens in a Storm: The Struggle for Global Tax Regulation*. Ithaca: Cornell University Press, 2006.

Shorrocks, Anthony, James Davies, and Rodrigo Lluberas. *Global Wealth Report*. Zurich: Credit Suisse Research Institute, 2019. https://www.credit-suisse.com/about-us/en/reports-research/global-wealth-report.html.

Sides, John, Michael Tesler, and Lynn Vavreck. *Identity Crisis: The 2016 Presidential Campaign and the Battle for the Meaning of America*. Princeton, NJ: Princeton University Press, 2019.

Sillerman, Karen Perry. "The Midwest's Food System Is Failing. Here's Why." *Blog: Union of Concerned Scientists*, 17 July 2018. https://blog.ucsusa.org/karen-perry-stillerman/the-midwests-food-system-is-failing-heres-why.

Slobodian, Quinn. *Globalists: The End of Empire and the Birth of Neoliberalism*. Cambridge, MA: Harvard University Press, 2018.

Smith, Adam. *An Inquiry into the Nature and Causes of the Wealth of Nations*. Glasgow Edition of the Works and Correspondence of Adam Smith. Edited by R. H. Campbell and A. S. Skinner. 2 vols., vol. 1. Indianapolis: Liberty Classics, 1976 [1776].

Smith, Adam. "The Theory of Moral Sentiments." Edited by D. D. Raphael and A. L. Macfie. Indianapolis: Liberty Classics, 1984 [1759].

Smith, Adam. *The Wealth of Nations*. New York: Bantam Classics, 2003 [1776].

Smith, Merritt Roe, and Leo Marx. *Does Technology Drive History? The Dilemma of Technological Determinism*. Cambridge, MA: MIT Press, 1994.

Solberg, Emily G., Edward Diener, and Michael D. Robinson. "Why Are Materialists Less Satisfied?" In *Psychology and Consumer Culture: The Struggle for a Good Life in a Materialistic World*, edited by T. Kasser and A. D. Kanner, 29–48. American Psychological Association, 2004.

Song, Hayeon, Anne Zmyslinski-Seelig, Jinyoung Kim, Adam Drent, Angela Victor, Kikuko Omori, and Mike Allen. "Does Facebook Make You Lonely? A Meta Analysis." *Computers in Human Behavior* 36 (July 2014): 446–452.

Sornette, Didier. *Why Stock Markets Crash: Critical Events in Complex Financial Systems*. Princeton, NJ: Princeton University Press, 2002.

Stampler, Laura. "Amazon Will Pay a Whopping $0 in Federal Taxes on $11.2 Billion Profits." *Fortune*, 14 February 2019. https://fortune.com/2019/02/14/amazon-doesnt-pay-federal-taxes-2019/.

Stansbury, Anna, and Lawrence Summers. "Declining Worker Power and American Economic Performance." Brookings Papers on Economic Activity, BPEA Conference Drafts, 19 March 2020.

Staples, Clifford L. "Board Globalisation in the World's Largest TNCs 1993–2005." *Corporate Governance* 15, no. 2 (2017): 311–321.

Steffen, Will, Johan Rockström, Katherine Richardson, Timothy M. Lenton, Carl Folke, Diana Liverman, Colin P. Summerhayes, et al. "Trajectories of the Earth System in the Anthropocene." *Proceedings of the National Academy of Sciences* 115, no. 33 (2018): 8252–8259. http://www.pnas.org/content/pnas/115/33/8252.full.pdf.

Stern, Nicholas. *Stern Review Report on the Economics of Climate Change*. London: H.M. Treasury, 2006.

Stiglitz, Joseph E. "Inequality and Economic Growth." In *Rethinking Capitalism: Economics and Policy for Sustainable and Inclusive Growth*, edited by Michael Jacobs and Mariana Mazzucato, 134–155. Chichester, UK: John Wiley and Sons, 2016.

Stiglitz, Joseph E. "Monetary Policy in a Multi-Polar World." In *Taming Capital Flows: Capital Account Management in an Era of Globalization*, edited by J. E. Stiglitz and R. S. Gürkaynak, 124–170. International Economic Association Series. London: Palgrave Macmillan, 2015.

Stiglitz, Joseph. *People, Power, and Profits: Progressive Capitalism for an Age of Discontent*. New York: W. W. Norton, 2019.

Stock, James H., and Mark W. Watson. "Has the Business Cycle Changed and Why?" *NBER Macroeconomics Annual* 17 (2002): 159–218.

Strange, Susan. "The Future of Global Capitalism; or Will Divergence Persist Forever?" In *Political Economy of Modern Capitalism: Mapping Convergence and Diversity*, edited by Colin Crouch and Wolfgang Streeck, 182–191. London: Sage, 1997.

Streeck, Wolfgang. "The Return of the Repressed." *New Left Review* 104 (March/April 2017): 5–18.

Summers, Lawrence H. "Low Equilibrium Real Rates, Financial Crisis, and Secular Stagnation." In *Across the Great Divide: New Perspectives on the Financial Crisis*, edited by Martin Neil Baily and John B. Taylor, 37–50. Stanford, CA: Hoover Institution Press, 2014.

Surowiecki, James. *The Wisdom of Crowds*. New York: Anchor Books, 2005.

Tainter, Joseph A. *The Collapse of Complex Societies*. Cambridge: Cambridge University Press, 1988.

Tainter, Joseph A. "Social Complexity and Sustainability." *Ecological Complexity* 3, no. 2 (2006): 91–103.

Tam, Fiona G. "Foxconn Factories Are Labor Camps: Report." *South China Morning Post*, 11 October 2010. https://www.scmp.com/article/727143/foxconn-factories-are-labour-camps-report.

Tepper, Jonathan, and Denise Hearn. *The Myth of Capitalism: Monopolies and the Death of Competition*. Hoboken: John Wiley and Sons, 2019.

Thatcher, Margaret. Interview with *Woman's Own*, Downing Street, 23 September 1987. https://www.margaretthatcher.org/document/106689.

Thelen, Kathleen. "Varieties of Labour Politics in the Developed Democracies." In *Varieties of Capitalism: The Institutional Foundations of Comparative Advantage*, edited by Peter Hall and David Soskice, 71–103. Oxford: Oxford University Press, 2001.

Turner, Monica G., William H. Romme, and Daniel B. Tinker. "Surprises and Lessons from the 1988 Yellowstone Fires." *Frontiers in Ecology and the Environment* 1, no. 7 (2003): 351–358.

Twigger-Ross, Clare, Katya Brooks, Liza Papadopoulou, Paula Orr, Rolands Sadauskis, Alexia Coke, Neil Simcock, Andrew Stirling, and Gordon Walker. *Community Resilience to Climate Change: An Evidence Review*. York: The Joseph Rowntree Foundation, 2015.

UNFCCC. "The Copenhagen Accord." United Nations Decision-/CP.15, https://unfccc.int/files/ meetings/cop_15/application/pdf/cop15_cph_auv.pdf.

Ungar, Lyle, Barb Mellors, Ville Satopää, Jon Baron, Phil Tetlock, Jaime Ramos, and Sam Swift. *The Good Judgment Project: A Large Scale Test*. AAAI Technical Report. Menlo Park, CA: Association for the Advancement of Artificial Intelligence, 2012.

United Nations. "Paris Agreement." https://unfccc.int/sites/default/files/English_paris_agreement.pdf.

US Department of the Treasury. "Treasury Secretary O'Neill Statement on OECD Tax Havens." News Release no. PO-366, 5 October 2001. http://www.treasury.gov/press-center/press-releases/Pages/po366.aspx.

US White House. "Remarks by President Trump Before Marine One Departure." 26 November 2018. https://www.whitehouse.gov/briefings-statements/remarks-president-trump-marine-one-departure-26/.

Van Boven, Leaf. "Experientialism, Materialism, and the Pursuit of Happiness." *Review of General Psychology* 9, no. 2 (2005): 132–142.

van Veen, Kees, and Ilse Marsman. "How International Are Executive Boards of European MNCs? National Diversity in 15 European Countries." *European Management Journal* 26 (2008): 188–198.

Varoufakis, Yanis, and Jacob Moe. *Talking to My Daughter about the Economy, or, How Capitalism Works—and How It Fails*. New York: Farrar, Straus and Giroux, 2018.

Vogel, David. "Taming Globalization? Civil Regulation and Corporate Capitalism." In *The Oxford Handbook of Business and Government*, edited by David Coen, Win Grant, and Graham Wilson, 471–495. Oxford: Oxford University Press, 2010.

von Humboldt, Wilhelm. *The Sphere and Duties of Government*. Translated by Junior Joseph Coulthard. London: John Chapman, 1854.

Wade, Robert. "Is the Globalization Consensus Dead?" *Antipode* 41, no. S1 (2010): 141–165.

Waldrop, M. Mitchell. *Complexity: The Emerging Science at the Edge of Order and Chaos*. New York: Simon and Schuster, 1992.

Wallace-Wells, David. "The Uninhabitable Earth." *New York Magazine*, 10 July 2017.

Wallace-Wells, David. *The Uninhabitable Earth*. New York: Tim Duggan Books, 2019.

Walmart. *Apply to Be a Supplier*. 2017. http://corporate.walmart.com/suppliers/apply-to-be-a-supplier.

Walmart. *Walmart 2103 Annual Report*. 2013. http://c46b2bcc0db5865f5a76–91c2ff8eba65983a1c33d367b8503d02.r78.cf2.rackcdn.com/88/2d/4fdf67184a359fdef07b1c3f4732/2013-annual-report-for-walmart-storesinc_130221024708579502.pdf.

Waterman, Alan S. "On the Importance of Distinguishing Hedonia and Eudaimonia When Contemplating the Hedonic Treadmill." *American Psychologist* 62, no. 6 (2007): 612–613. https://doi.org/10.1037/0003-066X62.6.612.

Watson, Matthew. "Ricardian Political Economy and the 'Varieties of Capitalism' Approach: Specialization, Trade and Comparative Institutional Advantage." *Comparative European Politics* 1, no. 2 (2003): 227–240.

Wee, Sui-Lee, and Paul Mozur. "Amazon Wants to Disrupt Health Care in America. In China, Tech Giants Already Have." *New York Times*, 31 January 2018. https://www.nytimes.com/2018/01/31/technology/amazon-china-health-care-ai.html.

Weinzierl, Matthew. "Popular Acceptance of Inequality Due to Innate Brute Luck and Support for Classical Benefit-Based Taxation." *Journal of Public Economics* 155 (2017): 54–63.

White House Council of Economic Advisers. "Labor Market Monopsony: Trends, Consequences, and Policy Responses." October 2016. 20161025_monopsony_labor_mrkt_cea.pdf (archives.gov).

Whitley, Shelagh, and Laurie Van Der Burg. *Fossil Fuel Subsidy Reform: From Rhetoric to Reality*. London: World Resources Institute, 2015. http://newclimateeconomy.report/misc/working-papers.

Wilkinson, Richard G., and Kate E. Pickett. "Income Inequality and Social Dysfunction." *Annual Review of Sociology* 35 (2009): 493–511.

Wilks, Stephen. *The Political Power of the Business Corporation*. Cheltenham: Edward Elgar, 2013.

Winner, Langdon. *Autonomous Technology: Technics-Out-of-Control as a Theme in Political Thought*. Boston: MIT Press, 1978.

Wolf, Martin. *Why Globalisation Works*. New Haven, CT: Yale University Press, 2004.

World Bank. *Gross Domestic Product 2015*. World Development Indicator Database, 11 October 2016. http://databank.worldbank.org/data/download/GDP.pdf.

World Commission on Environment and Development. *Our Common Future*. Oxford: Oxford University Press, 1987.

Wren-Lewis, Sam. "Well-Being as a Primary Good: Towards Legitimate Well-Being Policy." *Philosophy and Public Policy Quarterly* 31, no. 2 (2013): 2–9.

Wulfgramm, Melike, Tonia Bieber, and Stephan Leibfried, eds. *Welfare State Transformations and Inequality in OECD Countries*. London: Palgrave Macmillan, 2016.

Zeballos-Roig, Joseph. "Spain Is Moving to Establish Permanent Basic Income in the Wake of the Coronavirus Pandemic." https://www.businessinsider.com/spain-universal-basic-income-coronavirus-yang-ubi-permanent-first-europe-2020-4.

Zolli, Andrew, and Ann Marie Healy. *Resilience: Why Things Bounce Back*. New York: Simon and Schuster, 2014.

Index

www.ingramcontent.com/pod-product-compliance
Lightning Source LLC
LaVergne TN
LVHW040158080826
844660LV00001B/23

* 9 7 8 1 4 3 8 4 8 6 9 7 0 *